QUEER
COSMOS

QUEER COSMOS

The Astrology of Queer Identities & Relationships

COLIN BEDELL

CLEiS
PRESS

Published in the United States by Cleis Press, an imprint of Start Midnight, LLC, 101 Hudson Street, Thirty-Seventh Floor, Suite 3705, Jersey City, NJ 07302.

Printed in the United States
Cover design: Allyson Fields
Cover image: iStock
Text design: Frank Wiedemann

First Edition.
10 9 8 7 6 5 4 3 2 1

Trade paper ISBN: 978-1-62778-293-7
E-book ISBN: 978-1-62778-506-8

TABLE OF CONTENTS

INTRODUCTION

The contemporary queer identity is both compelled and qualified to steward the message of radical self-acceptance, authenticity, courage, and connection into today's culture. If you needed a permission slip, you have it now: you're compelled and qualified to steward the message of radical self-acceptance, authenticity, courage, and connection into today's culture.

Growing up with the unspoken knowledge that we weren't like other kids was our initiation to this lifelong assignment. We were exposed to shame too early for our young minds, while we were in the process of forming the adult personalities we hold today.

Words matter. So let's review the current semantics on shame. I appreciate Dr. Brené Brown's definition. She unpacks shame as "the intensely painful feeling or experience of believing that we are flawed and therefore unworthy of love and belonging—something we've experienced, done, or failed to do makes us unworthy of connection."[1] Though culture and times are changing rapidly, I would argue that the vast majority of queer people would pinpoint their sex, sexuality, and/or gender as ground zero for shame. Perhaps we didn't identify with the gender assigned to us at birth, or we realized we had an interpersonal sexual attraction that was not considered the social norm. For most, this silent realization of

---

1   Brené Brown. "Shame v. Guilt." *Brené Brown*, January 14, 2013, brenebrown.com/articles/2013/01/14/shame-v-guilt/.

"unworthiness" does not occur in isolation. Like shrapnel in a shame cyclone, reasons for our "unworthiness" pierce our skin—not having the race, social class, physical ability, body, sexual orientation, or theology that provides some people with an array of privileges, affording them unearned access to opportunity, dignity, and mobility.

While we were inside the closet, locked out of heteronormativity's life-defining moments, our shame tried to convince us that we would never find belonging because we were fundamentally flawed and therefore undeserving of meaningful connections. Our shame was no soloist. It screeched with a chorus of voices from our families of origin, classmates, bullies, school officials, and even romantic partners, reinforcing "You're not enough. You're not (insert privileged adjective here) enough."

Our pain around this feeling of unworthiness became perversely comfortable over time, in that it felt familiar. So we built defense mechanisms to honor this shame in adulthood. At least our shame never abandoned us. It stayed hidden within, surrounded in soundproof defects and dysfunctions—those coping mechanisms that allowed our shame to remain unspoken—like perfectionism, emotional stoicism, disengagement, and contempt. In isolation, it insidiously convinced us that we were the only ones who were carrying it around. So why on earth would we talk about it with those who could never understand? Shame builds its strength over us while we keep it in silence and secrecy.[2] But, like all life forms, shame has to fight for its

---

2   Lynn Okura. "WATCH: Dr. Brené Brown on Why Shame Is 'Lethal,'" *HuffPost*, August 27, 2013, www.huffpost.com/entry/ brene-brown-shame_n_3807115.

survival. So it urged us to develop behaviors and patholo-
gies to help keep it alive. Until we came out. For so many
of us, coming out felt like we could breathe for the first
time. The moment we wrapped language around our sex,
sexuality, and/or gender, we began to release the power
shame held on us. Since shame dies when it is spoken, the
speaking of our existential truths was the first step toward
unlearning the conditioning of shame. What stands before
us now is the task of cultivating authenticity and estab-
lishing meaningful connections with others. We're living
in a time when society's leading personal-growth experts,
psychologists, and even spiritualists unanimously agree:
"The quality of our relationships determines the quality
of our lives."[3] Yet shame tries to convince us that we
are fundamentally unworthy of relationships. So shame
remains the single greatest barrier between ourselves
and the experiences that most define our lives. Though
queer shame is highly individualized and nuanced, especially when lived and understood through the intersection
of race, gender, and class, it's important to note that the
need for connection is a universal experience for all of
humanity. So if the quality of our lives is dependent on the
quality of our relationships, yet shame poisons our technicolor queer minds with the black ink of "I'm unlovable.
I'm not enough. I'm unworthy," then we have a serious
crisis of connection on our hands.

At the 2017 convention of the American Psychological Association, Dr. Julianne Holt-Lunstad presented

---

3   Ruthie Ackerman. "Esther Perel: On How Our Love Lives Impact
Our Careers." *Forbes,* November 21, 2017, www.forbes.com/sites/
ruthieackerman/2017/11/21/esther-perel-on-how-our-love-lives-
impact-our-careers/#6e795f6323b5.

work on loneliness. She said, "Loneliness or perceived social isolation is a subjective experience relating to dissatisfaction with one's social relationship."[4] Loneliness is becoming an increasingly significant public health concern. A 2018 survey conducted by global health service Cigna found, "Nearly half of Americans report sometimes or always feeling alone (46 percent) or left out (47 percent)."[5] This loneliness percentage has doubled in the last fifty years. Loneliness is treated as an epidemic by some social researchers and health professionals, since it is linked to physical illness and to functional and cognitive decline. Studies show that loneliness is associated with an increased risk of developing dementia and chronic diseases, and also with a higher rate of mortality.[6] Of course, nothing is new under the sun. In 1928, a seminal fictional but perhaps autobiographical text published in Great Britain, *The Well of Loneliness*, follows protagonist Stephen Gordon, an aristocratic woman who lives with "sexual inversion," prefers to dress in a masculine fashion, and loves women. *The Well of Loneliness* follows Stephen from childhood to adulthood, while she negotiates her way around her "inversion" and gender identity and experiences a series of painfully familiar disappointments due to her unrequited love for other women.

---

4   Aparna Shankar, Anne McMunn, James Banks, and Andrew Steptoe, "Loneliness, Social Isolation, a Behavioral and Biological Health Indicators in Older Adults," *Health Psychology* 30, no. 4 (2011): 377–385, doi: 10.1037/a0022826.

5   Cigna 2018 U.S. Loneliness Index, Cigna, 2018, https://www.multivu.com/players/English/8294451-cigna-us-loneliness-survey/docs/FactSheet_1524071393425-302762795.pdf.

6   Shankar et al., "Loneliness," 377–385.

The Well of Loneliness is considered one of the first—if not *the* first—queer coming-of-age stories. Though it's close to a century old, the narrative of loneliness in queer lives is heartbreakingly timeless. Radclyffe Hall writes, "What remained? Loneliness, or worse still, far worse because it so deeply degraded the spirit, a life of perpetual subterfuge, of guarded opinions and guarded actions, of lies of omission if not of speech, of becoming an accomplice in the world's injustice by maintaining at all times a judicious silence, making and keeping the friends one respected, on false pretenses, because if they knew they would turn aside, even the friends one respected."[7] Countless of us in the queer community, like Hall's central character, ask, "What remained?" As a social species, we need connection to survive and thrive. Our lives depend on it—we're hardwired to need the joy and fulfillment that relationships bring us. And it's not just for our health. We need collaboration to dismantle the social structures that deny the bare minimum of legal protections to our community. We need connection to show up as accomplices in activism, community organizing, and social justice work. We need empathy-driven connection to detangle the internal emotional structures that shame survives on.

Modern society offers us a treasure trove of applicable secular and spiritual resources that help queer people set themselves free from the barbed wire of shame, develop skills to cultivate the personal practice of authenticity, and sharpen our tools to rise above loneliness while we build functional relationships in service to each other.

---

7   Radclyffe Hall, *The Well of Loneliness* (London: Penguin Classics, 2015), 221.

I believe astrology can be an antidote to this shame.

I believe astrology is also a powerful tool that fortifies connection.

I'm not speaking to an empty auditorium. In a 2018 study conducted in collaboration with Wakefield Research, researchers surveyed "1,000 Americans 18 years and older about their views on spirituality vs. organized religion." According to their study, "91 percent of Americans feel that some aspects of spirituality are more appealing than organized religion."[8] Organized religion theoretically was meant to be a space for others to find their belonging, continuity, and meaning. When many of these traditions failed to adapt to culture's progress, a mass exodus occurred, and the erstwhile congregations found other schools of thought for belonging, continuity, and meaning. In the same survey, researchers found, "Astrology is the most popular New Age practice taking hold. More than two in five (42 percent) Americans have read horoscopes."[9] Like no other metaphysical system, astrology can provide exceptionally precise insight into our essential spiritual nature. At the conclusion of *The Well of Loneliness*, Stephen cries to God, "Acknowledge us, oh God, before the whole world. Give us also the right to our existence!"[10] I believe astrology helps us acknowledge ourselves to the god of our understanding, the universe, or whatever language we use

---

8   PRNewswire, "Spirituality Could Appeal to Young Americans More Than Organized Religion, Research Study Reveals," January 23, 2019, https://www.prnewswire.com/news-releases/spirituality-could-appeal-to-young-americans-more-than-organized-religion-research-study-reveals-300782535.html.

9   PRNewswire, "Spirituality."

10   Hall, *The Well of Loneliness*.

to understand the divine. Astrology can help us acknowledge our essential existence within the world of our life experiences. Personally, I know astrology was the first language that successfully helped me wrap my head and heart around my reflection, without relying on the toxic masculine codes that prevail in American culture. I believe it can be a language for you, too. Astrology can be a miraculously helpful lens through which we look with starry eyes upon the areas of ourselves that shame deemed unworthy of love and belonging. It's a perception-correcting tool that can help us transform our wounds into our greatest gifts. In all the great wisdoms of the world, they teach the primary task of the human experience is a discovery and expression of our potential. Astrology is no different. Life is a hero's journey. And astrology is a resource with which we can deconstruct the shame and programming we developed while in the closet and reconstruct our most authentic expressions. Astrology is where we meet the self unchained by social shackles, where only the light of the divine shines from our unarmored selves.

Since it's a method to provide renewed personal insight, astrology can then become a tool that fortifies those experiences that determine the quality of our lives—relationships. It can be a resource to help us engage with the crisis of connection and the loneliness epidemic with a bit of magic. Since astrology has wonderful instruction on relationship preferences, mutuality practices, and compatibility, it can even articulate the special energy that exists between you and your partners.

For chronological context, astrology is argued to be one of the world's oldest metaphysical systems, with historical artifacts dated to ancient Babylonia. Thousands of years later, the Stonewall riots, which proved to be not the beginning but the benchmark of queer liberation in the United States, were set in motion by, among others, two trans women of color (Virgo Sun Marsha P. Johnson and Cancer Sun Sylvia Rivera) on June 28, 1969, at the Stonewall Inn in New York City. In 1973, "homosexuality" was removed from the *Diagnostic and Statistical Manual of Mental Disorders* because of the research contributions of Dr. Evelyn Hooker in 1956. Queer studies emerged in academic spaces in the 1980s as a challenge to the idea of identity-based knowledge—in other words, the idea that to be assigned female or male at birth then contributed to particular fundamental characteristics within that identity—and the assumption of a gender binary.

Today, with unprecedented digital access to data on astrology, history, identity, and queer theory, you can approach this intersection from as many vantage points as there are stars in the universe. Should you be looking to astrology to answer your existential questions? I don't think so. I think you, as Sagittarius Sun Rainer Rilke wrote, can approach queer astrology methodically, while being "patient toward all that is unsolved in your heart and try to love the questions themselves, like locked rooms and like books that are now written in a very foreign tongue. Do not now seek the answers, which cannot be given you because you would not be able to live them. And the point is, to live everything. Live the questions now. Perhaps you will then gradually, without noticing it, live along some distant day into the answer."[11]

---

11   R. M. Rilke, F. X. Kappus, and K.W. Maurer. *Letters to a Young Poet* (London: Euston Press: 1943).

Within queer is "queery." Which is why I chose this Rilke quote, since it inspires us to love the queries and questions themselves until we can live into and as the answer. No astrologer—especially myself—has a monopoly on these queries and answers. My book is only one in a constellation of brilliant queer thinkers on astrology, gender/sexuality, identity, and personal growth. Consider pioneer Jack Fertig, also known as Sister Boom Boom, or the queer astrologers and allies who launched the first ever Queer Astrology conference in San Francisco in July 2013. We are grateful for the contributions of Tony Howard, Jessica Lanyadoo, Danny Larkin, Gary Lortenzen, Chani Nicholas, Barry Pearlman, Christopher Renstrom, Laurence Joseph Thomas, Ian Waisler, Rhea Wolf, and all the other astrologers who have to come out as both an astrology believer and queer. I am blessed to be in the middle of my elders' legacy, collaborating with others I love deeply in the field, in service to the alternative possibilities for queer descendants. As are you now.

And so *Queer Cosmos* was written to be one of many comparative resources attempting to integrate the constellation of astrology, queer studies, universal spiritual themes, and skills for personal growth. These topics are as infinite as the very universe we study. So I decided to focus *Queer Cosmos* as imagining astrology as a metaphysical medicine for queer shame and a resource to help us transcend loneliness. Up first, I'll outline queer theory by discussing the variations between sex, gender, and sexuality, for a helpful foundation. Then I'll attempt to simplify how astrology works by illustrating the planets' themes and the helpful key qualities expressed through the elements.

Once you have that foundation, you'll meet the queer zodiac. Each chapter references the character patterns of the zodiac, carefully devoid of gendered constructions and heteronormative assumptions. I locate the meanings, experiences, behaviors, and mundane activities we all participate in that each sign has a rulership over, and how each sign's energy expresses itself in queer spaces. Since this book explores shame, too, I write about why each archetype is loved. None are loved more or less than the others. Since love is the only antidote to feelings of power-lessness and isolation, it is my prayer that readers feel a deeper sense of self-love and permission to honor the gifts they are divined to express.

I also touch on the blind spots of each sign, though I keep the analysis uplifting. I believe the more we embody the best of the archetype and turn on its light, the more we can cast out the darkness effortlessly. To individu-alize, I follow the queer meaning of each sign with the natal aspects from the Ascendant to Uranus, and for some signs I discuss the generational markings for Neptune and Pluto, where they are applicable to living generations. So you can see how the planets express the themes of the signs, free from norms related to dominance, submission, masculine, feminine, etc. If we investigate the meaning of all twelve, we can use each as a guidepost that helps us clarify our queer natal charts with sophistication and competence.

In an effort to preserve our history and help us feel connected to our legacy, I concluded each chapter with queer public figures born under the sun sign of the chapter. I highly recommend independent research into their lives, failures, and successes. "Meeting" them was a deeply meaningful experience for me, and I imagine it could be for you, too. Since ancestral work is a wonderful tool for texturing your metaphysical practice, consider these figures a part of your family tree. Many of them are still with us, too, so take the time to recognize their contributions and let their example be a field of possibility for you. If this is of interest for you, I leaned on research by Eric Marcus in both the *Making Gay History* book and podcast.

In the second half of this book, I've explored compatibility without the binary of "good" versus "bad" dynamics, but with an organization deeply inspired by a body of supportive literature that's changing the culture on connection. I've "queered" compatibility through the lens of exploring every combination without the traditional relationship structures like marriage and/or monogamy. Leaning on research by leading figures in the field of connection, I'll blend the metaphysical with the physical. I organize each sign with qualities they'll want to honor and qualities they'll want to integrate, and I've explored the signs in love through the paradox of love and desire, which is articulated beautifully by Esther Perel as the interplay of autonomy and closeness.

I'll outline key terms and relationship outcomes to help you navigate these life-defining experiences with conviction, values, and a helpful vocabulary. Then we'll describe the energy between the signs and the lessons they stand to potentially learn together. Since belonging is the place where we find the most meaning, it's important for us to find the right tools to engage with connection. In this process of finding the light in our essential queer nature, we can begin the lifelong process of dimming the darkness of shame, and emerge into relationships that give our lives fullness and meaning.

As a white, cisgendered, able-bodied gay man, I don't speak for the entirety of the queer community. So at the end of this book, I've included interviews with astrology enthusiasts and practitioners across the queer spectrum whose stories work as launchpads for you to understand astrology as a tool for self-discovery and relational insight.

A Course in Miracles (a self-studied program of universal spiritual themes) defines light as "understanding." It is with this light in our hearts that we can embody and steward the practices of radical self-acceptance, courage, justice, empathy, and authenticity within our culture. It's a mighty task that we're not alone in making manifest today. In moments of confidence crisis, I ask myself, "Would it be reasonable to believe we were given astrology without the means or opportunities to successfully implement it into our lives?" A high-minded approach to astrology allows queer-identified people to feel deeply supported in their pursuit of meaning, authenticity, and connection while recognizing the universe already ordains it. So together, let's get started.

QUEER THEORY:
A QUICK CHRONICLE

Since this book investigates astrology from a queer angle, an early summation on queer studies is helpful here to empower you to apply these ideas to astrological ones.

Queer studies in American academia dawned in the 1980s, as a challenge to the use of identity-based knowledge. Identity-based knowledge refers to the idea that the identities assigned to us at birth based on our genitalia somehow contribute to particular types of knowledge and characteristics fundamental to these assigned gender identities. Queer studies also challenged the male/female gender binary, an idea born of preexisting work by gender and sexuality academics that determined essential characteristics and expressions of the feminine and masculine.

Queer studies scholars examine the relationship among gender, sex, and sexual orientation. Contemporary thought on gender, sex, and sexual orientation is still complicated, dynamic, and flexible, since we are all in stages of unlearning falsehoods from a patriarchal system. As each of us have our highly individualized astrological charts, each of us have our highly individualized understandings and expressions of gender, sex, and sexuality in our lives.

Gender is a socially constructed conception of people's roles based on traits like masculinity, femininity, a hybrid of both, or a total rejection of both. Pisces Sun theorist Judith Butler in her 1990 work *Gender Trouble* deduced that masculinity and femininity are performances. They are not inherent qualities of our personhood, like, say, handedness or eye color. Gender is something we *do* because it's a socially constructed performance built on our cultural norms. Like the notion that "all men are emotionally stoic" or "all women are maternal." Meaning, the concept of male or female is a jointly constructed understanding born of shared assumptions about reality.

If all of gender is performance, we must sharply question those beliefs held by people in our culture about what is "real" regarding gender.

Referring to one's sex is speaking to one's physiology—their genetics and hormones—like XY chromosomes in male biology and XX chromosomes in female biology. It's important to note that genitals do not determine one's sex, and that intersex individuals could have a variety of sexual organs and/or varying levels of hormones.

Sexual orientation speaks to attraction and arousal on a romantic and physical basis. One's identification of their sexual orientation communicates what the speaker is romantically and/or sexually attracted to. Words like *pansexual*, *lesbian*, *bisexual*, *gay*, and *asexual*, to name a few, are all applicable ways of describing sexuality, since the speaker is identifying their preferred identity or the preferred identities of their romantic and/or sexual partners.

While examining gender, sex, and sexuality, queer scholars aim to facilitate dialogue across the schools of social sciences and humanities in order to update existing models about the relationship between all three. Additionally, to "queer" a school of thought is to inspect it for heteronormativity, which is defined as "of, relating to, or based on the attitude that heterosexuality is the only normal and natural expression of sexuality."[12] Like gender, to queer is a demonstrative action. To queer is to question, introduce skepticism, and resist societally imposed labels, identities, and expectations that aren't accurate for the human experience. I appreciate how academic Michael Warner, a Virgo Sun, defines the verb *queer* as a "resistance to the regime of normal."[13] With that in mind, how do queer astrologers resist the regime of "normal" that is present is the current dialogue? I don't consider astrology an inherently gendered or heteronormative metaphysical system. But I do think its practitioners are influenced by the patriarchal structures and conditioning that raised them. So queer astrologers can resist normalized assumptions on gender, sex, and sexuality in our field through questioning the norms and demonstrating the alternatives. I spoke with Sagittarius Sun Danny Brave, a writer and spiritual healer who identifies as gender transcen-

---

12   https://www.merriam-webster.com/dictionary/heteronormative

13   Michael Warner, "Introduction," *Fear of a Queer Planet: Queer Politics and Social Theory,* (Minneapolis: University of Minnesota Press, 1993), xxvii. https://it.wikisource.org/wiki/Lettera_a_messer_Benedetto_Varchi

dent and whose preferred pronouns are ze/zim/zir. Brave said, "If we are resisting or even rejecting the norm, then what are we saying yes to? What are the choices in relation to gender identity, expression, sexuality, etc., that are a result of the questioning? What does astrology that is queer say yes to?"

For example, we can actively reject monogamy as the "best" relationship model, giving it no hierarchical value above any other relationship model, like polyamory, for example. We can question the interpretation of a cisgendered Cancer woman as more, say, "inherently maternal" or of an Aries cisgendered man as more "direct and confrontational." Though we'll make space and support both if they arrive. I believe queer Astrologers can say yes to the multitude of gender expressions—from Venus, Mars, Mercury, Moon to Uranus—not only within the chart but within the lived experiences of our community.

No matter one's gender, race, sex, sexuality, or spiritual identification, all normalized assumptions accepted as inherently *true* are a straitjacket. Take one of the most popular assumptions as an example—"vulnerability is weakness." Many of us believe this as inherently true, which is why we try actively to avoid any expression of vulnerability. Yet according to Dr. Brené Brown's research, there is no single practice of courage that doesn't have vulnerability at its bottom line. So vulnerability isn't weakness at all—it is the prerequisite of courage, and of the experiences that determine our quality of life. Is it not courageous and vulnerable to say, "I don't identify with the gender assigned to me"? Is it not courageous and vulnerable to own our stories and practice shame resilience, to resist negotiating our worth or value for others?

For the purposes of this book, we have to examine cultural assumptions on sex, gender, sexuality, and other experiences of the human condition as shame's favorite feeding ground. These unspoken, "I thought it was just me" mythologies of the inner world are where shame can take shape, morphing into perfectionism, people pleasing, improper boundaries, and inauthentic gender performances. With that in mind, let us not forget that shame can multiply affects those people who are discriminated against not just because of their sexuality, but because of their race, as they are exposed to overlapping systems of both gender discrimination and racial discrimination. Danny Brave explains, "And so it oppresses trans people, queer people, people of color, and queer trans people of color disproportionately."

We will use astrology and its beautiful embodiment of universal spiritual values to detangle the knots in our hearts tied by shame, heteronormativity, racism, and patriarchal conditioning. I've also encouraged my clients who were born into abusive and/or highly dysfunctional families to allow astrology to reparent them, and to see the sky as their home. Michelangelo wrote, "I saw the angel in the marble and carved until I set it free."[14] You could liken your astrological inquiry to carving away the heavy marble within so your angel can take flight. Within you is a divinity ready and willing to take the skies. Takeoff starts now.

---

14 https://it.wikisource.org/wiki/Lettera_a_messer_Benedetto_Varchi

QUEER CONSTELLATIONS: HOW DOES ASTROLOGY WORK?

Given astrology's esoteric origins, one of the most rightful criticisms of astrology is its inaccessible language and bewildering techniques. I take this critique very seriously, since I believe identities on the fringes are the ones who need to know astrology's alternative possibilities the most.

Astrology is built on accessibility, acceptance, and understanding for all. So long as you have a birthday, you have a seat at this table. You matter. You belong. Therefore, the teachings on astrology should meet every reader where they are, with accessibility and practical solutions that help all of us navigate our personal contexts with universal wisdom in service to success. Like this anonymous quote reminds us, "If it's inaccessible to the poor, it is neither radical nor revolutionary."

The gateway to the study of astrology is usually one's understanding of the twelve zodiac signs. Most typically start with our own sign. The thirty or thirty-one days that determine zodiac sign seasons are not arbitrary, but prede-termined. The foundation of astrology is consistently the relationship between the planets and the zodiac. When we refer to the zodiac signs, we are referring to their constella-tions in the night sky. So the way in to accessing astrology is a twofold method—through planets and constellations.

At any given moment—from the second you took your first breath to the stars above you right now while this book is in your hands—the sun, moon, and every planet are all touring one of the twelve constellations of the zodiac signs. To explain, when we casually mention our sign, we are actually referencing the sun, because the sun transits each zodiac constellation for approximately thirty days. If one says, "I'm Christina and I'm a Sagittarius," Christina is saying she was born while the sun was *tran-siting* the constellation Sagittarius, because the sun tran-sits Sagittarius between November 21 and December 22 every year.

A skeleton key that helps you unlock astrology is understanding every planet as a thematic storyteller and every constellation (or sign) as a chapter. The planets tell their stories within the zodiac constellation they transit through. At any given moment, all planets will transit one of the twelve signs' constellations. Once again, planet as thematic storyteller and the sign as specific chapter. The story the planets and signs are telling in tandem is the evolution of the soul. One could interchange *evolution of the soul* for *personal growth, inner peace, mental health, deliverance, resurrection, enlightenment,* or *nirvana*—whichever term resonates with you. They're all different words for the same idea, which is the ideal outcome of any serious spiritual inquiry—the healing of the mind.

The moment you were born, the location of the planets transiting the constellations above you created your own hero's journey, an outline for the experiences in front of you. This story is your birth chart. Your birth chart does not abide by any worldly identity norms for gender, sex, class, or race, or the norms of comparison, scarcity, or shame that seek to keep your queer identity hidden.

Think of your birth chart as a circle. Within the divine circle is a map of the planets while they toured the zodiac constellations. The chart is divided into twelve sections, known as the houses.

The number twelve is a repetitive number in astrology —twelve signs, twelve houses. Each house in your chart is governed by a specific sign. So if each of your twelve houses in the chart is ruled by a particular sign, then you have all the signs present somewhere in your birth chart and thus . . . you have entire universe within you.

This idea does intersect with current thinking in astrophysics. Neil deGrasse Tyson wrote in his *Astrophysics for People in a Hurry*, "Every one of our body's atoms is traceable to the Big Bang and to the thermonuclear furnaces with high-mass stars that exploded more than five billion years ago. We are stardust brought to life, then empowered by the Universe to figure itself out—and we have only just begun."[15] Astrologers can interpret your birth chart in all its glory to help empower your decisions and find key themes, times, and opportunity periods that promote your maximum creative possibility. They do this through recognizing how each zodiac sign is a coded

---

15   Neil deGrasse Tyson, *Astrophysics for People in a Hurry* (New York, London: W.W. Norton & Company, 2017).

message, complete with specific and practical instructions for us to practice righteous living on our hero's journey.

Where would the queer community be without our chosen family? Cancer will teach you how to tend to those bonds and protect your network. Where would this same community be without Aquarius's activism and intersection? Queer identities also cherish the philosophical dimension of semantics and the flexibility of verbal communication. So does Gemini. No zodiac sign has a monopoly on merit. All twelve are necessary to speak to the multidimensionality of the human experience, and you have all twelve within you.

Since the rest of *Queer Cosmos* will explore the foundation of astrology, the planets, and the zodiac signs, now is the time to have your birth chart accessible so you can see how these energies exist in you. Remember, your birth chart is the map above you at your exact moment of birth, which provides the insight into the divinity within. To calculate your birth chart, you'll need your birth date, exact time of birth, and location (city/state/country). You can input this information into countless free chart-generator sources online, like Astro-Seek.com, Astro-Charts.com, Astrolabe.com, and others.

If your birth time or birth date is unknown for any number of reasons, you still belong to the school of astrological thought. I believe the soul chooses the chart. So there's no wrong way to calculate what the soul knows to be true. Simply enter sunrise for your birth time on your birth date as you define it, and your birth chart can be easily calculated.

THE SUN: YOUR IDENTITY & VITALITY

The source of life and power on earth, the sun is also the center star of your entire astrological story, shining its brilliance, strength, and focus on all the individual's values, personality traits, experiences, and relationships. The sun in our chart is where we want to be seen, validated, and understood. The sun in queer astrology is also the beginning of detangling heteronormativity's conditioning in the astrological system. It'll help you locate the spiritual energies and meanings that you are meant to express in the world, even if they repudiate what society deems appropriate of male- and/or female-identified people.

In order for this sun to shine from our charts and harness powerful experiences outside our bodies, we'll want to make sure the sun is fully embodied and expressed. In the chapters ahead, you'll read about the meaning of each sign, and the more you implement the meaning into your head and heart, the more you'll realize fantastic outcomes in your life. Determined by the month you're born, your sun sign is the generator of your life, power, and light (or "understanding") in your chart. It is the central organizing principle that vitalizes all other aspects in your chart.

Sun Transit Length: Thirty days
Rules: Leo

THE ASCENDANT: YOUR VISIBILITY & REPRESENTATION

Since all luminaries, planets, and constellations rise and set in one twenty-four-hour day from your vantage point on Earth,

there is always one zodiac sign ascending on the eastern-
most horizon for approximately two and a half hours until
the day is complete. The sign rising at our exact moment
of birth is our ascendant. You could liken the ascendant
to the cover of your queer astrological story. Given how
important the idea and practice of visibility and representation is for marginalized folks, we look to our ascendant
to instruct us on how our divine visibility and representation expresses itself. The ascendant contextualizes queer
themes in our life such as "realness," the aesthetic, and
how we perform our identity. Think of your ascendant as
your drag persona. Since it's the first impression we make
on others, the ascendant is the universe's first impression
on our chart. It textures the entire birth chart—all of the
other elements of our chart are expressed through this
sign. Additionally, experiences infiltrate our thinking
through the ascendant, which affects our interpretations.

 ## THE MOON: YOUR VULNERABILITIES & SHAME

The cherished home of your chart, your
moon sign shapes all that you are emotionally receptive to in the human experience.
It is the temple of your needs, vulnerabilities, sensitivities,
and intimacies. Think of the moon as the mother of your
ballroom house. It's your moon energy that shapes how
you experience the family you belong to, whether that's
your family of origin or the queer one you've chosen.
Your moon sign is the energy that helps you feel emotionally safe, born from the programming of your childhood
conditioning and/or family of origin. Your moon sign also

stylizes your preverbal responses and emotional reflexes. Therefore, your moon sign is how you reach for empathy from trusted confidants, and/or how you write your shame stories and live your defense mechanisms. Tuning in to the nature and safety of your moon sign is easily one of the most valuable emotional regulation tools you could ever learn, since the moon sign is how you express your highest levels of shame and emotions.

Transit Length: 2.5 days
Rules: Cancer

MERCURY: YOUR MENTAL HEALTH & LANGUAGE

Look who's talking! That's easy—it's your Mercury sign. The planet of active intelligence and the "persuasive tongue," your Mercury sign is how you apply your intellectual faculties while you pattern find, research, move about your life, listen, and communicate—both nonverbally and verbally. Your Mercury is how you mobilize and socialize with your friends. It's also your primary tool to queer ideas and connections, which is evidenced by its symbolism—a gender-nonconforming icon, with its receptive, Venusian foundation and its dynamic, penetrating crescent helmet, nodding to the divinity who wore it. The symbol's crescent receives high-minded intelligence, synthesizes all data through the circle's orbit, then dynamically sends that data through the cross, which applies it to the material world. So we can use Mercury to receive intelligence beyond this world, and that'll help us make sense of our queer experiences in relationship to our other experiences,

then find a sense of dominion over worldly beliefs and structures that prevent us from flying at full wingspan.
Transit Length: Three direct weeks
Rules: Gemini and Virgo

VENUS: YOUR VALUES & ROMANCES

Follow Venus's rose petals to discover your values, styles, financial literacy, sensuality practices, and how you relate to romantic relationships. Regardless of gender, sexuality, or sex, your Venus sign is your feminine principles, embodied by magnetism, receptivity, and seduction, and it rules how you cherish and receive the feminine energy outside you. If you need a tool for navigating this side of yourself, just look carefully into Venus's mirror—which is the symbol of the planet itself—to find your "divine feminine," liberated from misogyny and expressed with the power of the universe. This reflection will also help you see the values that inform the choices that shape your life. In order to rise above your shame stories, you need to outline a list of values that will guide you to unlearn shame's programming and find your worthiness in righteous places instead. Most popularly, your Venus sign is how you'd like to see or feel your desired bids for connection. Venus rules desire. It influences your technique for reaching and receiving the beloved energy you crave. In a romantic culture where opportunity, uncertainty, and choice can overwhelm us, your Venus sign will ground your decisions with divine direction and a successful outcome.
Transit Length: 3.5 weeks
Rules: Taurus and Libra

MARS: YOUR SEXUALITY & CONFLICT TRANSFORMATION

Grab the spray bottle! I need to mist my face a bit, because Mars gets me hot and bothered. The fiery, dynamic, and passionate ruler of your sexual stamina, ambitions, and conflict transformation strategies is expressed by your Mars sign. Additionally, your Martian sign is how you embody the sacred masculine energy, which is dynamic, generative, autonomous, and active. Remember, healthy Martian energy isn't a "power-over" energy based on unhealthy dominance and submission, which is a root of toxic masculinity. Your Mars sign is "power-with" energy, meaning power achieved through collaboration. Your Mars sign will help you find what self-generated energy you possess, so you can then collaborate with others in the sheets and streets. So look to your Mars sign when exploring sexuality paradigms and/or relationship structures like polyamory, monogamy, and everything in between. To aid your activism and/or community organizing efforts, your Mars sign helps you understand what you're fighting for on behalf of the collective. It also helps you implement healthy personal and interpersonal boundaries, since it's the planet that helps you transform conflict. So long as you're operating with your Venus-informed values and your nonviolent communication from Mercury, Mars will work its mojo in the battlefield for you to come out victorious.

Transit Length: Two months
Mars: Aries and Scorpio

JUPITER: YOUR WISDOM & EDUCATION

Bigger is better? If you're asking the zodiac's most prolific size queen, Jupiter, the biggest planet in astrology and the planet that enlarges anything it touches, the answer is 100 percent yes. Your Jupiter sign rules your big capacity to think out of a vision. Where would our culture be without the visions of queer ancestors who considered the possibility of community organizing, disproving homosexuality as a mental illness, or mobilizing for legal protections? Your Jupiter sign is the container where these ideologies are explored. When your ideologies change, conversations change, and when conversations change—so does the world. Your Jupiter sign shines some light on your preferred higher education system, too. Colleges and universities can provide spaces of life-defining importance for queer identities, and your Jupiter sign will show you which campus is the queerest fit for your talents. With the right diploma hanging on your wall, you'll understand the only thing that expands anything it touches is an intelligent mind. So it is with your Jupiter sign. How can you apply your brilliance to live out of a vision and not live in the purview of worldly microcircumstances? Your Jupiter sign will show you the way to make your ideas and conversations ideological containers from which new possibilities can emerge for us all.

Transit Length: 11.5 months

Rules: Sagittarius

SATURN: YOUR DISCIPLINE & RESILIENCE

To live is to suffer. All the great wisdoms, biographies, and theologies teach us this existential truth. It's not an easy principle to absorb, but it cannot be denied, either. So Saturn asks us to find the meaning and resilience within the suffering. As queer people, most of us don't have to think too hard to remember shameful experiences or moments of suffering. So your Saturn placement asks you, "Who are you going to be in the space of your suffering?" What's happening to you does not determine your life's outcome, but your choices do. The lessons in your Saturn sign hold the key to your queer resilience, righteous discipline, commitment, integrity, and radical responsibility. These might be rather unpopular values, especially in a society constantly encouraging us to be self-indulgent. But Saturn is always reminding us that a meaningful life is not a popularity contest, but one achieved through the willingness and effort to live life differently. So your Saturn sign shows you how to harness its energy to learn more about personal growth and the higher consciousness that helps us all find meaning, empathy, and more compassion while in the suffering. That way, if we've transformed our own lives, we know how to help others do the same. If you know what changes a heart, you know what can change the world, and this moral authority is the gift of Saturn's resilience and discipline.

Transit Length: 2.5 years
Rules: Capricorn

URANUS: ADAPTABILITY & EMANCIPATION

Greek philosopher Heraclitus teaches us that change is the only constant—otherwise known as the Law of Impermanence—and so unusual Uranus helps us adapt to these changes, spark the electricity of innovation, and wrap our arms around uncertainty with the right strategy, even if it's surrender. Uranus rules ideas on freedom and liberation, which is why Uranus is theorized as the queerest planet, since our queer identities are not supported by the status quo. Like us, Uranus is the status quo's public enemy number one. Your Uranus sign gives you intelligent insight into a wealth of queer ideas like: your technological prowess, freedom, relationship to personal autonomy and gender-nonconforming attitudes, willingness to engage with activism, community organizing, rule breaking, and mobilizing. Uranus knows the minority's radical but better ideas tend to usurp the majority's outdated modalities, so it gives an added dose of power to queer people who are courageous and outrageous enough to speak up and act those ideas out.

Transit Length: Seven years
Rules: Aquarius

NEPTUNE: YOUR SPIRITUALITY & IDEALS

On the ocean floor, Neptune's song for creativity, spirituality, universal love, and fantasy welcomes queer identities to its sanctuary and helps us express its power through our contributions to the world. Your Neptune sign rules your relationship to mysticism, divinity, artistic prowess, and the highest ideals that guide you to your most righteous living. If you consider spirituality as the path of the heart, without religious doctrine or dogma, then Neptune is the song you sing while you follow that path. As unlimited and timeless spiritual beings who probably chose to have a very queer human experience in this incarnation, we rely on our Neptune sign to give us the psychic techniques to engage with both the physical and nonphysical worlds. Neptune helps you dissolve the boundaries between the physical and nonphysical. You can honor Neptune by following your spiritually informed path and expressing your creative skills. Through artistic or metaphysical systems, your Neptune sign helps you capture queer experiences through a range of mediums. While helping us realize we're not alone in our shame and struggle, Neptune delivers us from it.

Transit Length: Fourteen years
Rules: Pisces

PLUTO: YOUR FOCUS & POWER

Before you call NASA and report this book a fraud, Pluto is still a major planetary player in astrology. Rather perfectly suited to the mythological story of belonging and then abandonment, Pluto rules the two-sided power of beginnings and endings, elimination, the destroyer and creator. You could liken the queer power of Pluto to the moment of coming out. It was a death for you and those who knew you. In this mourning and grief process, the burden is on you to live the new life you're trying to create. The only answer to death is life. Though it's reasonable to wonder how opposing themes are ruled by the same, singular celestial body, you must remember that the Pluto-ruled subconscious mind is still a mystery to us all. Swiss psychologist Carl Jung wrote how the paradox is one of the most cherished spiritual possessions.[16] So Pluto is a powerful tool for queer folks trying to let die what needs to die within their personal, relational, and or national spheres, while holding space for the new to be born. In Pluto do we take the deep plunge into discovering our universal potential. In Pluto we end our attachment to social conditioning; eliminate people-pleasing, performance, and perfectionism; and discover and fulfill the ideas of the essential self within.

Transit Length: Ten to twenty years
Rules: Scorpio

Now that you're familiar with how astrology organizes itself, remember our analogy of the planets as storytellers of the specific experiences within your chart. Exploring the planets as storytellers will help you arrive one step closer to accessing the stories of the zodiac. In the chapters that follow, I invite you to consider the function of each sign, none of them more or less important than the other, as a template to help you discover and express your divine potential. But before we move on, I want to disclose my favorite master key that unlocks the themes of the zodiac.

---

16   Carl G. Jung, "Aion," *Collected Works* (Princeton, N.J.: Princeton University Press, 1959), 9.

Every zodiac sign is a specific pair of what is known as modality and element in astrology. The three modalities in order of appearance in the zodiac calendar are: cardinal, fixed, and mutable. This sequence of cardinal, fixed, and mutable repeats itself four times from the beginning to the end of the zodiac's calendar. The four elements in order are: fire, earth, air, and water.

When astrology students liken the modality to the function and the element to the form of the sign, they can easily access the meanings of each sign.

The four cardinal signs are Aries, Cancer, Libra, and Capricorn. When the transiting sun enters a cardinal sign, a solstice or equinox begins. So where we have cardinal planetary aspects and/or cardinal-ruled houses in our chart, they herald new beliefs, experiences, locations, and relationships. When we need to find initiation, direct momentum, new beginnings, or new assertions, our dynamic cardinal sign energy can give it to us. The word *cardinal* is born from the Latin word *cardinalis*, which means "pivotal" or "principle." So the cardinal signs are astrologically obligated to lead, as are you wherever you have cardinal signs in your chart.

After the cardinal signs initiate new seasons, the four fixed signs follow through with the momentum that was set forth. Taurus, Leo, Scorpio, and Aquarius signs put the money wherever the cardinal mouth is. The fixed energy in our charts, whether that's our planetary aspects, fixed-ruled houses, or both, helps us stabilize and concentrate our values. Fixed signs loyally turn theories into practice, and demonstrate their validity in our life experiences. Their time of year is often in the middle of each season, holding up the purest form of the season. Your fixed signs highlight your perseverance, self-containment, convictions, and tenacity in translating your heart's desire into your life's achievement.

The four mutable signs, Gemini, Virgo, Sagittarius, and Pisces, tend to what needs to end, while holding space for the alternative possibilities to begin. They're essentially two energies for the price of one. These eight, I mean, *four* signs can pivot like no other. The word *mutable* mutated from its Latin origin *mutabilis*, which means "change." Where you have your mutable-governed houses and/or planetary aspects, you have boundless curiosity, wonderful adaptability and innovation, and a healthy detachment to an outcome. Knowing when it's time to let go is your mutable energy working to help you strengthen the depth of your spiritual seeking.

Remembering each zodiac sign's modality as their function, now we individualize the signs even further by conceptualizing their element as the form by which they express their modality's function. The zodiac calendar begins with an explosion of fire, as did the universe a few billion years ago in the big bang. The three fire signs are Aries, Leo, and Sagittarius. The meaning of fire is expressed in these powerhouses as they demonstrate bravery, courage, passion, and worthiness. Where we have fire in our chart, we have the introduction of our confidence, which helps us dismantle shame. Shame cannot live in the presence of a fire element, as these elements deem us all essentially worthy of belonging and purpose. This confidence comes from knowing what we deserve because we are all divine. Fire is also how we share our wisdom with others, because we know experiences change when conversations change.

Emerging powerfully from the center fire, the earth signs Taurus, Virgo, and Capricorn are our chart's security system. The earth signs are bodyguards, as they teach us to honor the material, tangible experiences of the physical world. Your earth signs demonstrate where you are dependable, sensual, and self-mastered. Where we have earth in our chart, we have clarification of timeless values that ground queer lives, a desire to be of intelligent service to others, since our community is born of relationships, and the work ethic to effect structural change in glorious ways.

Verbal communication is often at the heart of all of life's most meaningful experiences. So where you have air in your chart, you have the right thinking and accurate words to negotiate, compromise, question, disagree, and agree. Ethereals Gemini, Libra, and Aquarius have the cognition and communication repertoire to stay light on their feet while they're airborne in an effort to gather the data for communication. Where you have your air signs, you have the mental agility to shatter the binary, to share your existential world meaningfully with others by carefully developing trust given and received, and to build a community from a committed vision of access and equality for all.

Where there is water, there is emotion. Where you find Cancer, Scorpio, and Pisces in your chart, you have access to tenderness, sensitivity, intimacy, and spiritual surrender. The water signs help you feel and experience all that's nonverbal. Meaningful moments can't always be theorized or read about. The water signs motivate us to feel an experience so deeply that words can't dwell in its depths. From family belonging, to intimacy, to our spiritual practices, the emotions that underpin our experiences are so powerful, it's difficult to wrap our heads around them. These emotions are the homeland of the water signs.

Congratulations! You've nearly finished the most technical chapter of *Queer Cosmos*. You now know why the constellations shine, what themes the planets tell us about, how a birth chart offers individualized insight, and the understanding of each sign's modality and element as further insight into your otherworldly nature, free from worldly unworthiness. Now we will discuss the zodiac signs and share their directions on righteously living our hero's journeys.

Since we all have twelve sections (or houses) of the chart, ruled by the twelve zodiac signs, the next chapters explore a *cumulative* inquiry into the meaning of each zodiac sign. We won't go into specifics regarding houses in the following chapters, but for those who are curious, I wrote a grid on my favorite topics for the houses (see following page). With your chart you can find which sign rules the content of the house. Starting with your ascendant as the ruler of the first house, you move in chronological order until you get to the sign before the ascendant, which rules your twelfth house. Your natal planets show the what of your story, the theme of the signs express the how, and the houses show you where it will happen. For further information on the houses, I recommend *Houses of the Horoscope* by fellow queer astrologer Alan Oken.

First House	Identity, Ambition, Charisma & Divinity
Second House	Clarity of Values, Finances, Security & Conviction
Third House	Observation, Curiosity, Communication & Active Listening
Fourth House	Vulnerability, Home, Family & Emotional Safety
Fifth House	Courage, Worthiness, Grandeur & Lovability
Sixth House	Inner Peace, Health, Wellness & Routine
Seventh House	Negotiation, Romance, Partnerships & Balance
Eighth House	Intimacy, Eroticism, Desire & Transformation
Ninth House	Expansions, Education, Optimism & Travel
Tenth House	Integrity, Discipline, Responsibility & Life Purpose
Eleventh House	Friendships, Activism, Community & Shared Humanity
Twelfth House	Closure, Surrender, Fantasy & Illusion

It would best serve you to read the chapters of this book in order and in completion. In doing so, you'll be able to identify the experiences that each sign rules and understand that they all serve a meaningful expression—no more or less important than the others—in our lives. Once again, I invite you to consider—an astronomical invitation, since the Latin root of "consider," *sidereal*, means "from the stars"—the function and/or meaning of all twelve signs as a template to help you discover and express your divine potential. I believe all the zodiac signs have a particular direction on how you can unlearn the programming of shame, cultivate authenticity, integrate a practice for more righteous living, and earn relationships that vitalize the meaning of your life.

There's wisdom in every single zodiac sign. And each sign carries the lessons of the one before, fortifies its strengths during its transit, then passes the torch to the next in divine timing. So it's very helpful to see the chronological evolution from Aries to Pisces and all the ways the signs in between help us live with more meaning and love in the present moment. In so doing, we can learn to love the meaning of all signs, embrace the energies we once had difficulty with, and self-actualize using astrology's underlying ethos, which is radical acceptance for all. And so it begins.

ARIES—THE HERO

March 21–April 20
Modality: Cardinal
Element: Fire
Ruling planet: Mars

Before there was time, there was fire . . . and Aries. Emerging in the radiant blossoms and unparalleled joy in the days that follow the spring equinox, Aries energy is the invitation to begin again. The fires of Aries set us from free from cruel winters and mistakes of the past. In Aries, we begin the hero's journey. In Aries, we reconstruct the essential aspects of our queer nature. In Aries, we begin the greatest adventure any one of us can ever take—the journey of self-discovery.

Where you have mighty Aries presiding in your chart, you have a conflagration of all kinds of powerful inspiration, innovation, and bravery that helps you directly combat heteronormativity. But the hero's energy doesn't stop there. Aries is the boxing gloves we can put on while we combat people pleasing, socially constructed performance, and innovation's kryptonite—perfectionism. Where we need queer Aries energy, we can set fires behind the direct action, confidence, and security that gives us the impulse to step out of the closet in bravery and candor.

When any transiting or natal planet shines behind the ram's constellation, it brings forth the passion that resides inside the hearts of the children of Mars and makes it available to everyone on earth. The lifelong work of shame resilience, authenticity, and courage begins with the question "Is there another way to live our lives?" Like the big bang—boom!—Aries energy appears on the scene and yells, "Hell, yeah, there is!" In its fires, Aries energy happily highlights what you need to surrender to win this hero's journey. Reach for your resilience, for it's invaluable weaponry while cultivating authenticity as a practice and the energy to achieve the wholehearted living required for meaningful relationships.

Queer Aries energy is embodied by the choice to step out of the darkness of fear and shame. Queer Aries energy is found in the willingness to withdraw from that which shame told you is inherently true, and in the bravery to start again. Not only the zodiac's very first sign, Aries is the first and only cardinal fire sign. So the high-minded Aries make strong project initiators and strong asserters of identity, for they are emotionally and mentally driving onward. As the hero, Aries energy helps us become the heroes of our lives while we own our desires, passions, and curiosities.

As the first cardinal sign in our calendar, think of Aries as the commander in chief of an army of all twelve signs. While in command, Aries is generally very well meaning—though sometimes a little tactless. These fire benders come alive when they're leading their soldiers toward a common outcome. Their confidence and disarming sense of humor, loyalty, bravery, spontaneity, and passion make rams formidable opponents and beautiful lovers. Their token animal, the ram, blesses Aries energy with the focused, headstrong power to charge ahead and not linger on past mistakes. But remember—a ram is a still a little lamb.

Give these self-directed souls the space to burn their fire, and they'll pull you right in so you can shine beautifully, too. Their self-love is contagious. When the Aries is on, *everyone* is on. But every redeemed Aries battles a few shadowy enemies, too, which manifest themselves in characteristics like: bratty, selfish, ego-driven, demanding, domineering, aggressive, and unrelenting. Another important blind spot for Aries to remember is that not everyone possesses the same amount of self-starting, motivated, confrontational, and confident energy as Aries does, so the Aries would be very wise not to take it personally when their partners battle self-esteem issues. Interpersonal relationships won't always unfold exactly as Aries thinks they should. To combat this, Aries energy can be a powerful space of becoming. They'd be smart to create a space where they invite others to rise to their creative possibility through words of affirmation and action.

In our community, the queer Aries is the hero because they have no reservations while leading the charge to disrupt the heteronormative, binary, patriarchal status quo with their Martian energy. That's why we need their energy at full power so desperately. So every queer activist group would benefit from the outspoken Aries on their side, since they embody the movements throughout queer history that proved that a little upset—a riot in New York City, a protest that can wield the power to correct history. Aries energy nods to movements like ACT UP at the Food and Drug Administration, the patrons who threw money at the police in the Stonewall riots, and other places in our history where the power was in the people. Give them the space to explode in technicolor disruption, and you'll be amazed at how Aries shows up to the party in all their Mars glory. Like a panoramic firework show in the night sky, Aries energy is hard to miss and beautiful to watch. You'll never be the same again.

NATAL PLACEMENTS IN ARIES

Ascendant in Aries: When you walk into a room, the temperature rises. Since Mars rules Aries, having Mars as the ruler of your chart gives you the fire and passion to make heat waves wherever you go. Some may be uncomfortable around your energy's bold, powerful directness. But that's on them, not you. The last thing queer people need to do is shrink to help others feel taller. When it comes to navigating shame, you'd benefit from recognizing the physiological components, like your blood boiling or temporary loss of breath. That way, you'll avoid impulsive behavior, instead questioning your anger story and then wrapping your head around solutions that can help you.

Sun in Aries: The hero's here! You incarnated because you are demonstrating to the zodiac what a life mostly set free from fear and insecurity looks like. Your self-love is the greatest gift you have, and you teach it to the queer community through demonstration. You are loved because of your bravery, gumption, and passion for seizing opportunity. As a leader, you take responsibility for finding the potential in others, and you hold space for that potential to express itself, which inspires profound loyalty from your loved ones.

Moon in Aries: Your heart's on fire. Born while the sensitive moon toured through Aries, your emotional center is outspoken, authentic, and unafraid to pursue what gives you joy. You are loved because your self-generated bravery is contagious, and the zodiac gathers around its fires to learn what it means to be wholehearted. Your deepest psychic need is autonomy. Your independence is your blood. When emotionally hijacked, you can become hyperconfrontational. Try to learn strategies on conflict transformation and negotiation.

Mercury in Aries: Straight talk leads to straight understanding! You always know where the point is, and you try to get right to it. Your words can be windows into the soul or weapons against others, if too impulsive. Speak in service of daring self-expression, while inspiring others to find their voices and use them to practice authenticity.

Venus in Aries: When the goddess of love joined with the god of war, Cupid was born. A closeted romantic, you love the adventure and joy of falling in love. Never afraid of bold gestures of affection or sharing your feelings, you love to love boldly. You're bidding for connection with those with charisma, confidence, and social elegance. The values that inform these relationship bids are mutuality, autonomy, and joy.

Mars in Aries: Daddy's home! You've inherited his grit and confidence in the pursuit of your self-actualization. You play to win each and every time. You love the adrenaline rush of competition, adventure, and play. When the lights go out, you're not afraid to pursue your erotic desires. Dynamic, direct movement is your comfort zone. You enjoy the chase. In conflict, you can wield boundaries quickly with your warrior-like assertions.

Jupiter in Aries: The universe ordained you as the leader. Use it well! You're supported when you take the lead and share your perceptions in a way that helps others feel like they're not alone. So dare greatly, take the risk, start the business, and speak truth to power. In education, consider independent studies or self-directed curricula where you are given the freedom to explore your academic interests.

Saturn in Aries: You're C-class! Think CEO, CFO, or CMO. You have all the skills to manage others in positions of authority or to demonstrate profoundly physical gifts like athleticism. Your lesson is to learn how to follow through on the ideas you imagine. Do some learning on how to focus and commit to strategies and structures without abandoning them because they're boring or too long.

Uranus in Aries: Hey, trailblazer! With Uranus in Aries, you'll boldly go where no sign has gone before. Particularly when it comes to the disruption of norms that limit identity expression and freedom—so have at it! With this placement, you can pioneer breakthroughs the world needs with your daring risk taking, courage, and enthusiasm. If it's tried and true, don't bother. If it's brand-new, give it a go!

Neptune in Aries: Jump first, ask questions later—right? With Neptune in Aries, your spiritual visions are bold, brave, and disruptive. You'll impact the spiritual ethers with your willingness to understand how the divine uniquely shines through you. With this placement, your spiritual and artistic practices are more self-directed. You find your higher self through meaningful alone time and self-inquiry.

House of Aries Suns: Rosie O'Donnell (Comedian/actress), Robert Mackie (fashion designer), Jim Parsons (actor), Elton John (musician), Margarethe Cammermeyer (activist), Camille Cabral (trans activist), Richard Chamberlain (actor), Rachel Maddow (journalist), Linda Hunt (actress), Cat Cora (chef), David Hyde Pierce (actor), Anthony Perkins (actor), Janis Ian (musician/author), Marc Jacobs (designer), Cynthia Nixon (actress/politician), Kristen Stewart (actress), Harris Wofford (politician), Amy Ray (musician), Magda Szubanski (activist/actress), Ole von Beust (politician), Luke Evans (actor), George Platt Lynes (photographer), Bessie Smith (musician), Amelia Atwater-Rhodes (author), Raymond Chan Chi-chuen (politician), Dusty Springfield (musician), Maria Bello (actress), Dick Sargent (actor)

TAURUS—THE LOVER

April 21–May 21
Modality: Fixed
Element: Earth
Ruling planet: Venus

Like their divine mother, the queer Taurus can't help but seem to descend into all spaces they're in like the goddess of love herself right off Botticelli's seashell. Taurus embodies and emanates sensuality and beauty in all forms and has a light in their eye on love. And you can feel the ground get stronger underneath you while it supports the bull who just walked in. Grounded by values, unfailingly kind, and socially gracious, Taurus energy is the crown jewel every comprehensive group needs to shine. Descendants of Venus, Taurus energy expresses itself exceptionally well in many queer-dominated spaces that are ruled by Venus, like the theater, art and design, writing, fashion, and music.

As the zodiac's first earth sign, Taurus energy introduces the universe to the qualities that make earth so beautiful—Taurus provides consistency, sensuality, dependability, and romance in an effort to preserve and protect what they love. As the only fixed earth sign, Taurus energy throws itself all in by wholeheartedly committing to their passions. This Taurus passion is often attached to industries of service, like health and wellness, and to the aesthetic arts, of course.

Few can understand and communicate those mesmerizing worlds like the gifted children of Taurus. Taurus finds the divine, the god of their understanding, in art and design, and all the methods they use to connect to the aesthetics and create their very own personal Eden—from music and visual arts, to scent and taste—are miraculous to witness. Everyone is blessed to join the Taurus there.

The shadow side of the bull is equally forceful. When their space is left unchecked, Taurus energy can be *over*whelming; they'll overtalk, overeat, overspend, overdrink, over-(insert verb here). When unredeemed, the Taurus energy often does everything in excess. I like the words *blind spot* for Taurus's shadow side, because they don't mean any malice. They just don't know what they don't know.

Without question, Taurus energy excels professionally in the beauty, aesthetics, music, culinary, entertainment, art, or design industries. With a gifted understanding of these worlds, they can professionally rise easily and quickly. Outside of careers in the spotlight, Tauruses can take direction and authority well. It's all in the delivery. Like my mother says, "You do more with honey than you do with vinegar!" Express gratitude for their follow-through, and you'll find yourself with one of the most formidable and loyal connections in your life.

If Taurus supports the cause, they work efficiently in a one-on-one partnership, large groups, or solo. The Taurus method of work is slow and steady but extremely efficient. Their tenacity will surely win legions of admirers who acclaim their work. And given their wide network, they will channel the gifts of the Venus homeland and connect people to others who can be of service.

Taurus energy and queer identities are a perfect match. Free from restricting heteronormative patriarchy, queer Taurus can proudly express the gifts of Venus and wherever they feel the call to do so. You can easily spot Taurus writing poetry about heartbreak or the bliss of falling in love, performing, making others laugh, cooking extravagant meals, singing from the Taurus-ruled throat chakra, dancing, eating, drinking, and just being merry.

Taurus is at their absolute happiest when they are surrounded by whatever their heart deems beautiful. Don't confuse their highbrow enthusiasm with superficial materialism—they only live to earn . . . so they can share. That's why Taurus is the Lover. Consider yourself lucky if they share their bounty with you, because you've been carefully chosen and deemed high quality enough to receive their earnings. On that note, Taurus is often relegated to conversations on personal wealth and material gain. But I don't think that's the most meaningful interpretation we can extend to our bull brethren.

What Taurus teaches us about a meaningful life is the necessity of clarifying our values. If you imagine your values as the philosophies that ground you internally while you're bombarded by the chaos of the outside world, you can see how these touchstones can provide you with Taurus-ruled security. It's not money that queer Taurus is pursuing, but meaning. As we all are. Clarification of your values becomes the terra firma beneath you, and with choices born of these values, gardens of emotional security, happiness, and virtue bloom around you. We'll have Taurus to thank for the protection they provide.

NATAL ASPECTS IN TAURUS

Ascendant in Taurus: Hey, beauty queen! With Venus as your chart ruler, you are serving all the angles and looks for us. When you walk into a room, you bring forth tranquility, dignity, and material/sensual beauty. Your first impression is often bearing a smile, a compassionate gaze, and the latest chic fragrance—you're magnetic. You help the zodiac see glamour, fashion, and cosmetology differently, in a way that inspires them to see it all as extensions of their self-expression.

Sun in Taurus: You're a fine artist of love. And love is the energy that operationalizes the universe. Using this power system of love, you can focus your intention and will in service to quality connections among people, especially through the art and design industries. You incarnated to help the zodiac understand the pleasures of commitment, closeness, and owning our passions without apology. You are loved as the high priest/priestess of happiness. Joy is an uncomfortable emotion for many to experience, but you can soften right into it, and you take your loved ones with you so they can share in its effects.

Moon in Taurus: Let's get cozy! Born while la luna toured through a constellation she has a special affinity for, your essential emotional nature is calm, stable, and looking for what can keep you there. You are loved because you show up with a generous spirit that wants to share joy. Your deepest psychic need is security. You want to receive the commitment you're willing to give. If shame hijacks your moon, try to avoid writing a conspiracy in your head. Embrace the vulnerability, and ask the right questions before you make up your mind about a situation causing you stress.

Mercury in Taurus: Does it work? Your technical mind is concerned with efficiency and practical application. A focused, methodical learner, when you're interested in something, you learn everything about it and put it right to the test. When it comes to verbal communication, you only speak on what you know. On listening, you can guide others by asking open-ended questions and mirroring back what you hear to show the speaker you paid attention. A careful thinker, you don't rush to the finish line or to conclusions impulsively. So give yourself permission to move slowly while you master your favorite topics.

Venus in Taurus: You're a hopeful, not hopeless, romantic. With a deep knowing of love given and received as a peak experience of life, you approach matters of romance with excitement. You'd be wise to move slowly while you discern who has earned and who can match your high-quality connection skills. You're looking for suitors whose values are a bit romantically classic—like old-school dating without the outdated norms. Flowers, gifts, courting, and openhearted excitement are meaningful to you. Along the way, your gifted ear, hand, and eye for art and design allow you to showcase your skills. Your creativity is served best while you try to capture the feelings of the collective and help them feel more seen.

Mars in Taurus: You're a lover, not a fighter. But when you see red, your red planet comes out. Before that happens, you're motivated to pursue sensual experiences that make you feel completely embodied. You also long to find your divine in the details, especially around the aesthetic industry, which feels like home to your soul. When the lights go out, your sexual desire is fueled by what feels comfortable, beautiful, passionate, and luxurious. You want sexuality to be an extension of the feelings you have. If your feelings are rage or anger, you won't be available for socialization. Take steps back, emotionally regulate though healthy strategies, and return when you've figured out which value was broken or which need wasn't met, so you can maintain your integrity.

Jupiter in Taurus: Go hug a tree. No, seriously! If you want higher wisdom, all you need is to be around the nature that birthed this archetype in order to receive the intelligence it's ready to give you. Or you can surround yourself with whatever feels glamorous, because your temple needs to be beautiful. With the peace of mind bestowed to you in these spaces, you'll get the best hits. When it comes to higher education, your experience should be hands on, and you'll want to enroll in a university that deeply supports its students not just with its faculty, but with advisers, assistants, and mentors. A specialist, you should find the right academic spaces that will get you started on your interests quickly so you have the time to really master your curiosities.

Saturn in Taurus: What do you value? Your lesson is centered on making sure your decisions reflect these core touchstones, like authenticity, creativity, and integrity. Your follow-through is already legendary, but your self-starting could use a bit of a push. Yes, it's scary and vulnerable to begin without a guarantee, but this lesson is pushing you to show up without it anyway. Just start before you're ready and edit the plan as you go along, because perfectionism does not deserve to corrode your success here.

Uranus in Taurus: Slow and steady changes the race. With Uranus in steadfast Taurus, you're happy to change what needs to be changed, but slowly and deliberately. Especially when it's applied to practical values, income, and security. With this placement, you'll usher in new changes with your logic, focus, and aesthetic skills.

House of Taurus Suns: Toller Cranston (Olympian), Jessica Clark (actress), John Waters (artist), Roy Halston (designer), Dame Ethel Smyth (activist), Jean-Paul Gaultier (designer), Anja Pärson (Olympian), Ma Rainey (musician), Russell T Davies (screenwriter), Garrison Starr (musician), Onir (filmmaker), Alice B. Toklas (activist), Romaine Brooks (artist), Lesley Gore (musician), William Inge (playwright), Sandra Toksvig (comedian), Keith Haring (artist), Angélica Lozano Correa (activist/politician), Tom of Finland (artist), Alan Bennett (author),

Valentino (designer), Robbie Rogers (athlete), Magnus Hirschfeld (activist), Liberace (musician), Adrienne Rich (writer), Howard Ashman (composer), Felicia Pearson (actress), Sam Smith (musician)

GEMINI—THE SPEAKER

May 22–June 21
Modality: Mutable
Element: Air
Ruling planet: Mercury

I f you want to see a trail of fire behind someone's sprint after they ask your sign, just say with a smile, "I'm a Gemini." Exceptionally misunderstood because of the hollow interpretations on the Internet, and stereotyped because its easy, the firstborn children of Mercury arouse intensely polar opposite reactions, much like the polarity of the mythological twins they embody, Castor and Pollux.

The zodiac's first air sign, the Gemini energy is textured with Mercurial mystery. Like the element air, you can't immediately hold, touch, or see the Gemini, but you can always hear them coming from the accelerated speed of your heartbeat. As a mutable sign, Gemini Suns were born while seasons were transitioning—a spring fully blossomed emerging into the summer solstice. So their essential nature is the middle point between two different forces. The Gemini introduces the great paradox into the collective lexicon, defined as a "statement or proposition that seems self-contradictory or absurd but in reality expresses a possible truth."[17] We've seen the Cardinal Aries initiating queer identity, the fixed Taurus embodying the values of queer identity, so now the queer Gemini must fly forward and adapt to whatever is necessary for the benefit of their self-actualization and the greater good.

Gemini introduces the value of "both/and" or "Not only but also..." to the zodiac. They're the first dissenters to the paradigm of either/or. It's always both/and. If anyone can wrap their head and hearts around this idea, it's queer people. Because we recognize its sincerity as a survival and success strategy.

Parented by planet Mercury, the winged messenger of communication and intellect, Gemini can lift their thoughts and language to the absolute highest levels. Just like the final destination of Mr. Mercury when he delivered messages to Zeus on Mount Olympus. Alternatively, high-minded Gemini can messenger consciousness and communication to the depths of discomfort, authenticity, and the unknown. After all, Mercury was the only divinity given the liberty to fly between the higher and lower worlds unharmed. So can all his Gemini children.

Without proper consideration, Gemini's level of curiosity and agility seems hard to pinpoint, thereby propelling

---

17   Dictionary.com, "paradox," http:// www.dictionary.com/browse/ paradox.

skeptics to project insincerity onto Gemini. This notion is false. Gemini is spiritually obligated to embody and teach divine detachment. Buddha taught that the second noble truth is "Attachment is the root of suffering." We often get ourselves into mental, spiritual, and emotional trouble when we're too attached to one result. Imagine the inner peace we could all feel if we had a balance of strategy and improvisation in our lives.[18] And so it is the Gemini function to stay unattached to rigidity and certainty, and to demonstrate radical self-transformation. So often we think we cannot change our circumstances, but not Gemini. With two twins battling for authority, the Gemini is always evolving because of this friction and contest.

When left too scattered, too detached and frantic, Gemini lacks consistency and integrity. Within the realm of too much possibility, Gemini neglects to stick around long enough to understand that there are some truths that are eternally true. Overeager, overstimulated—Gemini can overcommit. Their quicksilver brains are easily excited, so they answer "Yes!" instead of "I don't know. I'll tell you when I get there." So the Gemini must find the right values that help them locate the twins' tender spot between conflicting experiences—values that honor their need for mystery, excitement, trust, and reliability.

Gemini is the Speaker because, as descendants of the universe's messenger, the Gemini's premier function is to master the techniques of curiosity and communication. Like it or not, verbal communication is at the heart of

---

18   Buddha, Bodhi, and Ña n amoli, *The Middle Length Discourses of the Buddha: A Translation of the Majjhima Nika ya* (Oxford: Pali Text Soc., 2001), 888.

the most meaningful experiences in our lives. Everything worthwhile in the human experience is born from a request, agreement, boundary, or negotiation. So the Gemini is tasked to ask the right open-ended questions, reply from informed observations, find consistent patterns, and speak wisdom from all the intelligence they gathered. Within every Gemini is not only the brilliant orator, but the master listener. Gemini can listen from a place of understanding, not replying—which is what makes Gemini the master speaker. As I've said, the world changes when conversations change, and the Gemini has the pen, the microphone, and the audience hungry to hear their ideas.

NATAL ASPECTS IN GEMINI

Ascendant in Gemini: I have so many nicknames for Gemini rising because you're constantly reinventing yourself. Ruled by Mercury, you're speed racer, quicksilver, chatty Cathy, most talkative—you get the idea! Hungry for information and meaningful conversation, when you walk into a room, the air changes because your curiosities electrify it. This gives you a spirited first impression. Your Gemini ascendant helps the zodiac understand the power of self-expression and the glory of naming the parts of ourselves that demand to be understood.

Sun in Gemini: We've often defined *light* as "understanding," and the light of your Gemini Sun beams brightest when you're understanding complex ideas and communicating them in a way the masses can understand. Your intelligence and language skills are a gift to the zodiac—others are watching the way you think and speak because you're the master of both. You are loved because your cognition helps people feel seen, heard, and understood. As the twin, you can't help but mirror others back to themselves, which helps the people around you feel cherished.

Moon in Gemini: Whoever coined the term *emotional intelligence* was probably a Gemini moon. With the home of our emotions touring through eloquent Gemini, you can quickly name the emotion you're feeling. You are loved because you guide others to understand their emotional lexicon, and you help them feel less shame as soon as you say, "You're not alone." In order to feel psychically safe, you need people around you who are clear communicators and acute listeners, particularly while you discuss expectations, ideas, and plans. When uncomfortable, logic and reason become a defense mechanism, and you can be careless with your words. So give yourself permission to be emotionally exposed and sit with your vulnerability with an open heart until it passes.

Mercury in Gemini: An advantageous position, Mercury is right at home with Gemini. Your thinking, reading, analytical, writing, and language skills are supreme among the stars. You hardly struggle with finding the right words to say or write at opportune times. And you're teaching the zodiac how it's done. On listening, you'll want to make sure you can hold space for the talker long enough to help them feel understood. To honor this placement, you'll want to speak about speaking and learn about thinking. So many struggle with communication, but not you. So be proactive around spaces exploring dialogue and language to use this placement beautifully.

Venus in Gemini: Write a love letter. When the goddess of romance is in Gemini, you tend to love through beautiful language, intelligence, mental chemistry, and words of affirmation. Make sure you share how you feel about partners, not just what you think of them. You approach matters of the heart with your mind first. Shakespeare wrote that love does look with the mind and not the eyes, after all. Once you've found a suitor who can keep up with you intellectually, then they receive your heart. So you're looking for partners you can talk with, who are exiting to listen to because you're intellectually inspired by them. Once you find them, you're not afraid of commitment. So long as they honor your need for a bit of freedom, you're happy to get close.

Mars in Gemini: You don't need the sword to win wars. Just your pen. With fiery Mars in Gemini, you prefer to talk out your conflicts with others. A reactive planet and sign, you'll want to respond responsibly—rather than react—to harness the power of your pen. Look for common points of interest between you and your opponent first, then search for the win/win. Mars rules your sexuality, too, and this placement gets your blood flowing for partners who give you a run for your money. You run right for those who are intelligent, witty, a bit cheeky, and scandalous. It keeps your aggressor entertained and, so long as you're not bored (a hard task!), you're so happy.

Jupiter in Gemini: The zodiac's bookworm, you connect to the divine, to the higher wisdom, through literature. Your favorite "Aha!" moments were likely bestowed by the pages of a book. So your Jupiter ensures you don't need to learn the hard way. You can implement the wisdom from other people's writings or experiences and apply them to your life seamlessly. When it comes to choosing the best academic opportunities for you, look for universities that esteem the humanities, research, and campus community as part of their culture. You learn through discussion and other people, so a school that emphasizes both is your sanctuary.

Saturn in Gemini: Edit less, practice more. With Saturn in Gemini, you're striving for perfection when it comes to getting the words and social connections right. Try to rein in your investment on flawless analysis and language, and invest more in authentic communication born of consistent practice, which comes with inevitable mistakes. In so doing, do you posses the moral authority on communication because you're not working for what's unattainable, but for what's genuine. You'll use your words powerfully in service of helping others with the gravitas of Saturn!

Uranus in Gemini: What a whirlwind! With Uranus in ethereal and electric Gemini, you'll find your comfort while in flux. Boredom is the most painful torture chamber for your progressive, disruptive, quicksilver thinking. You'll implement new changes on a broad, big scale through your communication skills and in the communication arenas.

House of Gemini Suns: Tom Daley (Olympian), Anika Moa (musician), Kathleen Wynne (politician), Harvey Milk (activist/politician), Steven Morrissey (musician), Lea DeLaria (actress), Maya Marcel-Keyes (activist),

Greg Berlanti (director), Sir Ian McKellen (actor), Anette Trettebergstuen (politician), Alan Hollinghurst (novelist), Sally Ride (astronaut), Marijane Meaker (writer), Chris Colfer (actor), Laverne Cox (actress), Rupert Everett (actor), Melissa Etheridge (musician), Walt Whitman (poet), Brandi Carlile (musician), Zachary Quinto (actor), Wentworth Miller (actor), Josephine Baker (icon), Anderson Cooper (journalist), Alla Nazimova (actress), Federico García Lorca (writer), Suze Orman (host), Troye Sivan (musician), Sandra Bernhard (comedian), Harvey Fierstein (playwright), Parinya Charoenphol (athlete), Bülent Ersoy (musician), Dustin Lance Black (activist/ writer), Mario Silva (politician), Djuna Barnes (writer), Boy George (musician), Neil Patrick Harris (actor), Jenny Shimizu (actress), Phyllida Lloyd (director), E. Lynn Harris (author).

CANCER—THE MOON CHILD

June 22–July 21
Modality: Cardinal
Element: Water
Ruling luminary: The moon

As I've said: no sign has a monopoly on merit. But only Cancer can claim "belonging" as its home. Ask any social worker or theorist and they'll tell you human connection is an essential need. Belonging determines the quality of our life. So the experience under Cancer's roof is the single greatest determiner of our life's meaning. No sign has a monopoly on merit, but Cancer's function demands to be understood. Our lives depend on it.

While the sun transits Cancer in the Northern Hemisphere, the summer sunlight shines longer than the summer moon. Though the sun is the star of the season, the moon holds all the power for the first water sign in the zodiac. When we think about the moon's symbolism, we often consider our relationship to our emotions, home, motherhood, and family of origin. As sure as the moon will wax and wane, the Cancer's feelings are forever in flow while they search for home, family, safety, and belonging. Again, these concepts define the meaning of our lives. So given the preciousness of this search to understand "belonging," the universe gives its Cancers a protective shell to keep those who distract them from this purpose outside its boundaries, and to protect those who tend to it within.

This protective mechanism strengthens Cancer's inner world, which is powered by an emotional undercurrent illuminated by the most beautiful pearls of wisdom. Guided by the moon's feminine mystique, the Cancer's reflective instincts are to nurture and to protect their chosen and/or biological family, as well as their home. Protected by loved ones while in the safety of their home, the crab feels most comfortable to swim in the emotion ocean. Which is why Cancer's empathetic skills are legendary. Cancer initiates belonging, and the Cancer empathy mantra is "I feel this with you."

As the first water sign in the zodiac, Cancer energy initiates the experiences natural to the water elements, like our feelings, intuition, creativity, emotional bonds, and longing for home. It's important to note that whereas other signs share planetary parents, Cancer is the only sign mothered by the moon. Which is why the moon is the heart of our charts, and why Cancer leads with their heart. Of course they can wrap their heads around complex ideas, but it's the heart Cancer feels most comfortable wrapping around complex emotions.

What's particularly compelling for queer Cancer

energy is examining their divine mother and fiercely protective feminine archetype as instrumental for the liberation of identities. Without suffocating heteronormative values, Cancer energy is theoretically given the freedom to develop their divine emotional intelligence and use that wisdom to honor home, belonging, and family.

In our communities, the queer Cancer is the house mother. The most sacred authoritative figure in ballroom culture, and in our lives in general—what's holier than motherhood? Like the mother, Cancer loves to listen to your joys, your sorrows, and every emotion in between. Their quality of listening inspires profound loyalty, protection, and love from the family Cancer chooses as its own. When you think of what it means to be strong and powerful, all we need to do is look at mothers and their connection to their chosen families. The common characteristic of mammalian mothers when they sense a threat to their children or home is fierce, aggressive behavior. Nobody says, "Watch out for the papa bear!" It's the mother than inspires awe.

The blind spots that may create the most pain in Cancer's life are indirect communication and hypersensitivity. Yes, Cancer is blessed with seeming emotional telepathy drawn from their fluency in empathy. Cancer can feel the emotions of others without verbal language. It's entirely intuitive and a gift to sense the nature of others' hearts, but that's only a fraction of communication. So Cancer's life can greatly benefit from having the courage to (1) ask specifically for what they want, (2) be proactively vocal and clear about their expectations, and (3) succinctly vocalize their emotional reactions to circumstances that cause them victim-minded thoughts and behaviors. A few boundaries, a little full disclosure, will go a long way to protect them.

There's no higher art than living a good life, and there's no higher responsibility than the force of divine motherhood. For that, our hearts bow in gratitude for the Cancer energy that teaches us what it means to belong, and to create belonging in service of something greater than ourselves. Cancer energy is why "Welcome home" inspires a range of emotions when we hear it. Hopefully, it's a Cancer that flings the door open and greets you with what we all long to hear and feel within our hearts.

NATAL ASPECTS IN CANCER

Ascendant in Cancer: Moonlight shines from your heart. Ruled by this luminary, your first impression is magnetic, alluring, and felt deeply. When you walk into a room, people know there's a depth, a knowing, an enchanting quality that shines and resonates from your being. The same curiosity we have with the moon, people have with you—wondering both how and why you move around the world so differently. You teach the zodiac the answer, which is the power of following the path of your heart.

Sun in Cancer: Moon child, we salute you. Receiving the intuition, sensibilities, and magic of the moon, your heart is searching for emotional safety first and the people/places that feel just like home. You'll likely find these experiences when you give them away. Treat everyone like family and approach everywhere as home proactively in order for the universe to give you the people and places that provide emotional safety. You are loved because you make sure everyone around you is protected, tended to, and cared for. That's why mother is the highest archetype for queer folks, and if you follow the moon, embodying the value of the mother, the universe will lift you to divine places of peace and success.

Moon in Cancer: A happy homecoming, the moon loves to tour through its signsake.

Though it may feel like a curse, you are blessed to feel your feelings first and strongly. Your robust sensitivities make you a heart-centered soul who uses this intelligence in service of finding true belonging. You are loved because your empathy intuits what others need to feel safe and cherished before they do. Your deepest psychic need is security. Rightfully unwilling to accept carelessness, you need extensive consideration in order to release the beautiful waters of your heart to another. You'll want to develop practices of healthy emotional regulation and curiosity when in discomfort or shame, so you don't damage your connections through impulsive emotional offloading.

Mercury in Cancer: More than 90 percent of communication is nonverbal, and you're fluent in the energies, body language, and cues that comprise all of unspoken communication. A blend of heart and head, you can name your sensitivities and quickly locate them in another. A creative, intuitive thinker, you likely feel drawn to more artistic expressions that communicate the human experience. So balance your pursuit of the nonverbal, aesthetic communication styles with research into verbal communication. In so doing, you'll honor your heart and head blend by both sensing energies and finding the right words when you need them.

Venus in Cancer: Home is where the heart is for your Venus placement. Your romantic bids for connection are lighthearted but deeply meaningful, substantial bids for long-lasting romantic belonging. Move slowly when opening your heart, and ensure your partner has earned it, since you're looking for partners who feel like family and remind you of the best of home. The front door to your heart is opened through consistent compassion, safety, and sensitivity. In exchange, you'll gift powerful Cancerian loyalty, emotional support, and the security of intimacy to your partners.

Mars in Cancer: Your red-ruled sexual desires are expressions of how you feel about partners. Which is why, in your Mars placement, you'll need careful discernment before casual sexual activity. Without first discerning whether or not the dynamic is a container of trust and/or commitment, you're betraying yourself. When you have this trust, your sexual experiences are deeply meaningful, intimate, and healing for you and your partners. When it comes to conflict, you don't shy away from expressing which particular need is not being met. Emotionality will run high when you're enraged, so excuse yourself until cognition returns. When it does, calmly articulate which value was broken or need was unmet, declare a boundary with a generous assumption about your opponent, and engage them in a new possibility.

Jupiter in Cancer: Your wisdom is ancestral. With Jupiter in the sign of home and family, your divine understanding and spiritual practices need to be deeply rooted within cultural, ancestral traditions. Your heart soars at the notion that your ritual and spiritual practice is tied to the healers, the women in your family who allowed you to be you. When considering the right educational opportunities for you, make sure you visit the campus first and register whether or not it feels like a home away from home. Check the emotional pulse in the atmosphere and let your intuition tell you if it's safe. Focus on academic programs and topics that align with your values, because if you don't feel emotionally invested in it, you won't totally unlock your highest learning.

Saturn in Cancer: Is tough love helpful? For this sign placement, though it's uncomfortable, the answer is yes. Your lesson is overcoming emotional self-indulgence and hypersensitivity to achieve emotional mastery. You may cling to home, family, and mommy a bit too much, so you're avoiding any situations that can cause you discomfort. In doing so, you're not an emotional master but an emotional avoider. So tough love is a tough pill to swallow, but it's your way to achieving the lessons of this Saturn placement and taking your life back while you practice resilience, responsibility, and discipline.

Uranus in Cancer: You're an empath of divine order. With Uranus in emotionally intelligent Cancer, you feel the feelings of others, and that's how you'll know what needs to change. You'll strive for progress and equality because you can feel the majority of the collective's emotions. So you'll know the pain points and find solutions to those issues.

Pluto in Cancer: There's no place like home! The Pluto in Cancer generation (1914–39) transformed the relationships to family, home, and lineage. Your transformative power lies in how you reach to protect that which is important to you—from chosen family, to family of origin, to your homeland.

House of Cancer Suns: Meredith Baxter (actress), Lana Wachowski (director), Alan Turing (scientist), Larry Kramer (writer), Sean Hayes (actor), Sunil Babu Pant (politician), Sylvia Rivera (icon), Johnny Weir (Olympian), Orlando Cruz (athlete), Jean Cocteau (writer), Megan Rapinoe (athlete), Frida Kahlo (artist), Silvia Modig (politician), Kelly McGillis (activist), Angel Haze (musician), Alexandra Hedison (photographer), Marcel Proust (writer), Fiona Shaw (actress), Giorgio Armani (designer), Michelle Rodriguez (actress), Kyrsten Sinema (politician), Mary Emma Woolley (activist), Jane Lynch (actress), Olly Alexander (musician), Tony Kushner (activist), Lillian Faderman (historian), Rufus Wainwright (musician), and Emily Saliers (musician).

LEO—THE SUN GOD

July 23–August 22
Modality: Fixed
Element: Fire
Ruling luminary: The sun

I'd bet a million and a half dollars that the first-ever Miss Fire Island winner was probably a Leo. You see, these kings and queens can't help but live their lives like drag queen royalty. Leos beam with sunlight charisma and an irrefutable nature of ease and leadership. Ruled by the sun, the brightest and most centered point in our solar system, Leo lives like our galaxy's ruling star: absolutely larger than life. Leo, whether they like it or not, is constantly at the center of our attention. Often approached with a kind of timid, shy wonder, the bright Leo energy is felt as initially intimidating, but worth a close look. Just don't stare too directly.

Like the moon has sole ownership of Cancer, the sun

has sole jurisdiction over Leo. Just as the sun is a fixed force of fire, Leo is the zodiac's fixed fire sign. So the queer Leo can focus their eternal flame of life, giving force and enthusiasm to whatever project or person they have their powerful heart set on. When considering their fixed flame as a symbol for shame resilience, Leo represents worthiness. According to Dr. Brené Brown's research, the only qualifier that determines a life of courage, love, and belonging is the *belief* that one is worthy of courage, love, and belonging. When you see a high-minded Leo, you know you see a person who believes they are worthy of relationship success, happiness, and joy. It's an incredible cosmic gift to witness, because Leo is a possibility model for us all. How would our lives be different if we believed right now—without qualifying circumstances like income or professional accolades—that we are already worthy of all of what gives our life the most meaning? Ask a Leo.

In astrological conversations, Leo is most frequently expressed through their association with celebrity status and regality. Understandably so. Star quality is captivating, sure, but it's ultimately meaningless glitz and glamour. What often gets overlooked is this Leo's tremendous capability for love and meaningful connection because they deemed themselves worthy.

No matter how hard they try to deny it—though they often won't—the Leo is the zodiac's consummate romantic. Longing for a love story, they will surrender to their heart's every wish if romantic love is on the horizon. The brightest star in the Leo's constellation is the lion's heart—named Regulus—and a Leo's heart is the star that divinely guides them to magical experiences of romance and meaning in life.

But even royalty has their blind spots. For the Leo energy, they inevitably focus on the self because they've been allowed to their whole life. They wonder: *How can this benefit me? How can this person help me? What do I have to gain from this?* Leos have no issue talking, seizing, and behaving first, without a thorough analysis of how the consequences could affect others.

The most redeemed Leo energy shares their cosmic spotlight, which is why they are the sun god. Remember, flame doesn't lose its value when it is shared. Like Marianne Williamson said, "As we let our own light shine, we unconsciously give others permission to do the same. As we are liberated from our own fear, our presence automatically liberates others."[19] Self-love improves us all. Brave and wild Leo energy can ignite the flame of self love in many people . . . but only if they step off the throne, empower others, and invite someone else to sit on the red velvet hot seat every once in a while. Queer Leo energy *is* life force in some spaces. So many queer icons are these high-powered, high-energy, strong, charismatic, and courageous characters. That's Leo's kingdom. Leo lives a life of such tremendous romance and glamour, you can't help but understand how being larger than life is truly the right size. Born with the universe's crown on their head, worthiness shines so deeply from their heart. When a Leo dares greatly, shows up to the runway of life both ready and willing to be seen, they inspire us to set ourselves free from fear. Leo's light shines away the darkness of

---

19 Marianne Williamson, *A Return to Love: Reflections on the Principles of a Course in Miracles* (New York, HarperOne, 2012) 190-91.

our crisis of confidence, insecurity, and fears. When they claim their worthiness of a courageous, creative life, they will take the zodiac with them to the kingdom of the wholehearted.

NATAL ASPECTS IN LEO

Ascendant in Leo: Did it just get brighter in here, or did a Leo ascendant walk into the room? Radiating from the sun as the ruler of the chart, when you—a Leo rising— walk into the room, the crowd stops, looks, and listens. Beaming with charisma and radiance, Leo on the ascendant gives you significant attention. You help the zodiac by using this social popularity well, speaking with depth, and contributing service from your royal platform.

Sun in Leo: In the peak of summer, you were born. While the sun blazes through the royal constellation, you celebrate another year on your throne. Follow the sun as a north star and learn how to incorporate its life-giving power, radiance, and glory into your heart. You are loved because you already believe you're worthy of love in your heart. And your life has no choice but to organize itself around your convictions on confidence, romance, and personal success. Your courage annihilates worldly barriers, and you leave the road bit more paved, inclusive, and inviting to those who follow your lead.

Moon in Leo: You live and love loudly. When la luna tours in Leo, your emotions burn with the heat of a thousand suns. And so your hopes, wishes, and dreams are lifted to the highest levels. You are loved because you radiate joy, drama, and a magnificent sense of humor to those who love you. With Leo as the ruler of your feels, you protect your right to feel whatever you want unapologetically. And you'll fight any battle to make sure others are allowed to honor their emotions. Your deepest psychic needs are affirmation and loyalty. You're no dumb-dumb—you know what contributions you can make in another's life. So you appreciate when they know it, too. And you appreciate when they're willing to prove a sense of loyalty so big, they'll show up for you with happiness each and every time.

Mercury in Leo: Courage comes from the Latin root *cor*, translated into "heart," and when Mercury tours in Leo, it means the brave act of telling the story of your whole heart. Your Mercury sign gives you the bravery, so write and speak the story of your whole heart. You learn the most effectively when entertained and emotionally invested in the material. With a flair for storytelling, you touch listeners and audiences with enthralling anecdotes. You appreciate straight talk, and you do proactively disclose what is and what is not okay with your royal majesty. Given the power of your spoken word, spare no affirmation when someone is stuck in shame. Your generous kindness could change a life with one word.

Venus in Leo: Every monarch needs another. So your heart is always looking for the corresponding sovereign you'd like to rule your kingdom with. Openhearted, brave, and direct, your bids for romantic connection are displays of romantic grandeur that would make the best love story plot feel a bit flat. Make sure the recipient works to be confident, secure, and worthy. Otherwise they won't be able to contain all the love you want to give. Your ideal match is another king or queen equal in power, dignity, and authority. Otherwise you'll trample all over them, and secretly you want someone to challenge you. Where else would the drama come from?

Mars in Leo: Roar, baby, roar! Mars loves to burn in a fire sign, and when it burns in Leo, you have a head start on your practices with conflict and sexual desire. So long as you keep your confidence firmly protected, you'll be less likely to attack another's insensitive remark like a lion attacks its helpless prey. If someone scratches the crown, just remember: lions don't lose sleep over opinions of sheep. If you're still angry, have a cleanup conversation quickly. You're motivated by your dreams and your fearless courage. You want to make a big mark on the world, and with this Mars sign, you're likely to do it. When you're a cat in heat, you love a sensual, adventurous, sometimes romantic, sometimes carnal experience. So long as your heart's all in, whether it's recreational, meaningful, or both, you'll be thrilled in the castle boudoir.

Jupiter in Leo: Any spiritual path is a path of the heart. With Jupiter in heart-centered Leo, you're looking for a spiritual path that helps you understand what unique gifts and abilities are burning within. You want to "know thyself" so you can give your best self to others. Metaphysical and/or spiritual systems that provide dynamic self-awareness are a requirement for you. When choosing which academic curriculum is a royal fit, give your attention to schools that have a bustling arts and design program and/or that encourage cross-disciplinary studies between the arts, humanities, sciences, etc. You love finding the treasures within each department so you can transfer and apply them to your favorite areas of academic and personal interest.

Saturn in Leo: Heavy is the head that wears the crown. Your Saturn lesson is to understand the labor and sacrifice required to hold positions of charismatic authority. You were born with an innate emotional fullness, worthiness, and a proximity to advantageous circumstances. The universe wants to make sure you're not just using these aspects to serve your own needs as you define them, but rather, you're expanding inclusion and opportunity for everyone not born in castle walls. If you try to do this in the creative, artistic, and design worlds, your efforts will be lifted to the highest, while you learn to keep your heavy head high and the crown even higher.

Uranus in Leo: Make love, not war! Revolutionary Uranus in heart-centered Leo gives you a personality that protects the freedom to think, feel, and follow your passions so long as they harm no one. You'll usher in changes in the fields of entertainment, media, and the arts by owning your individuality and telling the stories of your heart.

Pluto in Leo: Your inner child's calling! The Pluto in Leo generation (1937–58) transformed the creative, entertainment, and pleasure industries by holding on to their childlike wonder and enchantment. Your transformative power is found in how you retain your confidence, courage, and individuality.

House of Leo Suns: Anna Paquin (actress), Christine
Quinn (politician), Nikki Sinclaire (politician), Judy
Grahn (poet), Paul Taylor (choreographer), Sean Maloney
(politician), Barbara Gittings (activist), Yves Sant Laurent
(designer), James Baldwin (author), Sapphire (artist),
Carole Pope (musician), Gladys Bentley (musician),
Radclyffe Hall (writer), Herb Ritts (photographer), Andrea
Gibson (poet), and Miguel Vale de Almeida (activist).

VIRGO—THE MAIDEN

August 23–September 22
Element: Earth
Modality: Mutable
Ruling planet: Mercury

Did you wake up #flawless, Virgo? Just like this? Yes, you did. Just like your house mother, Beyoncé. Don't take our word for it. We're not biased—we're just stating the facts. You're in the same solar family as Queen Bey and the cofounder of queer liberation, Marsha P. Johnson.

The second earth sign in the zodiac, Virgo Suns were born between summer and fall, which matches their second earth position. Within each Virgo is a paradox, delicately managed, between structure and detachment, consistency and spontaneity. As such, their orientation is both carefully organized and comfortable with uncertainty. Intuitively, Virgo knows when it's time to put their most efficient foot forward and when to fall in surrender to life's mysteries.

The second planet ruled by messenger Mercury, the Virgo soul leaps in joy while it honors attention to detail, literature, verbal communication practices, and the written arts. Some of the most beautiful expressions of Virgo come from the intersection they nurture between communication and the physical body. Whoever was the first wise voice to say, "Just listen to your body" was probably a Virgo. When they're elevated, they make sensational experts on personal growth, health, wellness, nutrition, and physical fitness, because their inner senses can hear the messages of the body. Of course, they're happy to give what they own, and so Virgo helps others find their specific internal guidance system.

The Virgo mythology is more nuanced than just the maiden. I'll explore the maiden next, but first let's consider seeing Virgo's mythology as connected to the themes of the season they are born under. The Virgo archetype is the goddess of the harvest or the great earth mother. In this way, Virgo is of service while they allocate resources carefully to make sure everyone gets equal share throughout the winter.

The great earth mother as Virgo expresses herself in the children of Virgo through this service-oriented love language. Their gifts shine when they're applying Mercury's intelligence to problem solve for others. So if you're lucky enough to have Virgo allies in your corner, cherish their impeccability, intelligence, and dependability. When they say they're going to show up for you—they mean it.

Which is why you'll find Virgos in activism, social justice, and community organizing—they can't rest unless they're helping others. When they do, their minds focus on where the personal, societal, or structural inadequacies are and quickly find the solutions for them. Virgo's focus is a lesson for us all. Find the problem and identify with the healing.

Latin for *Virgo* doesn't strictly mean "virgin" (or "sexually untouched"), as the symbol of the maiden suggests. It could be argued it means "self-contained," and therefore free from unnecessary external influence. So Virgo is not easily influenced or triggered because of their earthy self-containment. But if you want to force them to smile, all you need to do is show up for them with the same reliability they do for you. Try to say what you mean and mean what you say when talking with a Virgo. Ruled by messenger Mercury, their minds need clear communication. And express meaningful gratitude when they come to your rescue. It will send their heart a-flutter and guarantee they'll do it again.

As with all of us, our gifts can be double-edged. Virgo children must be careful not to enable others. Their worth is not born of putting the needs of everyone else before their own, nor of fixing everyone's problems. Sometimes all a friend needs is a listening ear and empathy, not an immediate problem-solving strategy. With their lightning-fast mind, Virgo would also be wise to get a grip on shame's impulse of inflicting emotional self-mutilation. Perfectionism is unhealthy, dysfunctional, and not conducive to a life of meaning. It's shame masquerading as ambition. And it tells Virgo the lie that if they act perfectly, they're immune to criticism. This is patently false, so the sooner Virgo stands on the value of authenticity, rather than overaccommodation and perfectionism, the more likely they'll achieve their highest goals for good.

What Virgo can teach us about shame resilience is that it's a daily, consistent practice. At their best, Virgo goes out of their way to put in the effort to make their life work. Virgo confronts us all with the question *what daily practices can I commit to in order to ensure I'm operating at my best?* They hold themselves to a high but not unreachable standard when it comes to personal and relational success. Their commitment to these practices speaks well of them. Virgo teaches us the value of consistent, thoughtful, and intelligent choices that help us increase shame resilience, cultivate authenticity, and find the right foundation for meaningful connection.

NATAL ASPECTS IN VIRGO

Ascendant in Virgo: Don't hide your beautiful eyes behind those glasses. The first trait people notice about you are your eyes while they scan the room, looking for patterns and searching for answers in the mundane. Ruled by quicksilver Mercury, your mind's agility, your one-liners, and your analytical prowess are second to none. You teach the zodiac the value of finding the divine in the details, where you'll provide clarity on what you observed and give us all a laugh with your rich sense of humor.

Sun in Virgo: The action that centralizes the universe's power is service. We see this organizing energy in nature, in all the ways the various parts of the ecosystem are in service to the collective survival. The universe is always in service to life rising to its maximum possibility. Your ruling star and the universe are one and the same. When you follow your psychological imperative to help and serve others, you and your efforts will be a triumph. Your power lies in your curiosity, practical intelligence, and sense of responsibility. You are loved because you're a keen thinker, an intelligent speaker, and a careful listener. The greatest gift you can give to someone is awareness, and your mental strength helps others feel validated.

Moon in Virgo: The typical element for the moon is water, and Virgo is an earth sign. So the power of your emotions is more contained and is slowly revealed as trust is carefully earned. You are loved because it's not all about you, but how you can use your emotional and intellectual strength to help others. Your deepest psychic need is reliability. You have a wellspring of energy to give, but you can't give it until or unless you find reliability in the words and actions of others. Be careful not to lean on hyperfunctioning or enabling behavior for those who refuse to help themselves. See yourself as an empowerer, not an enabler. When shame washes over you, use your critical awareness and ask yourself what you really know for sure. Chances are, there's little evidence to support that shame. Then speak to a trusted friend to share your story and heal from it.

Mercury in Virgo: Hey, valedictorian! Mercury loves bookworming with Virgo. Your thinking, speaking, and listening styles are textured by excellent intelligence, rationality, and practicality. This foundation is so helpful in the communication, personal-growth, and technically focused industries, which your mind is best served to contribute to. Slow to feel total mastery of topics, you're a methodical learner, not an overnight expert. You can use your language well by discussing strategies and solutions for more righteous living. When you offer suggestions, people listen. So speak to that listening with topics around self-care, self-love, and personal development.

Venus in Virgo: You don't profess your love. You practice it. Sure, you might say "I love you" when you're called to, but you prefer to practice love in action and duty to your partner. Your Venus sign shows your love through acts of service and presence of mind. Given your more intellectual, behavioral expressions of romance, you need a partner who will inspire a deeper emotional inquiry into romance, but match you on verbal communication. Since your demonstration of love is centered on improving, you'll want to make sure you also take the time to identify what your partner does well already and vocalize gratitude for it.

Mars in Virgo: You're a superhero. With the red planet touring through Virgo, you were born with the capacity for extreme multitasking and efficiency. In matters of conflict, you may arrive late to the party. Since you're often in motion and in service, you may not register when a boundary was broken or when you're avoiding the conflict altogether. Practice your tolerance level with discomfort by practicing conflict resolution with situations you consider unjust. You're happy to take your follow-through to the bedroom, where you love to give pleasure. You're happy to initiate it and you're just as happy to receive it. You can intuit your partner's preferences and make it happen.

Jupiter in Virgo: Transcendentalists believed in the accord of nature and how nature's harmony lives within us. So does your Jupiter sign! You find your higher wisdom when paying attention to the self-organizing and self-correcting forces present in nature. And since you are one with it, so can you find a spiritual path that helps you invoke nature's power in your life experiences. When it comes to choosing the right educational opportunities, choosing an environmentally conscious campus surrounded by natural beauty would be wise. A small campus focused on professor/student dynamics will give you the collaborative dynamic you crave.

Saturn in Virgo: You're the new Pandora. With this Saturn lesson, your goal is to find hope, possibility, and optimism in the face of chaos, randomness, and despair. When you harness this power effectively, you will implement a kind of purity, a light in dark spaces, where it's needed the most. Since you can find solutions so quickly in the face of disaster, your moral authority is called to engage with despair so you can transform it. Set aside perfectionism and people pleasing in the pursuit of being a vision of hope that can help us find transcendent living in the worldly circumstances of suffering.

Uranus in Virgo: Do we live to work or work to live? Uranus in Virgo asks this question. With the change-maker planet in the dutiful sign, you'll usher in social changes in the labor, technology, and health industries. This placement gives you the ability to examine how society improves work/wellness and how work/wellness can improve societal norms.

Pluto in Virgo: Make the subconscious conscious. This Pluto in Virgo generation (1956–72) transformed the conscious mind through psychological insight and analysis of shame. Your transformative power extends itself through practical, logical, and insightful steps around all types of healing.

House of Virgo Suns: Stephen Fry (comedian), Marsha P. Johnson (icon), Leonard Bernstein (musician), Tom Ford (designer), Meshell Ndegeocello (musician), Jeanette Winterson (author), Jeffrey Buttle (Olympian), Leslie Feinberg (activist), Lily Tomlin (actress), Freddie Mercury (musician), Jane Addams (activist), Sylvester (musician), Michael Feinstein (musician), Paul Iacono (actor), Valerie Taylor (writer), Evan Rachel Wood (actress), Paul Goodman (writer), Alison Bechdel (artist), Leslie Cheung (entertainer), Claudette Colbert (actress), Pier Vittorio Tondelli (artist), Ann Bannon (writer), Greta Garbo (actress), Tegan Quin (musician), Sara Quin (musician), Riyad Vinci Wadia (filmmaker), Anne Burrell (chef) and Fannie Flagg (actress).

LIBRA—THE JUSTICE

September 23–October 22
Modality: Cardinal
Element: Air
Ruling planet: Venus

The section ruled by Libra in the chart is the west-ernmost hemisphere on Earth. So it's where the sun sets. Libra is a cardinal sign, so it does hold a theme of initiation, but the sunset's symbolism of an ending is still accurate. The moment the sun enters Libra is the moment when personal development in isolation ends and trans-formation through relationship experiences begins.

Libra invites us to experience love and mutuality with one another. Which makes astrological sense, when looking at Libra's symbol of the balanced scales, symbol-izing equality. The sun in Libra marks the halfway point in the astrological calendar, beginning on the autumn equinox, which is the astronomical moment of equal daylight and nighttime. The theoretical idea is that signs from Aries to Virgo help the zodiac understand action, values, mindfulness, emotionality, worthiness, and service on the personal level. Then Libra teaches us how to love another.

When we meet Libra, their Venus-ruled elegance, charm, and grace disarm even the most defended among us. Without our armor, we understand love. Libra shows us we don't need armor whenever they are with us, since they truly come in peace and ask the same of us in return. Arriving in kindness, Libra uses the mirror belonging to their ruling divinity—which is the symbol for the planet Venus and the icon for the feminist movement—to accurately reflect the most noble, beautiful qualities in others. Libra demonstrates the first step in falling in love—the realization that we are seen by our potential partner.

In addition to romantic love, Libra energy is deeply focused on making sure everyone feels seen and invited to have a seat at the table. Since Libras effortlessly facilitate inclusion, connection, and conversation with such ease, you would have no idea they're concealing an inner anxiety that urges them to focus on justice.

If you look at the state of the world, we could all use a bit more of that Libra love. Libra Sun John Lennon wrote "All You Need Is Love" for a reason. Libras intuitively understand the importance of kindness and amnesty for wholehearted connection to flourish. When left undisciplined, an off-balance Libra uses relationships as an opportunity to avoid themselves. Their biggest nightmare is being alone, because their astrological responsibility is making sure they're connected. So some tools to strengthen their relational gifts are intensive alone time and effective boundary declaring to better ascertain who has earned their love and why.

Aesthetically inclined, Libra can express itself intelligently and beautifully in queer identities. Without heteronormative conditioning, queer Libras can express Venus's magnetic energy as artists, relationship coaches, designers, and healers. Their lives can demonstrate multidimensional approaches to not only the aesthetic industries, but to social advocacy and relationship theory in a range of mediums, like literature, music, film, and other forms. Through their connection to these spaces, they uplift their environments to their divine right order, and the world falls in love with them.

The contemporary research into romantic desire and longing aligns beautifully with the Libran archetype, first articulated over three thousand years ago. There are many ways we can understand just what the Libran balance is actually balancing, and if you ask a Libra, they'll say "It's me and we" with a smile.

This aligns with the principle of desire as a paradox of closeness and autonomy, as explored by Esther Perel. Libra can manage this paradox well and, when complemented with a queer nature, Libra doesn't have to abide by typical notions of monogamy, ownership, desire, or any other oppressive relationship structure that doesn't let this nuance speak for itself. Libra both knows and demonstrates that value of "me and we," of predictability and excitement, of mystery and certainty, etc. Libra gives us the skills to manage this anomaly with—you guessed it—balance.

There's a popular impulse in culture that encourages extensive inner exploration and personal success before we can show up to romantic relationships. Libra won't enroll in this. These descendants of the goddess of love know that there is no coming into conscious contact with our individual self except through romantic involvement and relationships. What basis do we have for self-love if we don't know how to love others? Balance being the operative outcome, of course, between me and we. Libra teaches us that romance, love, and partnership hardly sabotage our personal success, but instead fortify it. And when we know we love, we know ourselves.

NATAL ASPECTS IN LIBRA

Ascendant in Libra: Hey, glamazon! Your aura is enchanting, inviting, and lovely. Regardless of what your insecurities tell you, you're immediately adored by those who see you. When you walk into a room, people can sense your thoughtfulness and sincerity. You have a beautiful interest in others, and when you listen to them, you find yourself standing in front of a mirror. Which is why people love you—you help them feel like they're not alone in their struggle.

Sun in Libra: Born after the autumn equinox, the sun is teaching you to initiate new structures and practices on aesthetics and relationships. An artist of the senses and of love, you shine when you're creating something beautiful in the material and romantic dimensions. You are loved because you love to love. You express the power that exists between two people when they feel deeply connected. And if love casts out fear and shame, your function is needed desperately in the world today.

Moon in Libra: Beauty is internal, and so your internal moon shines with virtue. When the moon tours through Libra, your emotionality is defined by the quality of your relationship connections. So your deepest psychic need is harmony. You long for environments and relationships that are mutually supportive and where the rule is love and kindness, not the exception. And you are loved because you are so generous with your affirmations and support for others. Shame will try to convince you to please people and abandon yourself in favor of the needs of others. But balance is still the goal here. So make sure you're balancing your need for harmony and authenticity with your desire to reach out to others, so you don't end up accommodating others at the expense of your integrity.

Mercury in Libra: You're an artist. So if you wanted the validation—now you have it. When Mercury flies through Libra, the messenger divinity gives you the creative and artistic sensibilities that allow you to engage with art and design in a significant way. You'll feel more comfortable expressing your thoughts through aesthetic and creative mediums, and you'll learn a great deal through these modes of education. Use your gifts in service of exploring love in the human experience to have your work uplifted to public arenas.

Venus in Libra: Honey, I'm home! Since Venus naturally rules Libra, this placement blesses you with profound romantic techniques and the capacity to soften into love, vulnerability, and creativity with ease. Your ideal match is a partner who strives for love as much as you do. They'll hopefully keep you a bit grounded while you soften their edges, because you have a soft spot for the tough ones. You bid for connection in subtle, sincere, and romantic ways that remind us of the value of meaningful courtship.

Mars in Libra: World peace, please? With the planet of war burning in the sign of peace, you are ambitious for a world that ends all wars. You're focused on creating a culture where diplomacy, harmony, and design can revolutionize civilization. When it comes to conflict transformation on the personal level, you'll want to be up front about declaring when you're uncomfortable, why, and what you'll need to feel more safe in particular spaces. On the erotic level, your sexual desire is deeply romantic, sensual, and lovely. You'll want a partner who can pursue you with adoring directness and make love to you when they catch you.

Jupiter in Libra: Your divine is always in the design. You connect to a higher power though artistic, creative, and design mediums. After all, what is art but a divine visitation from the muses? Your peak spiritual experience is, of course, the giving and receiving of love. Do so with a spiritual strategy over a worldly one. When it's time for higher education, find curricula that treasure activism and social justice, and do so in decidedly creative ways—with a focus on community organizing and relationship building—to get the most out of your academic adventures.

Saturn in Libra: So often we say "serious relationship," but are we really thoughtful about it? Your Saturn lesson demands serious thought prior to relationship commitment. With this placement, you'll want to approach connection and relationships with serious consideration, since your ideal partnership is enduring, empowering, and founded on high-quality loyalty. That takes time to determine, and this Saturn placement gives you the psychological skills to discern the difference between casual and meaningful. Use it well, and your relationships will flourish.

Uranus in Libra: Till death do us part, or until love dies? Uranus in Libra helps you know. With the freedom-passionate planet in the relational sign, this placement helps you know when the relationship harms freedom. And when too much distance harms the relationship. You'll usher in changes in relationship structures, norms, and expectations with this intuitive knowing.

Neptune in Libra: Divine design! With Neptune in beautiful Libra, this is a generation who finds their spirituality in beauty, design, aesthetics, and relationships. You'll impact conversations on spirituality by exploring relationships and art as a spiritual practice. With this placement, you can't access the divine but through beauty and romantic partners.

Pluto in Libra: The Pluto in Libra generation (1971–83) transformed the state of committed relationships through the destruction of outdated norms. Your transformational agency manifests when you identify and destroy whatever isn't in balance, mutuality, or justice.

House of Libra Suns: Manvendra Singh Gohil (Indian prince), Sir William Dobell (artist), Pedro Almodóvar (director), Carrie Brownstein (musician), Annie Leibovitz (photographer), Jóhanna Sigurðardóttir (politician),

Kristanna Loken (actress), Wade MacLauchlan (politi-
cian), Jerome Robbins (director), Matt Bomer (actor),
Eleanor Roosevelt (politician), Isaac Mizrahi (designer),
Ben Whishaw (actor), Michel Foucault (philosopher),
Jenna Talackova (activist), Oscar Wilde (author), Mont-
gomery Clift (actor), Mark Gatiss (actor), Laura Nyro
(musician), Uzi Even (politician), Brittney Griner (athlete),
Martina Navratilova (athlete), George Nader (actor),
Robert Reed (actor), Dale Jennings (activist), Andrew
Scott (actor), Brian Boitano (Olympian), Saffron Burrows
(actress).

SCORPIO—THE FINAL WORD

October 23–November 21
Modality: Fixed
Element: Water
Ruling planets: Pluto and Mars

Wouldn't we all love to lock ourselves into the dungeons of the zodiac's most sexual sign? But let's not sell Scorpios short now by relegating their analysis primarily to what goes on in their chamber of secrets. There are more critical layers to the eighth sign of the zodiac than their notorious sexual stamina and intensity.

Scorpio is irrefutably one of the most misunderstood and maligned signs in the zodiac. Everything their archetype lays claim to is what dominant social conditioning seeks to subvert, like unabashed authenticity, esoteric wisdom, sex positivity, brave confrontation, and even the idea of death.

The universe in its perfect architecture allows Scorpio

to be coruled by Mars and Pluto, through which Scorpio receives the warrior spirit necessary to destroy the illusions unfairly pushed against them. As the only fixed water sign in our zodiac, they harness the water element's powerful emotional strength and its ability to cleanse or destroy. So Scorpio can usher in its blessings or wrath wherever it deems necessary. When high-minded Scorpio energy has a true grip on the pulse of truth, they know immediately whether someone is living with or without integrity and can predict how situations will unfold, since there are certain metaphysical truths that are not confined to modernity's social codes, but are in relationship to the ages.

I've read Scorpios likened to "the final word," and I think that's an accurate description to describe such an enigmatic astrological energy. I imagine Scorpio as the universe's gatekeepers. Scorpio offers admission to those lucky souls who can move forward to the next signs, stories, and experiences of the zodiac and allows incredible transformation and self-actualization to those walking through the gate. If their final word deems you worthy to enter, consider Scorpio an ally to you now on your evolution.

Upon entering, Scorpio will celebrate and defend you on your mission forward. This gift they give to you is the same gift Scorpio always gives to themselves. Scorpio energy is often articulated as the mythological phoenix, regularly rising from the ashes of self-destruction and beginning again. So if you were met with thumbs-down, don't take it personally. Just do the personal growth work. Begin to understand what Scorpio stands for: self-transformation, overcoming shame, truth, and esoteric wisdom.

When Scorpio energy is unredeemed, the gifts of Mars and Pluto can become dangerous weapons against them and those they claim to love. Scorpio's focused consciousness can actively seek evidence of guilt and betrayal, sometimes at the expense of rational reason. They can live in the imagined wreckage of the future and, as Scorpio Sun Dr. Brené Brown says, "dress rehearse tragedy."[20] They'll wield swords of manipulation and unchecked emotional violence because it helps them numb themselves while they emotionally offload. Look at their title animal's defense mechanisms for context. When we think of a scorpion, we know they inflict serious damage. So could a wounded Scorpio who hasn't learned mechanisms of trust, resilience, empathy, or connection. Scorpio magic can be conjured in queer identities so powerfully because they are prolific truth tellers and status-quo disrupters. Scorpio is also astrologically hardwired to question the intersection of sex, sexuality, and gender, which is one of the most valuable ideas for the spiritually seeking queer person to grasp.

Most of the conditioning that keeps queer people living in dishonesty is the question of, "But what will people think?" That's not Scorpio's modus operandi. They are bound to tell the truth, whether viewers or listeners like it or not. Since the truth is often uncomfortable and nuanced, simplistic thinkers would rather criticize or dismiss the Scorpio truth teller, rather than wrestle their heads and hearts around the issue.

---

20 SuperSoul Sunday, "Dr. Brené Brown on Joy: It's Terrifying," Oprah Winfrey Network, March 17, 2013, https://www.youtube.com/watch?v=RKV0BWSPfOw.

Scorpio earning its sexual badges of honor is no accident either. But I think Scorpio is the most intimate, not the most sexual. Most everyone loves sex. What Scorpio does differently is continue the paradox of desire introduced by Libra and develop it into intimacy. Or, as Esther Perel says, "into-me-see."[21] Scorpio energy wants the most accurate insight into their partners. Scorpio craves the good, the true, the beautiful, the shame, the anger—if it belongs to their beloved, they want it.

When considering deepening our practices with intimacy, we have to examine our comfort levels with our personal experiences of joy and pain. Some of us are more comfortable with one than the other. Scorpio can hold space for both. This is another reason why Scorpio is considered so honest—because life is both heartbreaking and joyful. When it comes to intimacy, Scorpio joins with their partners to tend to both. From there, transformation begins. We are reborn when we are fully accepted and embraced by another. Scorpio is the arms. You are new again.

NATAL ASPECTS IN SCORPIO

Ascendant in Scorpio: Hardly subtle or delicate, the energy you walk into a room with is rightfully intense. With Mars and Pluto ruling your identity, you don't concern yourself with the comfort level of a crowd or party. Your magnetism and strength is felt immediately because authenticity is your bottom line, and when that value is in someone's

---

21   Mindvalley Talks, "How to Find the Sweet Spot between Love and Desire," Esther Perel, October 2, 2017, https://www.youtube.com/watch?v=ierRipP-7JA.

resonance, it announces itself. You show the zodiac the importance of forthright self-expression as an example of self-love and relationship health.

Sun in Scorpio: Born in the dead of autumn, the sun is your star to follow for ideas on intimacy, transformation, realness, and the mystical arts. You're fascinated by the unseen world that may be inspiring the seen world. You are loved because your loyalty, commitment, and comfort with the realities of life make you seen as an emotional bodyguard. You're easily trusted, confided in, and relied upon to help others navigate meaningful experiences.

Moon in Scorpio: When the moon tours through Scorpio, your heart is motivated to understand the most meaningful, powerful, and strong emotional waters that nourish us all. You can handle high and low ranges with ease, both personally and with others. You are loved because you bear witness to pain with empathy, and you generously affirm with honesty. Your sincerity takes your connections to a new depth of trust. Your shame triggers around betrayal and dishonesty are justified, but you will need to learn the mechanisms of trust. It will help you uplift the quality of your relationship connections.

Mercury in Scorpio: Hey, Sherlock! With the planet of thinking and speaking in the sign of truth, you're a natural detective and walking polygraph test. Your perception and communication skills are highly intuitional and emotionally charged, which can both protect and complicate you. Work on developing verbal skills that complement your hunches, instincts, and raw responses. As a learner, you are fascinated by hidden truths, the occult, and/or psychology.

Venus in Scorpio: Till death do us part! With the love goddess in Scorpio's lair, you want to forge romantic connections with permanence, meaning, and quality. If you're romantically invested, people can just feel it. It's in your resonance. So don't bother trying to hide it. Soften into vulnerability by allowing your emotions to be seen and heard with potential partners. It'll be scary and messy, but such is life's work. Make sure you find reliability, virtue, and consistency in your partner first, before you open up, and then you can pour your love into this container with trust.

Mars in Scorpio: The French call the orgasm "the little death," which is the nature of your Mars sign. Your sexual desires are powerful, life giving, and drawn to transform you and your partners through intimacy given and received. This power needs the right platform, so discern, discern, discern. Look for partners who use sexual experiences as continued communication for their feelings so you can let your Mars burn. On the battlefield, you are an unyielding opponent and highly strategic about winning. Err less toward ruthlessness and more toward finding the win/win deal. If anyone can find the place where you and your opponent are both trying to get the same need met (which is often at the bottom line of conflicts), it's you.

Jupiter in Scorpio: You're not here for the manicured, polished woo-woo. Your higher wisdom sign is looking for a theology or spiritual source material that helps you engage with grief, heartbreak, and suffering and transform them into recovery, healing, and peace. When you're interested in the academic words, try to find schools that have curricula that advance conversations around sex, gender, and sexuality. This is a focal point where you're called to serve, so you need a space that helps you contribute meaningfully.

Saturn in Scorpio: When wild buffalo see a storm, they run through it. They know they can't outrun it. This is your Saturn lesson. Experiences of pain, discomfort, and risk cannot be outrun. They need to be engaged with, so you must develop the discipline and values that allow you to engage with difficulty from a place of worthiness, which helps you transform the storm. On the other side, you'll be more resilient, merciful, and tender, with an open heart instead of the pain from a closed one.

Uranus in Scorpio: Know thyself! Intelligent Uranus in subconscious Scorpio gives you a placement that treasures the discovery of the personal unknown through mental and sexual health. This placement also gives you a very healthy skepticism of traditional sex and intimacy practices. Along with psychology, you'll steward in changes in the sexuality and identity arenas.

Neptune in Scorpio: New Age, Now Age? With Neptune in occult Scorpio, this is a generational marker that brings the hidden, the mystical, and the mysterious to the arts and to meaningful spiritual conversations. You'll impact dialogue on spirituality by ensuring the talks and practices are deep, authentic, and transformative.

Pluto in Scorpio: The Pluto in Scorpio generation (1983–95) were born into the AIDS crisis, and thus they will transform the societal views of sexuality, death, the occult, and transformation. Your transformational power is harnessed through a deep inquiry into the deepest truths.

House of Scorpio Suns: Jean Acker (actress), Chely Wright (musician), Glen Murray (politician), Caitlyn Jenner (public speaker), Frank Ocean (musician), Michelle Brooke-Marciniak (athlete), Ann-Marie MacDonald (writer), Timothy Findley (writer), Natalie Clifford Barney (writer), Sophie B. Hawkins (musician), Tom Waddell (athlete), k.d. lang (musician), Luchino Visconti (director), Darren Young (athlete), Robert Mapplethorpe (photographer), Michael Cunningham (writer) Agnès Maltais (politician), Marie Dressler (comedian), Phyllis Lyon (activist), Heather Matarazzo (actress), Roland Barthes (philosopher), Adolf Brand (activist), Louise Brooks (actress), Wendy Carlos (musician), Aaron Copland (musician), Jamie Babbit (director), Glenn Burke (athlete), Rock Hudson (actor), RuPaul (Unknown), Christian Siriano (designer), Jodie Foster (actress), Robert Wagner (actor), Timothy Conigrave (activist), Grace Darmond (actress), Noel Mewton-Wood (musician), Cherry Jones (actress), Benjamin Britten (musician), Billie Jean King (athlete), and André Gide (writer)

SAGITTARIUS—STATE OF GRACE

November 22–December 21
Modality: Mutable
Element: Fire
Ruling planet: Jupiter

When the sun enters Sagittarius, the night begins earlier, but the light remains. Which is why light is a central theme of late November and December, with lights adorning homes, trees, and menorahs. The zodiac's accelerated heartbeats tell them that celebrations are coming and that a Sagittarius just walked in the door.

Ruled by Zeus, the highest sovereign of Mount Olympus, Sagittarius-born souls are immense. Just like the size of their ruling planet, Jupiter, Sagittarius does everything in enormous proportions. The only thing subtle about their personality is the light in their eye. Blessed with Jupiter's proactive optimism and a contagiously happy-go-lucky orientation that moves even the most critical of skeptics, Sagittarius energy leaves every room, conversation, and heart a bit brighter than how they found it.

Sagittarius's symbol, the centaur, is a bow and arrow–wielding mythological creature that's half horse and half human. As a mutable sign, Sagittarius is two identities in one. So Sagittarius can wander, explore, adventure, and discover while leaning on their animalistic nature, but still maintain the critical thinking and full spectrum of emotions available to humans. Sagittarius introduces the idea of an archetype that goes beyond petty worldly competition and scarcity, in favor of the spiritual reality of sacred collaboration and abundance, which occurs when we combine our animalistic and human natures to discover what's available for us all in the wilderness.

Born between fall and winter, Sagittarius is mutable fire—a generously available life-force element that they hold within their minds and in the array of spaces they are called to. You see, "The more, the merrier" is not just a fun quote to them; it's their very foundational philosophy. And remember, since their personalities are essentially immense, Sagittarius has enough room for the extravagance of circumstances, friends, romantic partners, and careers that come their way.

Their highest function is the mutable grace with which Sagittarius shares their social power generously. What's so awe inspiring about Sagittarius is how they are hardwired for hope, which produces social popularity. Think about it—who *wouldn't* want to be around people who assume the best out of life, assume the best out of you, and then give you the context to be your best self? All things big, remember—Sagittarius vision can see the big picture.

Aware of the universality of life and what humanity has in common, Sagittarius can communicate and demonstrate a wisdom to their community that inspires and uplifts countless people.

When left to wander too far, Sagittarius can overlook the small details, little things, microtasks, etc. When this goes too far, Sagittarius can find themselves feeling unfulfilled in areas like friendships, relationships, work, and even location, because they weren't paying close attention to the small moments that can define the meaning of their experiences. When Sagittarius can see how the little things create the big things, they're light-years ahead. So Sagittarius would be wise to slow down and rein it in every once in a while. Doing so will allow them to learn how to check in with their inner voice—the one that pays attention to the small details—and compare it to their external reality. This will help them see if their experiences match with their highest good.

The queer experience is textured powerfully in Sagittarius. With their affinity for activism, education, expansion, travel, and community building, queer Sagittarius is resourceful in expanding conversations on sexuality, gender identity, and relationship theory to be more inclusive. Higher education is Sagittarius's domain, and the clarity, resources, and dialogue that higher education spaces can theoretically provide to queer students looking for guidance can be life defining. Sagittarius's popularity, and the inevitable controversy they ignite through their truth telling, can contextualize ideas never before considered. And they take these conversations in the high-minded direction that their arrows, hearts, and eyes are always fixated on—toward the stars.

The last fire sign, Sagittarius represents the highest embodiment of the fire element in the zodiac. So what's the highest function of the fire element in Sagittarius? Remember, one of the cornerstones of spiritual seeking is radical inclusivity. So, in the queer community, the highest function of Sagittarius is the wisdom that we are not alone because we are a continuation of the stories of our queer ancestors, collaborators in the stories we write with our contemporaries, and creators of the narratives of our descendants.

In every story, in every experience, in every direction of time—this is eternally true. This is the fire of Sagittarius. Humans began as storytellers, and so we stay. Surrounding the mutable fire in the center of our camp, we tell the story of our journey, and we can hear our hearts in the stories of others. The energy of connection comes alive when we listen carefully to the lived experiences of others, and our belonging is found when we tell our own stories in these spaces. Sagittarius is the voice that says, "It's your turn now." And they invite us to tell our truth in spaces where we matter, where we are cherished, where we belong in the wilderness.

NATAL ASPECTS IN SAGITTARIUS

Ascendant in Sagittarius: Your energy practically kicks the door down for you before you even walk into a room. Direct, bold, and blazing with the heat of Sagittarius, your first impression is magnanimous. You meet others with laughter, a smile, and every other openhearted emotion in between. You teach the zodiac how to de-escalate social anxiety, because you lead with kindness and generous assumptions.

Sun in Sagittarius: Born while fall transitioned into winter, the sun shines for Sagittarius's multidimensionality and the treasure of knowledge found between two seemingly separate aspects of their personality: the centaur's half human and half horse natures. You never have to exclusively commit to one or the other—you make peace with the competing forces of human and animal within your centaur soul. You're loved because you're so free. Your liberation, courage, and kindness are contagious. You inspire the zodiac to find our freedom and our joy in the unknown.

Moon in Sagittarius: When the ruler of home travels through the sign of the wanderer, your heart is a traveler, looking for the people, places, and feelings that feel like an adventure. You're not looking to stay put too long, because you're hit by wanderlust and curiosity often. You are loved because you are relentlessly searching for joy and innocence. Your heart space becomes a space of possibility, because you live from a vision of what's possible, and not from your immediate circumstances. Shame will get you in a headlock if you feel unworthy to express disappointment, heartbreak, or pain, as if you always need to happy, happy, joy, joy. You just need to be authentic. The people closest to you can handle your pain and your happiness.

Mercury in Sagittarius: You're a visionary! When the messenger divinity tours through the centaur sign, you are always imagining new possibilities, realities, and paradigms that benefit the world. You need to be intellectually stimulated and enriched by strong verbal communicators.

Probably fluent in more than one language, and always ready to jet-set, your mind, passport, and communication skills are searching for that which lies beyond. Balance this curiosity with a focus on honoring the present moment so you don't miss important details.

Venus in Sagittarius: If you love someone, keep them free. When Venus rides on the Sagittarius horseback, you are a lover who loves to be free. You bid for connection with your dynamically mental interest in your partners, showing sincere enthusiasm to know about your partners' interior world. Once you feel like the lover won't tame you but will run wild with you, you're all in. You're a passionate, adventurous, exciting, and thoughtful partner who loves to create other worlds with your lover. Balance this exciting energy with the stabilizing force of security, reliability, and consistency to make this Venus placement soar.

Mars in Sagittarius: Mars loves to burn bright through a fire sign, and when the warrior god is blazing through Sagittarius, your ambitions are international, educational, and resourceful. You're motivated to learn what exists far beyond your comfort zone, and this Mars placement gives you the gumption to explore just that. On the level of conflict, your temper may flare, but you can be reached through dialogue and reason—and you're not one to hold a grudge. This is a transformative Mars placement that can help anger turn into compromise easily. In the bedroom, you're hungry for adventure, spontaneity, and passion. You want to imagine sexuality as place with no final frontier, because it is. Keep the imagination running wild, and you'll be happy again and again.

Jupiter in Sagittarius: Can you handle the truth? Yes! Jupiter rules Sagittarius, so with this favorable placement, you can handle the most rigorously honest spiritual wisdoms, giving you the tools to help you find deeper meaning. Your spiritual study would benefit from accessing the stories of Christ, Moses, Muhammad, Lahkshmi, Buddha, etc., more deeply because you see them as coded messages for righteous living. When it's time for higher education, keep it high. Your dream school should feel disruptive, visionary, controversial, and expansive. You want a college that sees ideas as contests, and may the best academic win!

Saturn in Sagittarius: Belief is meaningless. You're after the experience. Your Saturn lesson is about effectively applying beliefs to your experiences and seeing if they hold up as true for you. No more armchair philosopher, quoting from a book and proselytizing. You need to learn first, preach nothing, apply beliefs to your life, and watch what happens. To teach is to demonstrate. And you're running toward the lived experience, informed by righteous living.

Uranus in Sagittarius: Can you handle the truth? Brilliant Uranus in philosophical, religious, and academic Sagittarius gives you a placement where you're hungry to find the diamond of truth. You'll sharply question outdated norms of religion and intelligence in order to find the new alternatives that are more applicable to the times in which we live.

Neptune in Sagittarius: Hey, expat! With Neptune in worldly Sagittarius, this is a generation that wants to remove boundaries between countries and campuses.

You'll impact spiritual practices and conversations through exploring the universal themes in all the wisdoms, theologies, and myths of the world.

Pluto in Sagittarius: Bon voyage! The Pluto in Sagittarius generation (1995–2008) will transform how we internationally connect in order to make the world a more collaborative space. Your transformational power is found through higher education, travel, and publishing your authentic messages.

House of Sagittarius Suns: Robin Roberts (journalist), Rosa von Praunheim (activist/filmmaker), Tammy Lynn Michaels (actress), Jani Toivola (politician), Rita Mae Brown (writer), Matthew Shepard (icon), Gianni Versace (designer), Jason Collins (athlete), Cornell Woolrich (writer), Margaret Cho (comedian), Tom Hulce (actor), Willa Cather (writer), Brendan Burke (athlete), Norman Douglas (writer), Elvira Kurt (comedian), Emily Dickinson (poet), Tommy Kirk (actor), Raven-Symoné (actress), Mark Takano (politician), Brandon Teena (icon), Anton Hysén (athlete), Jobriath (musician), Amini Fonua (Olympian), Noël Coward (writer), Kanako Otsuji (politician), Paul Cadmus (artist), Sarah Paulson (actress), Christina, queen of Sweden (monarch), Brian Orser (Olympian), Jean Genet (writer), Elsie de Wolfe (socialite), and Michael Tilson Thomas (musician).

CAPRICORN—THE CAPTAIN

December 22–January 20
Modality: Cardinal
Element: Earth
Ruling planet: Saturn

As easy as it is to identify Saturn by its iconic rings, you can easily identify every Capricorn by the focus and deep contemplation that circles their eyes. If you seek the thoughts and ideas buried deep beneath their serious demeanor, you will have to soften into the practice of patience, for the gifts and virtues of Capricorn are earned slowly over seemingly mundane moments that are anything but.

Is it any wonder that the Capricorn, as our cardinal earth sign, would initiate their element earth slowly? Like the Earth itself, Capricorn is slow and steady. Capricorn is chronological, calculating, decisive, systematic, and seemingly immobile. Ruled by Saturn, the mythological ruler of time, discipline, integrity, boundaries, and commit-ment, Capricorn energy is governed by the most intimi-dating planetary deity and ideas. Given their intuitive understanding of timing, Capricorn energy is disciplined, militaristic, and restrained. They are the beginning and the end. Which is why they are born in the solar season that encompasses both the last and first day of the year.

Even at the youngest of ages, Capricorns have wisdom. They already understand the importance of tradition, honoring family, revering home and ancestors, and staying in service to their descendants. Far from emotion-ally impulsive, Capricorn energy is personally stable, observing the last thing standing—the truth.

Their calm orientation is often misunderstood as being cold, but when functioning at their highest, Capricorn exhibits emotional mastery. Remember, their patholog-ical animal—the seagoat—was the only fantastical being who could climb the top of the earth's highest mountain. The mountain is a symbol for the pinnacle of worldly success. On the ascent, the seagoat is only working with two climbing features, since its other half is a fish's tail. That tail also allows Capricorn to swim to the bottom of the ocean's depths and understand emotion, sensitivity, empathy, and even intuition. Though the seagoat is a mountain climber above all else, the fusion of goat and fish is representative of emotional mastery, which is the key to mastering worldly success.

That caliber of emotional impulse control is a gift to Capricorns, even though it sends the hypersensitive around them into spasms. But the truth is the last thing standing, and Capricorns don't ignore it. If neglectful of their duty to swim to the ocean floor and understand the emotional current that washes over us all, Capricorn energy will be brash, tactless, ruthless, harsh, unforgiving, withholding, and violently critical. But when they feel like they have accomplished what Lord Saturn is demanding of his children, a Capricorn will prove a steadfast and loyal ally to those who have earned it the good old-fashioned way: through classic manners, respect, kindness, and generosity.

At first glance, you might see Capricorn energy and consider it at odds with queer culture. But you could liken the connection between Capricorn energy and queer identities to the way winter stars light up the night sky. Rightfully, queer theory generally subverts heteronormative conditioning, extensively calling relationship models and gender norms into question. Capricorn energy, with Saturn's rings around their hearts and minds, asks us to consider, "But what *has* worked in the past? What is the function of structure, tradition, family, and home in queer lives?" Capricorns can reinvent the wheel and give traditions a contemporary relevance in beautiful ways.

In the current culture, we are experiencing a rapid growth in freedom and individualism. Theoretically, we can explore personal options, professional opportunities, and potential relationships like never before in history. We have freedom, but do we belong? This is what high-minded Capricorn can help us understand: that when it comes to personal success, of course the pursuit of happiness and liberty is important, but so is responsibility to others. Capricorn teachings are unpopular because the culture of today is self-indulgent and does not honor the wisdom that freedom and responsibility are both required. That's the contemplation buried deep within Capricorn—

how they can use their emotional mastery to build ideas, organizations, and structures that impact the world in a way that alleviates unnecessary human suffering. Next time you see one, ask, "How can I help?"

NATAL ASPECTS IN CAPRICORN

Ascendant in Capricorn: Ice queen? No way. You're just not easily won over with taskmaster Saturn as your chart ruler. When you walk into a room, people can feel you're in a position of moral authority. They know you take life seriously, so they approach you with respect while you walk with dignity. You teach the zodiac the value of emotional regulation, resilience, and maturity, whether they like it or not.

Sun in Capricorn: Born in the season of the winter solstice, your north star is asking you to incorporate structure as a tool to enable freedom and reminding you of the necessity of integrity in pursuing a higher path and career. You are loved because you're a counselor, a coach, and an empowerer of the highest level. You take on the responsibility of finding the potential in others, and you hold space for that potential to manifest.

Moon in Capricorn: When the warm and cozy moon aligns with her opposite archetype, you are an emotional fortress. Extremely slow to reveal yourself, heavily emotionally controlled, and grounded, you have gravitas. You are loved because you take emotional bonds extremely seriously and you're always ready to prove through acts of service how deeply you care. You'll be hijacked by shame when feelings around work, effort, and vulnerability strike. Remember, people want to see your sensitive side, and if you're discerning, you'll only reveal it to those who have earned it and won't use it against you.

Mercury in Capricorn: Let's talk facts and figures. When the planet of consciousness and communication flies through Capricorn, your technical mind is deeply focused on logistical, certain, and practical outcomes. If it doesn't work or make sense, get lost. When speaking, you make sure every word has a place. When listening, you're engaged to understand—not reply. You're a thoughtful and inspiring student around systems, techniques, and design.

Venus in Capricorn: Can we keep it old-school? This Venus sign, even in queer relationships, likes their dynamic a bit old-fashioned, classic, clean, and romantic. You bid for connection to potential partners who show you their responsibility, nobility, ethics, and success. You know that when you align with a partner, you take on their story. So you're careful about what coauthor you're writing this love story with. Try to incorporate a bit more romance and less contract negotiation so you can show your tender and practical side.

Mars in Capricorn: This is the commander in chief. Mars is focused, disciplined, and strategic in Capricorn. A gifted leader, you have ambitions that are long-term, prestigious, highly thought out, and likely to succeed with your winnable determination. When it comes to conflict transformation, you have exceptionally high standards. It's likely that you have conflicts with people who don't live up to the potential you've identified in them. So try to be patient and understanding and to meet people where they're at. When it comes to the erotic, you approach sexuality and intimacy very seriously—in the best way. You aim to please, to receive, and to make the exchange a deeply embodied experience in which both of you feel better than ever because you've earned the gift of each other's company.

Jupiter in Capricorn: Since *discipline* and *disciple* have the same root word, what are you a disciple of? This Jupiter placement prefers studying a disciplined spiritual source material that they can learn from every single day. Think transcendental meditation or a thoughtful spiritual path that promotes righteous living. In academic spaces, you prefer models of education that are tried and true. You'll love a college/university that fosters mentorship, because you appreciate learning from your elders, given your respect for the hierarchy.

Saturn in Capricorn: Your lessons are harder, but you're a bit more prepared with this Saturn placement because Saturn rules Capricorn. Your relationship to accountability, integrity, radical responsibility, and service are strengthened through a committed study. Your lesson is to see yourself as worthy of being an authority figure when you've proven yourself managing your own life well. Once you have that foundation of total alignment, you'll receive the validation you need to know that you are an authority on authority.

Uranus in Capricorn: Is freedom found in structure? With liberating Uranus in foundation-loving Capricorn, this placement helps you completely dismantle structures that oppress and build new ones that offer freedom for all. You'll impact changes in the government and other spaces where hierarchy reigns, building new, more progressive systems where equality organizes us all.

Neptune in Capricorn: If it ain't real, it's no deal. With Neptune in hardworking Capricorn, this is a generation that wants practical and ambitious application of spirituality. You'll change spiritual conversations and practices by encouraging the study of a discipline that really works in all areas of life.

Pluto in Capricorn: Structure's decaying! The Pluto in Capricorn generation (2008–2024) will transform the structures in capitalism, hierarchies, and government. Your transformative powers are achieved through considering how power structures affect the collective, and you'll be tasked with finding the solutions where structure gives us freedom.

House of Capricorn Suns: Brenda Howard (activist), Quentin Crisp (writer), Ismail Merchant (director), David Sedaris (writer), Marlene Dietrich (actress), Guido Westerwelle (politician), Elsa Gidlow (photographer), Katherine Moennig (actress), Lilly Wachowski (director), Jennifer Higdon (musician), Orry-Kelly (designer), E. M. Forster (writer), James Hormel (activist), Joe Orton (writer), Martine Rothblatt (author), William Haines (actor), M. Carey Thomas (activist), Dot Jones (actress), Michael Stipe (musician), Kate McKinnon (comedian), Nancy Ruth (politician), Gábor Szetey (politician), Christian

Louboutin (designer), Chester Kallman (writer), Michael Sam (athlete), Jack Andraka (scientist), Winnaretta Singer (socialite), Sal Mineo (actor), Patsy Kelly (actress), Kieron Richardson (actor), Edmund White (author), Nate Silver (writer), Holland Taylor (actress), Cary Grant (actor), Maulik Pancholy (actor), Patricia Highsmith (writer), Janis Joplin (musician), Cristóbal Balenciaga (designer).

AQUARIUS—THE GENIUS

January 20–February 18
Modality: Fixed
Element: Air
Ruling planet: Uranus

In the deepest corner of the coldest months, when the winter puts the world to sleep, the Aquarius born inhales their first breath. Is air only focused in breath? How does one hold and concentrate an element that is essentially everywhere, within, without, but impossible to grip? Ask an Aquarius. That's why they are the genius. The cornerstone of their fixed air personality structure is conviction. They are known as the greatest force multipliers. Utterly convinced (focused and fixed) of certain truths (air), the Aquarius energy elevates their brilliant thinking beyond mere personal opinion, to the convictions that are the handwriting of the universe.

Shallow astrology consumers assume Aquarius is a

water sign. "But they're the water bearers!" they cry. No, no. The water that Aquarius bears is not literally H_2O; the water is symbolic, not literal, and it represents the convictions that high-minded Aquarius cleanses the collective with. It cleans away the sins of the past and invites us all to (re-)cognize and remember the truth that social justice for all is the only way to move the world forward.

Spiritual convictions can be misused when they're applied only to personal issues, like romantic love or manifesting money. Aquarius energy seeks to remind us that unless we're advancing the collective, with access and equality for every single one of us, then we're not truly a part of the solution. Who cares if you're in a blissed-out relationship or living in abundance when people are suffering? Aquarius Angela Davis said, "We have to talk about liberating minds as well as liberating society." What do we all have in common? Thinking minds. How can we liberate society? Liberating minds. Changing the world is so much bigger than the all-about-me and all-about-mine conversations, and we can count on Aquarius energy to help us focus and find the path that includes the greater good for us all.

When left to wander too far in their own brains, Aquarius energy errs on the fanatical, the dogmatic, and the resolute. If lost in their sensitivity, Aquarius energy takes someone disagreeing with them as the capital crime. Fixed energy is focused and tenacious at best, but absolutely unyielding at worst. So for the Aquarius among us, it's important to ask, "Would you prefer to be right or would you prefer to be happy?" Aquarius energy is meant to liberate, not incarcerate. So it's important for their convictions to make room for nuance, uncertainty, and the vulnerabilities inherent in progressive thinking.

Aquarius energy is expressed very usefully and rather iconically through queer identities. Think about it— Aquarius born are not here to follow the rules set forth by Capricorn. Uranus ruled (har-har, laugh now), they are here to purposefully disrupt the dominant thinking of the status quo. And you'll see their influence in the list of public figures at the end of this chapter, who have changed mainstream culture because they had the courage to honor their convictions. These days, you can find brilliant Aquarius minds inviting radical conversations to expansive platforms like never before. So Aquarius gives access to all of us by not following the rules—rules that tend to give special, privileged treatment to the elite.

Since convictions are not inherently righteous, the task for Aquarius is finding the ones that can help us all. I've noticed that the greatest thinkers in higher consciousness and social justice are all pointing to the theme of shared humanity as the world's solution for the crisis we are currently in. With magnificent fixed air, Aquarius energy can find the place that all of humanity has in common. This requires deep thinking, contemplation, and research—three favorite pastimes for our last air sign.

In Jungian circles, the symbol of the collective unconscious essentially states that if we look deeply enough in the brains of every single human, we will find the same images, needs, desires, fears, and loves. If I could recommend a conviction to the queer Aquarius, it's that they use their brilliance to search for the collective unconscious and harness the energy that unites every single person alive, to cultivate their skills for shared humanity.

We are each other. And if Aquariuses let this conviction come alive in their minds and hearts, they can help usher in a world that is far less tolerant of warfare, injustice, and unnecessary human suffering. It would take a genius to reorder civilization around humanitarian values over economic ones. It would take a genius, and within the mind of every Aquarius is a genius ready to get to work.

NATAL ASPECTS IN AQUARIUS

Ascendant in Aquarius: You never meet a stranger! Because your ruling planet, Uranus, helps you connect to others quickly, they'll subconsciously feel an immediate sense of comfort, ease, and curiosity in your demeanor. With the sign that rules friendship on your ascendant, you are motivated to create meaningful, platonic bonds. So you approach everyone with the golden rule, treating others as you would want to be treated. This is what you teach the zodiac—the irrefutable belief that everyone is worthy of connection and kindness.

Sun in Aquarius: Born in the winter, you're not impressed by shiny, glittery, meaningless stimuli. Your thinking was born in harsh conditions, so you find the sunlight by searching for and speaking on topics with nuance, justice, intelligence, and depth. You can harness your power by giving yourself radical permission to be a rebel with a cause. You don't easily enroll in popular culture paradigms. Instead, you shine while you foster community, activism, and equality. You are loved because you make respect a routine habit of human interaction, and you embody the best of the beloved community.

Moon in Aquarius: What does it mean to truly belong, water bearer? When the home of belonging shines behind the Aquarius constellation, you're given an advanced education on connection, emotional safety, and belonging. In order to truly belong to others, you have to develop the capacity to stand alone. When you belong to yourself first, you can then find your tribe—those who never ask you to abandon self-belonging. Your deepest psychic need is liberation. You are loved because you accept others fundamentally and liberally, without condition. They feel it, and they love you for your radical acceptance. Shame will rear its ugly head when it tries to make you think you're too weird, too fringe to ever fit in. But you're not here to fit in. You incarnated to lead us to the wilderness where we all belong.

Mercury in Aquarius: Hey, mad scientist! When the quicksilver planet flies with the eccentric air sign, your thinking, speaking, and learning skills are anything but normal. An avant-garde brain and mouth were given to you so you can experiment with outdated norms and educational paradigms. So you can find resources that serve us all for the current moment in which we live. Use your consciousness to reveal what tools and practices don't benefit everyone, destroy them, and start again. Your mind searches for resources that inspire mental freedom and unbridled access for all.

Venus in Aquarius: Can we just be friends? No, really! Your love needs are deeply platonic. You bid for connection with the rare ones who embody the best of friendship and romance. Culture swears that's how the best relationships start! And you'll know. Search for suitors who talk to you like a friend but make you feel like a lover. Your ideal connection can honor both—they'll make your romances more friendly and your friendships more romantic. Find a partner with ethics, strong sensitivities, and a bit of grounding to keep your focus tethered to earth just a bit.

Mars in Aquarius: Make love, not war. You want nothing to do with impulsive, reactive conflict. You're much more inclined to engage with personal disagreement from a space of calm. The only broken boundary that sets you off into rage is a crime against humanity. Which speaks well of you. So get to the protest, call your politicians, and expand awareness! In erotic spaces, you're the initiator of the distance necessary to make your suitors feel like they haven't quite figured you out. There's still discovery left to be done, which keeps the spark, chemistry, and desire burning hot.

Jupiter in Aquarius: Look east. Aquarians shouldn't have too much in common, but if one pattern emerges, it's their fascination with eastern spiritual philosophies, largely inspired by Buddhism. Your spiritual path believes in unlearning the thought system of the world in order to reintroduce a more high-minded set of principles that honor the essential Buddha nature within. On learning, you'd be best served to enroll in a school that inspires disruptive, progressive, radical spaces of experimentation, utilizing technology as a problem solver. You're bored with tradition and legacy, much happier in academic spaces that can see toward the future.

Saturn in Aquarius: The nature of the collaboration determines the result. You'll learn this through experience while Saturn helps you find your tribe. This placement helps you develop the tools for community organizing and activism. You'll want to do this through all Aquarian-ruled forms, especially technology and social justice, and learn how to connect to others far and wide. This assignment helps you build a platform where others can pool their resources together and make the world more peaceful, tender, and equal for all.

Uranus in Aquarius: The electronic elsewhere! This is a natural affinity, since Uranus rules Aquarius, so this placement helps you revolutionize technology, the Internet, community, and the digital worlds that bind us. You're like the zodiac's premier mad scientist, and when you take daring chances, you'll see the rewards of your experiments everywhere. It's alive!

Neptune in Aquarius: Worldwide…magic? With Neptune in tech-savvy Aquarius, this generation learned spirituality on the Internet. This will impact the way you think, speak, and practice your divinities, because of the rate at which you consume information. You'll change the practice by ensuring our spiritual and creative abilities are used in service to social justice and equality.

Pluto in Aquarius: To infinity and beyond! The Pluto in Aquarius generation (2024–2044) will transform technology, the way we connect through technology, and space travel/research. Your transformative powers are achieved through evaluating technology as a problem solver. You'll be tasked with exploring cutting-edge frontiers through electronics and outer space.

House of Aquarius Suns: Lord Byron (poet), Elaine Noble (politician), Aya Kamikawa (politician), W. Somerset Maugham (writer), Virginia Woolf (writer), Ellen Degeneres (comedian), Eric Radford (Olympian), Colette (novelist), Gia Carangi (model), Sara Gilbert (actress), Tallulah Bankhead (actress), Portia de Rossi (actress), Patricia Velásquez (actress), Gertrude Stein (author), Helen Stephens (Olympian), Ramon Novarro (actor), Anne, queen of Great Britain (monarch), James Dean (actor), Ari-Pekka Liukkonen (Olympian), Amy Lowell (poet), Tammy Baldwin (politician), Patricia Field (designer), George Smitherman (politician), John Schlesinger (director), Peter Karlsson (athlete), Audre Lorde (activist), Jillian Michaels (trainer), Beth Ditto (musician), and F. O. Matthiessen (writer).

PISCES—THE GRAND FINALE

February 19–March 20
Modality: Mutable
Element: Water
Ruling planet: Neptune

Life as we know it began in a big bang. The entire universe emerged in an inferno. In our end, all that ever was, all that was ever born in the big bang, will return to the ocean, where time fades into eternity. On the sea floor, we will find Pisces welcoming us home. Descendants of Neptune—the ruler of the sea—the gentle Pisces heart beats passionately for the expression of creativity, fantasy, emotional intelligence, spiritual wisdom, and universal compassion.

With a wisdom in their eyes that whispers to us that they've been here many times before, Pisces energy is here to raise the collective consciousness with the highest quality of compassion. Embracing their role as the last function, the last sign of the zodiac, Pisces helps us look up and raise our hearts. Whatever you do, don't confuse their tenderness with timidness. There are two fish in every Pisces, and while one is more popularly known as the gentle one, the other Pisces fish can be a shark. They will sneak up on the opponents of love and compassion and take them out.

As the last sign in the zodiac, Pisces is the embodiment of mutable water. Born between sharply contrasting seasons, winter and spring, the Pisces soul holds two opposing fish swimming ferociously in opposite directions. One fish symbolizes the theme of completion and is bound by a divine cord to its twin fish, which symbolizes the promise of a new beginning. Considering Pisces as a sign deeply tethered to universal spiritual themes, you could see the commonality of themes like crucifixion/resurrection, enslavement/deliverance, and numbness/nirvana as all stemming from one primary theme: death/birth. Pisces *is* the water that releases and renews us. Pisces is the great existential ending and the beginning.

With this inherent gift comes enormous responsibility. Pisces's attunement to humanity, the healing arts, empathy, creative expression, and compassion present Pisces with exceptional opportunities. High-minded Pisces energy stands for the miracle, resurrection, deliverance, and nirvana. Given their strong connection to the divine and the abyss, their consciousness can receive higher thoughts, and if they are brave enough to speak them (which isn't always their responsibility, because it's a nonverbal sign), Pisces energy creates alternative paradigms of being free from fear.

With this prolific sense of feeling, Pisces energy will

need to recede from the earthly shores of material, economic, and meaningless consumptions and go within to dwell in the waters they call home. If they don't take the time to understand this alignment, the cord between the two fish—mythologically understood as the cord connecting lovers—then their consciousness will fall victim to martyrdom. Without a sense of integrity-driven personal growth, their resilience is low, their words sloppy, and their coping mechanisms dependent on self-annihilation.

Since Pisces is the only mutable water sign, it holds a gorgeous expression within queer voices and their relationship to the arts, otherness, and the sense that there's no need for attachment to prescribed rules of heteronormativity and gender. Since Pisces is the culmination of all identities, their highest actualization is the demonstration of how fluid identity, sexual orientation, and gender actually are. For many reasons, the aesthetic and theater industries have provided sanctuary for queer identities, and Neptune, the father of Pisces, is the divine father of those spaces. Pisces gifts shine in the liberated expressions of music, literature, design, and visual culture. The world is a kinder, gentler place in their honor, and my heart sings a sweeter song in their presence. The world and I are grateful.

When we're left unattached from the rigidity of body identification, the gender binary, and all the other oppressive structures that we grow up learning, we begin to reimagine self-perception from body to spirit. That's what an astrological education is: the training to see yourself not as a body, but as a spiritual being. Pisces begins this shift in self-perception. When we are soulfully, spiritually identified, we begin to know our essential nature is love. We are innocent souls learning how to give and receive love. Pisces is here to teach us that only this love matters. This is the truth, but life complicates it. Pisces knows only love is real. The practice of unconditional love given and received is the highest activity for us to experience. Pisces helps us walk on Earth but think the thoughts of the divine, so that we might make a little bit of heaven on earth.

NATAL ASPECTS IN PISCES

Ascendant in Pisces: You walk this world, but you're not of it. With the supremely otherworldly planet Neptune ruling your physical self, you exude an energy of mysticism and grace, blending divine empathy and strength. The brokenhearted find you because they know you have the elixir to heal. You are loved because you are a miracle worker and an artist of the soul. You feel a meaningful drive to shed light onto others' darkness, and you heal the world one conversation at a time.

Sun in Pisces: Born while winter turned into spring, your soul is the eternal paradox. Embracing the darkness and delivering us with light, you can use your creative, artistic, or healing skills to help the rest of the world overcome suffering and to deliver us from our pain. Your power manifests while you utilize your gifts to console others and work as a harmonizing agent for those in pain. You can do this effectively by embracing your intuition, and/or metaphysical and psychic capabilities, which inform your strengths.

Moon in Pisces: Hey, mermaid! When la luna swims with her Pisces, your emotional nature is deeply sensitive, unspoken, powerful, and highly imaginative. You can easily sense the emotions, energies, and dynamics around you. Your deepest psychic need is understanding. You want to feel seen, heard, and understood. You are loved because you respond with compassion, grace, and kindness. Shame will try to convince you that you're a failure because you're not (insert adjective here) enough. Practice self-compassion, identify your emotions carefully, and share them with the right spaces of empathy.

Mercury in Pisces: Daydream believer! When messenger Mercury swims with the mystical mermaids, your daydreams and language are rich with poetry, creativity, and imaginative insight. You learn the most through artistic mediums, fantasy, and emotion-backed teaching. If you're not emotionally all in, you're bored. Since your verbal planet is ruled by the most nonverbal sign, you'll want to work a bit harder to make sure you got the words right. Do a bit of research into emotional intelligence and learn the systems to help you wrap language around your sensitivities.

Venus in Pisces: It's meant to be! With this Venus placement, if your romance doesn't feel fated, deeply divined, and like true love—you don't want it. So be gentle with your tenderness and bid for connection to partners who have a soulful approach to love. Let your mystical romance be a space to give you the most healing and support. Be very discerning while you slowly reveal the depths of your heart's waters, and try to separate the

difference between love and need, lest you attract partners who love to need you but neglect to provide you with
support. Find a stable, consistent, and trustworthy soul
who can be the container of your waters.

Mars in Pisces: Let anger be your catalyst but not a best
friend. When the red planet tours through the tender
sign, you feel guilty when expressing discomfort or anger.
You're allowed to honor your anger, identify the behavior
that caused it, and create solutions to heal it. You too
are allowed to have your moments of direct confrontation and assertion of needs. When it comes to the erotic
space, all experiences with sexuality and pleasure need to
be highly meaningful, trusting, and beautiful. You want
your sexual communication to express how deeply you
feel about your beloved. So commune with others sexually who cherish the soulful, imaginative, and healing
possibilities of intimacy.

Jupiter in Pisces: Are you ascended, master? Pretty close!
With Jupiter in this favorable position, you are centrally
placed to receive all of Jupiter's higher wisdom through the
waters of Pisces. Consider a meditation practice or a highly
committed spiritual practice that helps you see, hear, and
feel with your inner senses over your physical ones. When
it comes to academic education, align with a college/univer-
sity that is focused on service. You'll want to enroll in an
education program that fosters using your access, resources,
and intelligence to be of service to those who need it.

Saturn in Pisces: You're not neurotic; you really were
born to be a healer. This Saturn lesson inspires you to

learn the practice of healing, which you can use most effectively to contribute the balm, harmonizing agent, or elixir needed to heal the broken heart or the broken world. Be careful not to enable too much fragility or emotional self-indulgence. Suffering is an inevitable experience in life, so the more you develop shame resilience around it, the more capable you are of transforming suffering to transcendence.

Uranus in Pisces: Divine rebellion! The revolutionary planet Uranus in spiritual Pisces reminds us that the best revolutions begin as internal ones. You'll use your gifts of progressive thinking to permanently set us free from past dysfunction. Particularly in theology, the arts, healing, and spirituality, you'll create alternative solutions wherever you feel intuitively called to.

Neptune in Pisces: We're one! With Neptune in its natural sign, Pisces, this generation inspires a deep quest for the highest outcomes of spiritual application and creativity. You'll change the conversation on spirituality through your prodigious understanding of peace, compassion, love, and forgiveness.

House of Pisces Suns: Hubert de Givenchy (designer), David Geffen (businessman), Ellen Page (actress), Jane Bowles (writer), Edna St. Vincent Millay (writer), Mabel Dodge Luhan (artist), Jenna Wolfe (journalist), Libby Davies (politician), Stephen Spender (author), Mercedes de Acosta (writer), Lytton Strachey (writer), Renata Borgatti (writer), Matthew Mitcham (Olympian), Perry Ellis (designer), Xavier Bettel (politician), Chaz

Bono (activist), Svend Robinson (politician), Pier Paolo Pasolini (artist), Eva Brunne (theologian), Bret Easton Ellis (writer), Wanda Sykes (comedian), Richard Adams (activist), Samuel Barber (composer), Vita Sackville-West (artist), Jean Wyllys (politician), the Lady Chablis (drag queen), Christopher Rice (writer), Bill Siksay (politician), Eudy Simelane (athlete), Edward Albee (artist), Vaslav Nijinsky (ballet dancer), Armistead Maupin (writer), Kwame Harris (athlete), Amir Ohana (politician), Donal Óg Cusack (athlete), Jon Hinson (politician), Alexander McQueen (designer), Stanley Bennett Clay (director), and Wilfred Owen (poet).

COSMIC LOVE

"Love is the only way to grasp another human being in the innermost core of his personality. No one can become fully aware of the very essence of another human being unless he loves him. By his love he is able to see the essential traits and features in the beloved person; and even more, he sees that which is potential in him, which is not yet actualized but yet ought to be actualized."[22]

Now that you've worked with the astrological principles that can liberate your most essential identity, worthiness, and lovability, you are ready for exploring relationship.

I'd argue that the topic astrologers are consulted on the most is love. *Always love.* The romantic in me is absolutely thrilled when people are curious about ideas beyond narrow self-identification. My excitement is interrupted

---

22 V. E. Frankl, *Man's Search for Meaning* (New York: Simon & Schuster, 1984), 134.

when I realize people believe that certain sign combinations are inherently good or bad, doomed or blessed. That's too simplistic. So I'm going to let you in on a little secret that I passionately ascribe to, and I hope it puts your mind at ease: every single sign is compatible with every single sign. When I say compatible, I don't mean that every partnership is easy, breezy, beautiful CoverGirl. When I think of compatibility, I'm thinking of energy between people that inspires—but not guarantees—the opportunity for the pair to learn how to love more deeply, authentically, and fearlessly.

Now who among us learns anything—particularly love—the easy way? Does that then make a seemingly "difficult" relationship inherently incompatible, just because it's not easy? Of course not. I think surface-level compatibility goes off the rails by pitching a fast, fun, cheap, and easy compatibility as the mountaintop of relationship success.

That thinking attempts to convince us that certain pairs are inherently compatible because they require less emotional and psychological labor, or because they can distance us from discomfort. But these dynamics can also provide self-indulgence and personal stagnation instead. *A Course in Miracles* posits the idea that every relationship is a teaching assignment. It explains how every relational assignment is orchestrated by central casting, the universe, God—whatever language you want to use.

So when Cupid's arrow hits you, it's the universe's way of getting your attention, because it just orchestrated a meet cute that begins a relationship assignment. It's intended to create maximal soul-growth opportunities for all people involved. *A Course* sees soul growth through complete love given and received and views intimacy given and received as the true mountaintop of relationships. Soul growth is messy. It's a painful birthing process, perhaps with a prerequisite of heartbreak, anger, and betrayal...but that does *not* mean the relationship is necessarily incompatible. Or that the entire experience was in vain.[23] If the lesson required for your soul growth is knowing when to leave "the room," to own your no, to let someone in, to extend forgiveness, to return to someone, etc., then the relationship is *still* compatible.

Most high-minded spiritual practitioners define relationship success by the quality of lessons learned—not by physical proximity, social frequency, or even the length of time the couple spent together. Two people can sleep in the same bed every night for decades while their hearts are thousands of miles away from each other. The opposite can also be true. Hearts can be joined even while separated at opposite ends of the world. We'd all be enlightened masters by now if everyone did exactly what we wanted them to—never pushed our buttons or pushed us out of our comfort zones. But that's not what happens in romantic relationships. Most of us have the emotional scars to prove it.

Relationships don't immediately remove our free-floating existential pain. If anything, they bring forth the existential pain through a reveal, don't they? We usually

---

23 Cases involving abuse are another matter entirely, and in no way do I condone any form of emotional, mental, physical, and/or sexual abuse. If abuse is present in the current dynamic, you do not have to experience this alone. I encourage you to reach out and share your stories with the queer-friendly National Domestic Violence Hotline— 1-800-799-7233.

learn about our personality defects when they clash against another's in a romantic or intimate context. So a relationship can theoretically inspire new reflections on what caused the pain to begin with—usually family of origin and/or past trauma—and then you can collaborate with your partner on solutions to fix it. When our defects come up in relationships, it's the perfect time to acknowledge our stuff and discuss with our partners how we practice forgiveness, apologies, and accountability. Because you love them deeply, you will reveal the worst part of yourself. So having a system in place where you can review forgiveness practices, apologies, and responsibilities allows the relationship's respect to stay in place.

The highest practice of astrology can give us language to help articulate the delicate compatibility process, if we understand that no one is inherently good or bad for each other. We're all in assignments to help heal one another through relationship lessons. I think it's particularly important for queer-identified folks to recognize the glory in writing our own scripts on relationships now, without hundreds of years of heteronormative relationship "values" to ascribe to. We can make our own rules when it comes to how we measure compatibility. So the next time you're consuming astrological material or engaged in a conversation on what sign is a "good match," remember—the zodiac is an awareness of our divine oneness. So every sign offers gifts and lessons to the other, and no pairing is less or more important than the rest. Whether or not you show up for that lesson is entirely up to you.

Writer on past lives Dr. Brian Weiss wrote in *Miracles Happen* that we don't choose when we meet our soul mate(s). We only choose what to do with them when they get here. I believe that. I can also guarantee that if you keep your heart open, your mind willing, your thoughts high, and your behavior tender, you will know that heaven is entered two by two, and you'll walk the road to paradise together.

Now that we've explored the more universal dimensions of relationship energies, we can get specific. In measuring astrological compatibility, there are only seven dynamics each sign has with the others. Throughout this compatibility exploration, I will discuss the seven dynamics without planetary associations. Doing so works better for queer compatibility purposes. But if you read the previous chapters about the natal aspects of your chart, and familiarized yourself with the signs you embody the most in relationships—from your ascendant down to your Saturn—you can design a love landscape. Identify your multidimensional preferences, desires, and needs; integrate them with your values; and align them with your relationship dynamics, expectations, and requests.

Heteronormative lenses view Venus and Mars primarily through their mythological affinities to each other, with Venus embodying the feminine and Mars embodying the masculine. Or they examine Mars and the moon for family-planning and pregnancy purposes. I'm sure you see the discomfort this might generate. So I think we can begin queer compatibility by integrating all energies into our charts beyond the Mars/Venus binary, masculine/feminine impulses, and assumptions on gender, sex, and sexuality in relationships.

The seven relationship matches between all planets/ luminaries are: conjunct, inconjunct, sextile, square, trine, quincunx, and polarity. So you have seven different assignments with other signs—no more or less compatible, special, or meaningful than the others. We'll review the seven dynamics in the sections ahead, but first, here's a helpful outline of their qualities, and of the secular and spiritual theorists

DYNAMIC	QUALITIES	THEORIST	SOURCE
Conjunct	Safe, Consistent, Securese	Don Miguel Ruiz	*The Mastery of Love*
Inconjunct	Loyal, Contrasting, Instructive	Dr. John Gottman Dr. Julie Gottman	*The Relationship Cure*
Sextile	Joyful, Supportive, Adventurous	Nan Silver Dr.John Gottman	*What Makes Love Last*
Square	Powerful , Transformative, Dynamic	Dr. Harville Hendrix	*Getting the Love You Want*
Trine	Harmonious, Sensual, Affectionate	Dr. Joanne Davila	"Relationship Competency" TED Talk
Quincunx	Surreal, Mysterious, Magnetic	Marianne Williamson	*A Return to Love*
Polarity	Completion, Romantic, Compromise	Esther Perel	*Mating in Captivity*

The conjunct assignment is present when the signs are the same. So you have only one conjunct sign. "Meet your match" takes on a whole new meaning! Love thrives on safety, consistency, and security. Your conjunction match often affords you those things because of the emotional fluency, ease, and comfort between you. Your relationship needs are very similar, your bids for connection very compatible, and you'll feel called to glorify your strengths when you merge. That being said, it's a mirror match because you're reflecting the same energies at each other, so your shadows can likely collude with each other. We often get triggered by people whose defects rub up against our own. So there's no hiding your gifts or shadows here! For a thoughtful analysis on spiritual love, author Don Miguel Ruiz's *The Mastery of Love* embodies the conjunct magnetism, security, and consistency beautifully, with actionable suggestions and helpful homework.

The second assignment is the inconjunct. We all have two inconjunct matches: the signs neighboring ours before and after. I've read that the signs after ours pick up where we left off. So tag—you're it! What's love's favorite neighbor? Hate. This match is love-hate. It'll make for hilarious shading, since we love to drag inconjunct signs, given how different we are. Under the shade, there's a magnetic sexual tension and a push-pull that creates the right friction for the soul growth to emerge. Since you're night and day, oil and water, try leaning on *The Relationship Cure* by Drs. John and Julie Gottman, who can help the inconjunct match's loyalty and contrasting styles come alive in the relationship by teaching how, when, and why our partners bid for connection. You'll see the specific actions that communication a reach for love, which will keep your hands and hearts held in trust with this match.

The two sextile matches are two signs before and after yours. This a complementary match, since the sextile matches' elements correspond to yours—these are pairs of fire/air or water/earth. They nourish each other. The sextile match lets a friendship blossom effortlessly. So the "container" of trust and verbal communication emerges easily, too. If getting too comfortable is an issue, it's likely in this pair. Pace yourselves carefully so you can reveal your existential truths slowly, which sustains the desire, the unknown, and the novelty. Introduce adventure and newness often so you can keep reintroducing yourselves to each other. For more on love's longevity, you'll want to learn from *What Makes Love Last* by Nan Silver and Dr. John Gottman, who provide the actions and conversation starters to help you nurture fondness, support, and admiration within the relationship.

On your feet! The square assignment doesn't let you sit still, and it's full of surprises. With two square matches three signs away, this dynamic's turn is a sharp left or sharp right from your relationships' conventional standards. Totally different from what you're used to, but the modality's the same: cardinal, fixed, or mutable. So identify the common point of interest for you both, born from this common quality. Then alternate roles—depending on what you're both more proficient at—between a dynamic-assertive role, where you take the lead, and a magnetic-receptive role, where you follow the lead and help where you can. Imago relationship therapy, developed by Dr. Harville Hendrix and Dr. Helen LaKelly Hunt, helps couples understand how family of origin and our caretakers influenced our relationship attachment styles, how we define safety, and how we manage conflict.

Welcome home! Four signs away on the left and right, you'll fall into pairs of arms waiting for you from your fellow element. Called the trine because there are three signs in every element, this assignment is harmonious, collaborative, and essentially understanding. You'll fall into an ease with each other so quickly that any need of working on practices like tolerance, compromise, and mutuality will fall to the wayside. But when does intimacy become intrusion? Incorporate appropriate levels of distance between you so that you never stop having to pay attention to each other. I appreciate Dr. Joanne Davila's research into romantic competency and find her TED Talk titled "Skills for Healthy Romantic Relationships" to be useful as a skill-based model of relationship functioning. Dr. Davila puts forth that romantic competency relies on the partnership's ability to demonstrate insight, mutuality, and emotion regulation. Insight is an accurate idea of who you authentically are, what your emotional needs are, what you desire, and your intention behind the things you do. Mutuality relies on the shared understanding that both people have needs, and that both sets of needs matter. Emotion regulation is a helpful skill that allows you to tolerate discomfort without getting too reactive, impulsive, or self-sabotaging.

The pronunciation of *quincunx* is a bit weird, and so is this assignment. Five signs behind and in front of you is a sign different from your essential nature. A balance of comfort with contrast is key, and if you maintain curiosity and a willingness to expand, you'll explore a world so beyond your own that you may never want to come back. Or you'll be begging for a one-way ticket home. You have the novelty of being unknown to one another, which increases the erotic, but you'll need a bit of practical help to maximize emotional closeness with each other. I'm recommending Marianne Williamson's *A Return to Love: Reflections on the Principles of A Course in Miracles* because, as *A Course in Miracles* suggests, we are assigned to each other in relationships. *A Return to Love* explores both the spiritual and practical skills and theories on relationships. Through Williamson's work, you'll have a meaningful context in this quincunx dynamic that helps you ask yourself and each other, "What are we here to learn from each other? How are we here to help each other heal?"

Opposites attract! They don't call this match polarity by accident, as the sign you're six away from is your polar opposite assignment. You only have one, and there's nothing else like it. Polarity signs are two halves of one whole. If you imagine love as the preferred outcome and make peace with your partner's opposite, seemingly clashing tools, you can make the match work beautifully. The chemistry is thermonuclear, and you'll bring out the best and worst of each other at the same time. When it's done well, it's heaven on earth. When fear reigns, it's hell. There's no in between with this match, so operate it well. For secular support in this match, you'll want to study Esther Perel's primary points in *Mating in Captivity* on the paradox of love and desire, which I've summarized in the sections ahead while applying this theory to compatibility.

There you have it! The seven matches, the seven assignments. They all have strengths and opportunities for growth. And when we view relationship dynamics with this both/and mind-set, and look at partnerships as managing clashing needs, then intimacy is ours.

One of the most valuable historical and social contexts to consider when reviewing compatibility is the fact that romantic and sexual culture is full of expectations that a single partner can give us what an entire community used to provide.

In Esther Perel's *Mating in Captivity*, she writes how

religious, communal, and family structures historically provided us with continuity, social support, and meaning at the expense of our individualism and autonomy. Dismantling these structures has left queer people and our allies with more free will and fewer shackles, but "we are almost more alone."[24] Our romantic culture has become the expression of a situation where we turn to one person for the protection and emotional support that an entire village of networks used to provide in prewar times. So the true flowering of relational intimacy has thus become constrained by heavy expectations. Then we accidentally transfer our free-floating expectations, unresolved trauma, and pain, already textured with potential queer shame, to our romantic relationships. As if connection isn't scary enough as it already is.

Loneliness, disconnection, and isolation are painfully perennial, it seems. But I think there's a bit of timeless truth in the idea of community-based intimacy, which queer people can invoke at any moment. In other words, if you don't want to overburden your romantic relationships with urgency, need, demand, or codependency, make your friendships and professional and family networks more romantic. It might feel counterintuitive, but if we bid for connection with more than one person throughout the day, the likelihood of emotional satisfaction is increased, because we're not asking our romantic partners to do that which it once took a village to do. Neediness is not a foundation for connection. Fullness is. So imagine ways that you can get full from others throughout the day, and you'll

---

24 Esther Perel, *Mating in Captivity: Reconciling the Erotic + the Domestic* (New York: HarperCollins, 2006) 9.

be overflowing with energy to give to romantic partners, in dynamics where it's emotionally and sexually appropriate.

I've organized the following compatibility sections by leaning heavily on Esther Perel's work, which understands love and desire as a paradox we can manage in relationships, not problems that need to be solved. If we understand love as needing closeness and trust to survive, while contextualizing desire as needing distance, mystery, and autonomy, we'll see which signs are more inclined to honor closeness or autonomy easily, and how they integrate its opposite. People often match with others who have their opposite inclinations—because the universe has a wonderful sense of humor—and this idea of opposite wounds and dysfunctions being matched in relationships is presented by the Imago relationship program, by Dr. Harville Hendrix and Dr. Helen LaKelly Hunt, discussed previously in the square dynamic paragraph. As both the Imago program and Perel's work point out, without the clash of opposites, the successful management of the paradox between love and desire, the tension across contrast, the relationship will feel like it's lacking something.

"Love enjoys knowing everything about you; desire needs mystery. Love likes to shrink the distance that exists between me and you, while desire is energized by it. If intimacy grows through repetition and familiarity, eroticism is numbed by repetition. It thrives on the mysterious, the novel, and the unexpected. . . . But too often, as couples settle into the comforts of love, they cease to fan the flame of desire. They forget that fire needs air."[25]

---

25   Perel, Mating, 37.

In this space of contrast between love and desire, growth can't help but emerge, if it's done well. So I've outlined here what qualities each sign offers in love, what they can happily offer in desire, and what they can stand to integrate more if they want to uplift their divine potential.

"Love is not something we give or get; it is something that we nurture and grow, a connection that can only be cultivated between two people when it exists within each one of them—we can only love others as much as we love ourselves."[26]

---

26 Brené Brown, *The Gifts of Imperfection: Let Go of Who You Think You're Supposed to Be and Embrace Who You Are* (Center City, MN: Hazelden Publishing, 2010) 26.

RELATIONSHIP COMPATIBILITY

ARIES IN LOVE

Audacious | Spontaneous | Direct
Honor: Autonomy & Distance
Integrate: Mutuality & Curiosity

Aries might be the first sign in the zodiac, often looking out for number one, but don't count them out on righteous coupling techniques! Sure, Aries can be a bit self-preoccupied, but when their heart's on fire for another, Aries can display some of the most magnificent expressions of romance, spontaneity, and novelty while showing up beautifully for their beloved.

Love is not always meant to be professed, but practiced. When an Aries loves you, they'll prove it through undeniably consistent behavior. Count on Aries for surprises that demonstrate how carefully they pay attention to your desires and grand gestures that make you feel like you're the only one for the number one sign in the zodiac.

The pursuit and practice of love is an *action* for an Aries, not just a conversation. In order for love and desire to sustain itself, Aries maintains separation and autonomy. All the research by Aries Sun Esther Perel points to the fact that desire needs distance. Since Aries can declare their individuality often, they can honor this astrological separation from others by protecting their emotional, mental, and intimate boundaries. To soften this distance, Aries can carefully integrate mutuality—the practice of balancing the needs of the relationship with the needs of the individuals who create it together.

ARIES & ARIES
Safe, consistent, secure

Tick, tick—boom! When Martians Aries and Aries collide in the fires of a big-bang love affair, this dynamic is exciting, passionate, brave, and highly stimulating for the relationship (and all those watching). Your conjunction match between two fire signs who love to explore autonomy and closeness is love in action. Love is a verb, and the zodiac's taking careful notes from Aries on how to practice, not just profess, connection. In this conjunction conflagration of alpha personalities, the questions are "Which Aries leads? Which Aries receives?" This dynamic assignment is trying to teach two rather impulsive and spontaneous rams to slow down a bit and dance the waltz together. If you want this match to keep the power, you'll want to know when to step up, move right, move back, and move left. By that, I mean identify each partner's specific gifts and opportunities for growth as early as you can. It won't take away the chemistry, because proactive disclosure will work as a container that holds the safety, trust, and integrity between you.

With the right conversations at the beginning, which is when you build the foundation of the dynamic, you two rams will learn more about each other's existential worlds and how to passionately cherish the values you bring to each other. Along the way, you'll empower one another to find solutions for your blind spots with shame-free, confidence-building resolutions. That way, once you've developed the plan of action—knowing which partner does what, where, when, and why for the right reasons—then you can accomplish the missions the universe has set for you.

ARIES & TAURUS
Loyal, contrasting, instructive
A magnetism between Venus-born Taurus and Mars-born Aries would inspire a quick attraction, and with the right tools, you're unstoppable. You're drawn to one another because you're intrigued by each other's different life-management techniques: Aries with their cardinal fire's relentless valor, and Taurus with their fixed earth consistent sensuality. This inconjunct match between neighbor signs helps you develop the right emotional impulse control, so you don't burn bridges or connections.

Your confidence will teach risk-averse Taurus how to simply get out of their own way and find a wellspring of bravery while they show up for all of life's most vulnerable and uncertain experiences. So long as the more romantic, relational Taurus enforces a bit of healthy distance between you, then the safety of love can still be honored while the flames of desire burn hot with intoxicating mystery and novelty. You don't need to overexplain or overdisclose to avoid relationship failure. In this space between two signs that already don't have a lot space between them, you will carefully develop tact, sensitivity, and depth from your more focused Taurus. The sensual bull has great wisdom to teach you on methodical approaches to life management and the consistency that inspires you to take goals from imagination to reality. With the blend of Aries's powerful fire and Taurus's earthy reliability in the space between you, this is a vibrant match for the Aries-ruled heart. Appreciate the helpful follow-through from your Taurus to make the couple's dreams a reality, with inspired strategy and action.

ARIES & GEMINI
Joyful, supportive, adventurous
You fell in love through laughter. As soon as you saw the light in Gemini's eye and the punch line falling out of their mouth, you were caught—hook, line, and sinker. Between Gemini's cheeky wit, which can level a room and your heart, and Aries's slapstick humor, this sextile assignment between the air of Mercury and the fire of Mars is highly joyful, entertaining, and on the move, where you both love to be. As a cardinal fire sign who loves to take action when inspired, you appreciate Gemini's mutable airborne ideas and how they're always ready to follow your lead. You carefully hang on their every word, and they cling to your every move. Between their brains and your brawn, this dynamic is ready for success.

To keep the love secure, make sure you demonstrate a willingness to listen to your Gemini's life experiences and observations with as much enthusiasm as you'd like them to listen to yours. Then have your Gemini use their gift of gab to verbally affirm you, so you feel cherished. The desire will burn bright, though the safety of love needs careful tending in this match. To help, your embodied approach to life will ask your twin to intellectualize less and feel/act a bit more. Gemini can suffer from analysis paralysis, and you'll break the pattern by telling them to just start before they're ready. "Let's do it now," you'll say, and they'll follow your lead after a bit of a fight, which inspires intimacy and compromise. There's no time like the present to be better together, and when you two sextile signs connect with this mission in mind, the laughter, adventure, love, desire, and support are given as long as you enjoy the ride.

ARIES & CANCER
Powerful, transformative, dynamic
Mommy's home! Or is it Daddy? Who knows! This square assignment between cardinal fire Aries and cardinal water Cancer brings out the nontraditional expression of both maternal and paternal energies in a romantic context. You feel immediately safer with your compassionate Cancer lover, as they tend to your needs proactively without invitation. Their heart becomes a home to you, and you know Cancer's loyalty is exactly the kind of ride or die you're looking for. It's a reflex when they're in love, which you're happy to relish in. Tender Cancer appreciates the way your strength is contagious, and it empowers, protects, honors, and shows up for them in true Aries spirit. The square dynamic keeps the mystery, novelty, and desire at a peak, since you're

always exploring new dimensions of each other, which inspires a fascination with each other.

You can contain this power by outlining what your needs are to protect the safety, reliability, and trust that sustains the love between square signs. Begin to build the container of love by consistently cherishing the feelings of your Cancer partner—pay attention to their moods and bite that tongue of yours!—while empowering them to verbalize exactly what they desire of you. If it's a bit more breathing room and distance that you need, you can gently express to the moon child that your alone time helps you love them more deeply, which is a win/win for the both of you. Balance the autonomy and partnership qualities with harmony, and this square match becomes a beautiful home between Mars and the moon that gives you both emotional support and empowered action.

ARIES & LEO
Harmonious, sensual, affectionate
Gather round the solar fire and listen to the story of how the hero fell in love with the royal. The mutual fire energy between you both sparked a quick bond between strong personalities. There is mutual appreciation and loyalty to each other, because you bring out the best in each other. You feel completely embodied and whole while you demonstrate your most powerful self to the Leo. This is an incredibly rare life experience, since you're used to setting off emotional trip wires, but the Leo's worthiness is theoretically unshakable. When the monarch of the zodiac finds you and notices how you put the "power" in the "royal power couple" their heart has been searching for, it's game over.

A romantic and demonstrative partnership between cardinal fire Mars-ruled Aries and fixed fire sun-ruled Leo, it's a trine match that offers harmony, closeness, and trust. The fire familiarity gives you the right foundation to keep your love safe, and as such, you can keep the desire burning stronger by making the familiar more unfamiliar. Gently encourage a bit of separation and distance between you so you'll never have each other completely figured out, and the curiosity will stay strong. Do new things together and stay mentally invested in each other's unknowns. Remember, too, that all people are flawed—even heroes and royals!—so keep your pride and defense mechanisms in healthy restraint while you carefully express apologies and forgiveness to each other. That way, conflict becomes a catalyst for growth and keeps you both becoming better versions of yourselves through the love you share.

ARIES & VIRGO

Surreal, mysterious, magnetic

You've always had a je ne sais quoi kind of feeling about finding the nerd with glasses in a library, am I right? Good thing, because brainiacs usually have an unspoken sweet spot for the more extroverted brave ones. You feel a meaningful respect for Virgo's intelligence and sensibility, which helps them take responsible, detailed care of not only themselves, but the people they love—a quality that your loyal heart adores. Erudite Virgo thinks your fiery enthusiasm, sense of humor, and innovative spirit help them see beyond the facts and figures of the head in favor of the dimensions of the heart, which is a destination they're striving to enter.

As a quincunx dynamic between cardinal fire Aries

and mutable earth Virgo, this match is between intelligent Mercury and action-oriented Mars. So if you both outline the right Mercury-ruled strategies and take Mars action on them in your romance, you'll find the terra firma that lets this campfire of love burn beautifully in trust, mutuality, and respect. The desire will be on high more often because you're both so unknown to each other, which is the biggest aphrodisiac. You'll have to go a bit farther to understand one another in intimacy, but don't give too much away in seduction. If you want to earn more of Virgo's trust, showcase your thoughtfulness and attention to detail to help them feel a bit safer around you. Communicate specific details of what you notice about their life, and they'll know how they matter to you. You're the cure they need to conquer the disease of people pleasing. While they take action, inspired by your life example, they'll reveal more tenderness to you, and you'll reveal more loyalty to them.

ARIES & LIBRA
Completion, romantic, compromise

Move over, Bonnie and Clyde! There's a new Aries/Libra Sun, "us against the world" couple in town. Hopefully you're a little less crime but a lot more power! Full disclosure: this polarity match is the framework that inspired the book in your hands. This match truly exemplifies the delicate balance between cardinal fiery Mars ruled me (you!) and cardinal air Venus-ruled we. Like so many, you were immediately enchanted by your Libra's social graces, elegance, and popularity. The charm Libra exudes while they move about the world and the positive impact they make on others' lives speaks so well of them. Libras were probably initially put off by, but secretly admiring of, your ram-ruled brashness, direct action, and confidence, which lights up all the rooms you work in.

Your exceptional polarity assignment is so valuable to help demonstrate to the zodiac the balance needed between your natural autonomy and Libra's relational closeness. So take Libra's lead when it comes to human connection and belonging. They know exactly how to harmonize, negotiate, and treat the needs of the individual as no more or less important than the needs of the relationship. You'll inspire Libra to tend to their needs with as much enthusiasm as they lovingly serve others. You'll be their bodyguard and their coach on authenticity over perfectionism and people pleasing. This is the me versus we paradox that drives my entire compatibility analysis. Your Libra and you are the teachers of this balance, and the zodiac is blessed by your lead.

ARIES & SCORPIO

Surreal, mysterious, magnetic

Love is a battlefield! Though this match is a surreal quincunx between cardinal fire you and the fixed water Scorpio, some astrological schools of thought remind us that you're both coruled by the planet Mars. So with substantial curiosity, negotiation, and acceptance, you can see what you have in common with your Scorpio partner. For one, you're deeply inspired and sometimes intimidated by Scorpio's authenticity, which inspires bids for both love and desire. When Scorpio shows their fearlessness, loyalty, and truth telling, they light the match to your heart and set it on fire. Though they don't want to admit it—because emotional exposure is hard for these souls—Scorpio is secretly romanced by your bravery, confidence, and passion to seize the best of life.

Mutually supported by action-oriented Martian energy, you're both discerning whether or not your partner is emotionally and psychologically strong enough. You know you can't push each other over, which is why you love and desire one another. Skeptical and secretive Scorpio can learn more about softening into the risks of vulnerability and trust from your inspiring lead. You have kindness always ready to be given to others, whereas Scorpio assumes guilt before innocence. Meanwhile, their methodical focus can help you find more meaning in the mundane, and their concentration will help you finish the ideas you start. Aligning your behavior with their ideas on intimacy and commitment, this match is a Martian force to be reckoned with, and I shudder for any opponents standing in your way.

ARIES & SAGITTARIUS
Harmonious, sensual, affectionate
Run wild! When the fellow fire signs and animalistic natures—Aries as ram and Sagittarius as half horse—align in the wilderness, this pair is a perfect trine match. Since you both crave adventure, independence, freedom, and joy, as the cardinal and mutable fire signs join together you'll stop at nothing to make them happen. Sagittarius's fire burns hot around your childlike enthusiasm, Martian leadership potential, and inherent confidence. They love that you practice self-love. You adore Sagittarius's Jupiter-ruled intelligence—their comfort level with your freedom and zeal for making their exciting visions manifest in their experience.

You'll want to show more proactivity to hold Sagittarius's attention span by keeping up with their interests. Ask a lot of questions, maintain curiosity, and let them lecture every once in a while. To keep you feeling cherished, Sagittarius will have to include you more in their mental and international adventures, so you feel valued while you contribute to their dreams. Your centaur will have to watch their carelessness, because you're a bit more sensitive than you let on. One wrong word will send you charging. On protecting love, honor the practice of equality, so you're both doing the supporting and being supported. Proactive boundary declaring on what's yours and what's your centaur's could help desire's distance breathe here. You can easily merge too far if you're not careful. So separate the fires a bit with trust, boundaries, and outlining expectations, and you'll be aflame in glory.

ARIES & CAPRICORN
Powerful, transformative, dynamic

C-class, baby! Between your innovative leadership skills and Capricorn's responsible management, you two high-ranking officers can run this relationship like *Forbes*'s greatest CEO, CMO, or CFO. You were likely a bit intimidated but very inspired by Capricorn's cardinal earthy ethics, outstanding discipline, and willingness to work at making the relationship thrive. Sometimes, it's really that easy! The seagoat of Saturn, on the other hand, was quietly moved by your confidence, your assertiveness, and your cavalier approach to rules. They love how you disrupt the norm, even if it's an inconvenience, since it inspires them to do the same.

Now the question is—who puts the C in CEO? This

dynamic is a square clash of the cardinal titans of earth and fire. This square dynamic keeps the desire strong, because you're both mysterious and yet highly reliable with each other. You won't have your partner's next move pegged. This keeps you on your toes and hungry for more interaction. Just make sure you're proactive about declaring what you'd like chief control of, and ask your Capricorn where they're more comfortable leading. If the proper identification of your strengths are agreed upon, you'll prove to be miraculous support systems of love, chemistry, adventure, and safety with each other. Just be very specific in outlining your love map, and listen to your Capricorn as they explain all the ways in which you both feel safe, trusted, and adored. Together, there's no mountain you can't climb or battle you won't win!

ARIES & AQUARIUS
Joyful, supportive, adventurous
Hey, individualist, meet the rebel! Both of your signs are focused deeply on personal identity, as the first sign Aries and the rebellious leader Aquarius. So the question is: Where's the relationship context? As a harmonious, supportive sextile match between fixed air Aquarius and cardinal fire Aries, this dynamic supports a joyful connection. Rebellious, Uranus-ruled Aquarius laughs wildly at your candor and appreciates your passion for self-exploration. They love that you're not afraid to smash the rules with your Martian power and follow the beat of your own drummer. You're intrigued by their calm, cool, and detached demeanor, even while they claim to be romantically interested. How dare they not give you attention!

Aquarius already knows you're special, but rebels won't fawn. Show how secure, intelligent, and curious you are about their sensitive eccentricities, and only then will Aquarius finally give you the affirmation you crave. This will sustain the loving energy of trust, loyalty, and safety you both share.

Your rapid-fire energy will inspire the water bearer to put the pedal to the metal and dare greatly. They can easily get stuck in the weeds and overthink things, which prevents them from showing up to the party when times urgently ask it of them. This contrast in your natures lets the spark of desire electrify you both. You'll explore new territories, places, and conversations together, where you'll realize that this Uranus-meets-Mars dynamic shines beautifully as long as you both help sculpt each other into the individualist and rebel you're born to be. So long as you push pride aside, this match will help you find your freedom and commitment.

ARIES & PISCES
Loyal, contrasting, instructive

The magic of winter becoming spring. This inconjunct dynamic embodies the two existential symbols in all the great spiritual teachings: the birth of Aries and the ending of Pisces. You're tethered to each other. This pair between cardinal fire you and mutable water Pisces can work if you accept each other's fundamental differences and stay focused on what you can learn from each other. You're enthralled by Pisces's Neptune-ruled contemplation, creativity, sensitivity, and mystery. Pisces is both entertained and charmed by your lightheartedness, sense of humor, and Mars energy. It lights a fire under their you-know-what. And their steady pace helps you avoid making brash decisions you'll regret later.

Given the existential distances between you, the unknown that textures desire and the mystical space of intrigue will keep you striving for meaningful practices of intimacy. But you'll need to be accepting of each other's radical differences and curious to know more about your partner. You'll want to align meaningfully on what contexts for love, safety, and trust look like for you both, and commit to implementing them. Be very clear and specific. You'll need a strong container to hold all the chemistry and power between Mars fire and Neptune water. If you can collaborate from the twofold question "What needs to start and what needs to end?" you'll be working with the two greatest forces in the universe, and your partnership can be a field of unlimited possibility.

TAURUS IN LOVE

Dependable | Protective | Sensual
Honor: Closeness & Romance
Integrate: Transformation & Depth

To be a Taurus is to always be in love. Ruled by the goddess of love herself, her Taurus born and influenced are intrinsically connected to closeness, romance, and pleasure. So they're always in love with an idea, song, place, or person. Is it any wonder that their number is two? No—they're always in relationships because they do it so beautifully.

In order for love to thrive, it needs safety and trust. Dependable, fixed earth Taurus offers both to their beloved when it is rightfully earned. When they are in love, Taurus provides a Garden of Eden for their partners, complete with devotion, safety, reliability, and pleasure. If you long for a love that's comfortable, seduce a Taurus. They'll combine the groundedness and the passion love loves.

In love, Taurus can honor their natural ability to bid for closeness and romance. In a world that prizes the rugged and tough individual, Taurus subverts this paradigm with their tenderness. They can offer emotional and physical closeness magnificently. Taurus also needs to trust that a partner who can cherish their romantic heart's power is on their way, or waiting to be asked. To integrate more fully with others, Taurus needs to heighten their ease with uncertainty, the possibility of change, and deep explorations of truth. They love to make others comfortable, but sometimes discomfort is necessary for intimacy and commitment. So go *there*.

TAURUS & ARIES
Loyal, contrasting, instructive

Hey, neighbor! Mars-ruled Aries and Venus-ruled Taurus have often stayed side by side in not just the zodiac, but in ancient mythologies and contemporary romantic dynamics. In this match between fixed earth you and cardinal fire Aries, there's definitely an endearing hurry-up-and-wait inconjunct energy at play. A stickler for high quality, you're certifiably impressed by Aries's fearless-ness, born from the powerful fires of Mars. Observing their behavior carefully, you slowly give the Aries trust when they do what they said they would. You love reliability given. Meanwhile, the ram is very comforted by the sincerely gentle, receptive, and glamorous energy you radiate when you're in love.

So this injunct match is a fun tension of push-pull, hurry up, slow down. If you want to turn up the heat of desire, show your fiery Aries you can give in to risk, spontaneity, and surprise. As the first sign in the zodiac, Aries is always on the hunt for the new and exciting. So it's your job to make the familiar more unfamiliar. It's a two-way street of encouragement, and you'll inspire Aries to stick with their divine inspiration. Your methodical, tenacious approach to life management will inspire Aries to develop careful impulse control and follow through so they don't short-circuit too soon or neglect to finish what they start. To secure the love's safety, make sure your Aries knows how you define and practice trust, commitment, and reliability within the context of your values and/or family of origin. Then you'll want to make sure you return the honor by asking about and delivering on their psychic needs, too, showing us the best of this classic Venus and Mars match.

TAURUS & TAURUS
Safe, consistent, secure

A little gluttony never hurt anyone, right? When you two Venusian signs wink, wink at each other and blend body to body, it's so hard to return to the harsher realities of the world, isn't it? Both fixed earth signs in this lovely conjunction, you're particular about how you would like your relationship to feel and look. In another Taurus, you've found a romantic who's just as nuanced as you, and who is fluent in the same love language. Venus victory! You adorn each other in romance, luxury, and full-bodied sensual experiences. Closeness is the ground love blooms from, which you two effortlessly create.

But distance is how desire stays alive, so you'll want to honor your penchant for proximity by integrating a bit of existential, emotional, and mental separation between you. That way, you'll feel like you're forever seducing and courting one another. You love to *have* a lover, so the idea here is to feel like you never quite have your Taurus yet. Also, remember to use your relationship to help each other handle the harsh realities of the outside world. Experiences with discomfort are unavoidable and necessary to engage with if we are to live meaningful lives. As two Venus-ruled signs who love their comfort, you may accidentally lower your mutual discomfort tolerance levels. So build this beautiful dynamic on life-sustaining values like shame resilience and emotional bravery. Then you can both focus on how you hold your sanctuary of love within you, while navigating the complexities and challenges of the world as an empowered and capable couple.

TAURUS & GEMINI
Loyal, contrasting, instructive

Explosive chemistry in the contrast? Definitely! These injunct neighbor signs are as contrasting as it gets. So the chemistry between you is rich with the best of a quick-silver Mercury and sensual Venus match—qualities like respect, humor, and loyalty. Often slow to fall, you were unusually quick to feel enamored with Gemini's intelligence and language skills. Your bull feet like to stay solid on the terra firma. Yet you couldn't help but notice how Gemini's Mercurial winged sandals keep them fun and light on their feet. This distinction between you is the spark and power of desire's dynamic, which keeps you both mysterious to each other and highly desirable.

A conscious effort between you both is needed to tend to the safety, reliability, and trust of love. Gemini will help wrap their words around love, and you'll demonstrate it. Make sure you're speaking the same language and practicing the same behavior to let love's container hold space for both energies. Explore your differences through curiosity in each other's emotional dowries, pasts, etc. Along the way, you keep the airborne Gemini on earthy solid ground, which they secretly adore, given how tenacious, committed, and dependable you are. Think of your Gemini as the visionary creative director— you're more comfortable in the project manager role, the person who gets the job done, anyway. Your practical consistency can help the Gemini follow through on their visions and practice impeccability with their word. Likewise, their adaptability helps you soften into ideological and emotional flexibility, teaching you to get comfortable with uncertainty and discomfort. This is a match of love both professed and practiced, which makes it an unforgettable and nourishing connection.

TAURUS & CANCER
Joyful, supportive, adventurous
Home, sweet home! This sextile match is textured with solace, safety, and trust between tender partners. A harmonious chemistry between your fixed earth sensibility and Cancer's cardinal water ideas, this match is the best of Venus and the moon, as it's so romantic and very comfortable. Your heart was moved by Cancer's sensitive and loving approaches to their meaningful relationships and family networks. Who doesn't love someone who loves others? Cancer is hardly unobvious in their affection. The moon-loving crab intuited that you could be the space for their next home, as the dependable and loyal earth element that can carry the emotion ocean deep in their heart. Blending complementary elements of your earth with their water, that beautiful space blooms and feels like home. Between your exceptional reliability and Cancer's loyalty, you're working with the best qualities that let love's safety and respect emerge.

But remember that comfort can be desire's antidote. So, though it'll be hard, make sure to slow the emotional pace and allow for healthy distance and the spark of mystery. As signs both capable of codependent behavior, you don't want to rush this relationship to have your partner fill a void. Your values and thoughtful approaches to life will inspire Cancer to tackle their emotional pain with critical, practical awareness. Then your Cancer will motivate you to be a bit more proactive around contexts that don't immediately serve you or your interests. Life moves fast, bull, so your Cancer will help you keep up. You'll help them slow down. That's why this match is divinely supported and divinely timed.

TAURUS & LEO
Powerful, transformative, dynamic

Though taking different forms, in the bull and the lion, you can find similarities between this square match of alpha animals. Not only are you both fixed signs—you as fixed earth and Leo as fixed fire—but you're loaded symbols of animalistic strength. So this square tension keeps the chemistry—and gridlocked conflict!—strong. You fell in love with the Leo because the universe is inspiring you with the monarch's worthiness, confidence, courage, charisma, and power, whereas the courageous lion values your clarity of values. They recognize the strength of your convictions and how these values keep you highly focused, trustworthy, and embodied in your whole self. This is how fixed energy respects other fixed energy. You can gently instruct the lion to invite others into their light and share their throne, since you're more relational. The lion, on the other hand, will empower you to show up to the world and to your life with more confidence and worthiness.

Square dynamics are textbook generators of desire, because they have a push-pull magnetism full of surprises, a bit of erotic rage, and adventure at every corner. So the passion and chemistry will remain. What needs work is the tending to love's structure, which can hold all the alpha power between you. Register how you bid for connection in different ways, and comfort one another by swallowing your pride and accepting those bids as a desire for closeness, not self-indulgence. Sooner or later, it'll look like the bull and the lion can corule the animal kingdom after all!

TAURUS & VIRGO
Harmonious, sensual, affectionate

Two little earth signs sitting in a tree . . . K-I-S-S-I-N-G. You two tree huggers are a supportive trine match, which helps this dynamic feel so classic and comfortable. Whereas you're fixed earth and ruled by sensual Venus, your beloved nerd is mutable earth and ruled by intelligent Mercury. You can immediately recognize Virgo's earthy, serene, and concentrated demeanor as the right resonance for you to stand with in love. You crave dependability and generously give it to others—Virgo is always paying attention, and when they register your dependability and consistency, they give it back to you. The intelligent Virgo deduced that your values of integrity, steadfast presence, and trustworthiness are exactly the ones they need to feel comfortable in love. With this trine match, your reflexes inspire closeness, trust, and safety with one another while you build love. It's an effortless construction.

Both highly relational and service-oriented signs, you'll want to temper the urge to merge a bit. For the roots of desire to grow, the two trees need breathing room between them. So incorporate a slower pace and mysterious seductions so you don't reveal everything too soon. Along the way, you can use your natural tenderness and sensuality to help your Virgo think a lot less and engage with their feelings more. You'll offer a wellspring of compassion to your sometimes self-critical lover. The perceptive Virgo can inspire you to take radical responsibility for the tenor of your life and can stoke your passion to play less and work harder. This is a complementary and romantic match made in the universe's enchanted, romantic forest.

TAURUS & LIBRA
Surreal, mysterious, magnetic

When the only two signs ruled by the goddess of love join in a love affair, it's a dynamic that beams with romance, comfort, glamour, and loyalty. This is a quincunx match, which is a bit strange at first, given your fixed earth sensibilities and Libra's cardinal air delicacies. But with the right willingness and effort, you'll easily find how Venus unites you. With your premier tastes, you were rightfully enchanted by the high quality of Libra's aesthetic, creative, and social skills. You find the divine in beauty, and your Libra is never in short supply of it. And your Libra quickly recognized the Venusian qualities in you, like sensuality, adherence to values, and artistic flair. In securing love, your natural reaching for each other creates the right container of closeness, security, and trust so that love can survive.

As you're both highly relational signs, tending to the more selfish, autonomous desire needs will feel a bit awkward at first. But if you approach the space between you as the space of uniting in intimacy, you'll understand how effective it is. Make sure you have structures and expectations in place that secure each other's autonomy. Your earth-ruled perception will help Libra focus more deeply on meaning over form, urging them to consider more substantial arenas over surface-level things, whereas ethereal Libra will help you expand your vision to allow people to disagree with you peacefully. You'll work hard to embed rituals, date nights, and romance in your relationship so you never lose the spark. Just make sure you help each other flex those resilience muscles so you can handle the highs and lows of life together in good form.

TAURUS & SCORPIO
Completion, romantic, compromise
This polar-opposite match has more in common than meets the eye, even if it's an alliance between light-filled, beautiful Venus and night-dwelling, intense Pluto. This is an oppositional energy between your fixed earth sensibilities and Scorpio's fixed water authenticity. You know intuitively that your Scorpio sees, feels, and understands things of profound intimacy and depth where your vision leaves off. And they see you deeply, too. Scorpio recognizes your visions of pleasure, art, consistency, and sensuality as the beautiful gifts they are. So both are valuable and necessary for each other.

The polarity dynamic is at peak desire status, as you're both constantly exploring, understanding, repelling, and attracting each other. So the chemistry is likely to be permanent! But you're both creatures of comfort, so training each other to manage discomfort is the context you'll want to honor if you want to generate love's security, loyalty, and transparency. You'll achieve this so long as you can inspire your Scorpio to soften into the present moment's joy and emotional exposure without living in the wreckage of the future. They want to commit and do right by you, but they're afraid they'll blow it. So be gentle and encouraging with these sensitive souls. Then your Scorpio turns off the light, which helps you cherish things you can't see, touch, eat, drink, or hear. They'll turn on a light in your heart instead, helping illuminate the deeper dimensions of intimacy. When you share your resources, existential arenas, and joy with each other, this match offers both novelty and comfort, adventure and security. You both deserve it all, so have at it!

TAURUS & SAGITTARIUS
Surreal, mysterious, magnetic
Bored by routine and self-indulgence? Look up to the stars, close your eyes, and whistle loudly for the Sagittarius! Immediately you'll hear their centaur's hooves galloping in your direction. You'll fall in love with Jupiter-born Sagittarius's relentless optimism, wanderlust, and thirst for knowledge. You know their adaptability and enthusiasm hold keys to wonderful personal expansion within you in this quincunx match. They'll appreciate not only your phenomenal whistling skills, but how your word is law. In their freedom-loving soul, they'll be inspired by your consistent Venus-valued integrity.

Between your fixed earth and their mutable fire energies, desire burns hot. You'll both be quick to explore and hopefully listen to each other's inner worlds, livelihoods, and histories because you're both so different that you'll be enthralled by the stories of your lover. In order to allow this desire to coexist with your loving Venus nature, you'll want to graciously allow your Sagittarius some breathing room. With your influence, your centaur will have become a bit more interdependent and will demonstrate skills and behaviors that validate how well they work with others, which matters to your interpersonal spirit. Thankfully, you can straight-talk with your Sagittarius, who loves direct honesty, and help them turn ideas into action. Meanwhile, your optimistic centaur will help you find a cure to the fundamentalism and dogma that keeps you stuck in fear, and teach you to explore the unknown with a gumption you never knew you wanted. This blend of fire and earth energies is both exciting and stable, which allows both love and desire to sustain themselves beautifully for you while you act on and speak the love you share.

TAURUS & CAPRICORN
Harmonious, sensual, affectionate

Forest, meet mountain! Triangles are strong geometric shapes that don't bend under pressure, and trines are supportive dynamics that don't bend under societal pressures. No combination honors this trine sturdiness quite like you two boulders of strength in the fixed earth forest and cardinal earth mountain. With Saturn-ruled Capricorn, you're completely in awe of their majesty—how they manage their lives and relationships with righteousness, discipline, and ethics. The Capricorn discerns that you're trusting and Venus worthy, and they're emotionally moved by your devotion to your passions and relationships. With trine matches, the stability, closeness, and harmony that allows love to become a home for the dynamic falls into place seamlessly. Earth signs need this level of security before revealing their love, and fortunately, it's given freely in this match.

Exchange security with risk by strategizing more ways to allow desire to develop as you journey into the unknown, the erotic, the unfamiliar. You can help each other become the people you're capable of being while still maintaining enough distance to keep you both on your toes and engaged in the experiences of your partner. To accelerate this process, you could relieve the Capricorn's workload by helping these ambitious folks pause and take in the joys of life, reminding them why they work so hard. Your Capricorn will help you begin to be vulnerable—a surprisingly difficult choice for you!—and lean into that vulnerability, so your follow-through energy can take over from there and finish what you started. Together, your love will reach the mountaintop's pinnacle and look over the forest in pride.

TAURUS & AQUARIUS
Powerful, transformative, dynamic
Seek understanding more than the feeling of being understood here. This fixed square match will do its wonders while you both go out of your way to stay curious, understanding, and accepting of each other—which doesn't necessarily come naturally to these rigid signs. You're curious about Aquarius's self-possession, how they move about the world with airy high-minded principles and Uranian detachment. It's like they belong nowhere and everywhere. Brilliant Aquarius knows you say what you mean and mean what you say in Venus-ruled earth style, so you've earned their trust and friendship. You're the beautiful romantic and they're the cool rebel. This clash is desire's homeland. It loves the power play, mystery, and tender sweet spot between two opposing forces. You'll enjoy the chemistry and intimacy for as long as you crave it.

The loving container will take a bit more effort, but your relational nature will inspire closeness, trust, and loyalty, so you have the right psychological container to hold this square energy carefully, should you ask about your Aquarius's attachment style, informed by family of origin. You can work toward this outcome by inspiring the Aquarius to negotiate and consider others more than they're naturally inclined to. The rugged individualist is a stereotype for a reason! Aquarius will likewise help you transcend your people-pleasing patterns and your avoidance of risk and uncertainty by coaching you on resilience and discomfort. The more you fight to avoid these things, the harder it sucks when they inevitably occur. The clash of these fixed earth and air signs can help you both emerge with skills that make you powerful in handing all the Uranian changes and Venusian consistencies of life with elegance and wisdom.

TAURUS & PISCES
Joyful, supportive, adventurous
Popular love talk says the best romances begin as friendships. This sextile match between your fixed earth consistency and Pisces's mutable water gives rise to surprise romances that don't begin in such a manner. But, ruled by boundary-dissolving Neptune, Pisces is looking for a partner who can offer both romantic and platonic energies to their beloved, which your earth structure can happily do. You likely fell for their soulful compassion, their passion for service, and your shared love of art, which means a great deal to your Venus-governed heart. The merfolk fall for those who are consistent, clear, and kind, and you deliver the jackpot. Earth and water matches create a beautiful "third" of sorts: a flower, growing from the earth and water, that blooms from the tender care you give and receive from one another.

This is a sextile match that can oscillate well between love and desire, surrender and autonomy, safety and mystery, because you enjoy the clarity of values in the match, and the Pisces gets the multidimensionality they crave. In learning to love you, Pisces will be challenged to commit and follow through to your high Taurus liking. You love when partners walk it (or in this case, swim it) like they talk it. I highly recommend the practice of nonviolent communication for this match to help with the structure around identifying needs, boundaries, and requests. Your dreamy Pisces will help you embrace the beauty in the mystery and mysticism of life, so you can enjoy the surprises together. Not everything needs to be figured out or answered, Taurus. But you'll never stop showing up for them, which will mean miracles to the tender Pisces. And they'll never stop surprising you with romance and fun, which creates a space where land meets sea and where desire, love, friendship, and romance are one.

GEMINI IN LOVE

Communicative | Inquisitive | Thoughtful
Honor: Paradox & Language
Integrate: Wisdom & Adventure

Come meet the twins! The first appearance of humans in the zodiac calendar, Gemini is represented by the mythological twins. Within each Gemini is a "both/and" energy, and their mutable air is expressed as a partnership between the twins. With most of modernity abandoning outdated norms and structures on relationships, expectations and rules are bygone. Without the binary, everything is a negotiation. Don't know how to negotiate? Meet the twins!

Nowadays, talk isn't cheap. It's rich! Ruled by messenger Mercury, Gemini knows how to speak and listen in love, making their contributions to connection invaluable. It's important to understand the astrological signs with their meaning in the zodiac's story. And the meaning of Gemini in love is: hold your beloved in curiosity, dialogue, and awareness, and love will grow.

In love, Gemini can honor paradox. It may feel like a toxin sometimes, but a paradox is love and desire's central organizing principle. So Gemini must demonstrate a comfort with the paradox of closeness and distance, or intimacy may become intrusion. So long as their language skills offer need-to-know details and a thoughtful curiosity, but not existential trespassing, love becomes partnership and not ownership.

Gemini would benefit from integrating more big-picture wisdom. They can utilize their microinformation as a match and let it grow into a larger narrative on love like a bonfire. When Gemini zooms out of their relationship context to learn what their relationship has in common with other partnerships, they'll find wisdom in the shared qualities and help others navigate relationships more effectively. If they see love as an adventure, their journey can inspire others to be brave, outspoken, and optimistic.

GEMINI & ARIES
Joyful, supportive, adventurous

Light it up, babies! When high-flying Gemini and fire-born Aries lock eyes across a room, the spark is lit and it's on. You'll adore the Martian Aries's enthusiasm, confidence, and humor, which is the only way their cardinal fire souls know how to live their lives. A passionate match, Aries will appreciate your mutable air—given conversation skills, intelligence, and jokes—especially if it's at their expense! Who knew? This is a sextile connection that is powerfully charged by the loyal laughter between you, the ease of friendship, and a wellspring of joy. With sextile bonds, the righteous love born of communication, trust, reliability, and respect occurs rather effortlessly, which is a wonderful by-product of this fire-meets-air dynamic. With just a bit more, but not a ton, of effort, you'll want to pace yourselves so that the desire between you stays strong and consistent.

This match can err on the side of a hit-and-run style if you're not careful, instead of a more gradual reveal of intimacy. So be patient while you maintain the mysticism of mystery and the right amount of proximity. You'll inspire your Aries to think more deeply on the ideas they're passionate about, helping their attention focus on the right strategies so the visions of their success inevitably come true, whereas your Mars-ruled ram will give you an occasional *Moonstruck* moment—"Snap out of it!"—so you'll be less in your head and more in your bona fide action. Analysis paralysis is no laughing matter. Together, you'll have not only the power but the happiness and intelligence to make your personal and professional dreams come true. And you'll celebrate every milestone along the way.

GEMINI & TAURUS
Loyal, contrasting, instructive

Slow and steady! When the twins and Taurus romance, it is a connection that can provide both reliability and novelty, provided you move at the right speed. Inhabiting the best of both the Mercury and Venus worlds, you'll want to move slowly, steadily, to handle this strongly magnetized inconjunct match. Forever curious, you'll be deeply impressed by Taurus's specialties and focus. You realize they're masters of their passions, which keeps your interests piqued and inspires intellectual deference where appropriate. Your bull will be a bit nervous around your energy's speed, but completely spellbound by how light and efficient you are on your feet. Your adaptability is elegant, and they love to surround themselves in it.

Inconjunct matches are two conversions of very different energy, which gives this dynamic the right distance to keep the erotic longing, seduction, and interest at its highest. You're looking at each other like puzzles without solutions, but you're not going to give up. So the container of love needs the right tending, and you'll want to follow your Taurus's lead on this, because affection, consistency, and dependability are their domain. This will be built carefully while you gently coach your Taurus, with that mutable air brain of yours, on ways to soften into flexibility and uncertainty. They'll appreciate your gift to them, and you'll see their softening as a qualifier for trust, because you're never a fan of rigid, constricting dogma. At the same time, your fixed earth Taurus will help you take off the winged sandals and commit to plans, places, and strategies that improve the personal and professional lives of you both. A solid match of Venus values and Mercury strategy, you'll stay deeply joined, forever transcending the mundane together.

GEMINI & GEMINI
Safe, consistent, secure

Put it in writing! Or a love letter. When two—or is it four?—Geminis fly together in a love story, this is a conjunction match of Mercury minds. Two—no, four!—Geminis joining their intelligence and connection skills beautifully. The personification of the quote "Love looks not with the eyes, but with the mind," you fell in love with each other's minds first and started the journey of intimacy and desire from intelligent origins. In this conjunction match, and in each other, you finally found someone who doesn't take themselves too seriously. Too many sticks in the mud really put a damper on your romantic optimism. Your Gemini can hold their own in dialogue, ask the right questions, and gladly introduce you to helpful resources that clarify your personal and relational experiences.

This match needs to work on theory application, not just theory integration. You know the right books, TED

Talks, and podcasts—but if you're not applying them to your love life, what's the point? On love, you'll want to honor how easily you afford each other safety, trust, and loyalty. The ease of your communication provides understanding both given and received. Dare I say, for desire's sake, you'll want to temper your inquisition skills and let mystery stand between you. Once you've figured each other out, the laziness could set in. So incorporate novelty in the mundane as often as you can. This partnership is a romantic think tank where you're always solving problems and helping others lighten up. If you inspire each other to use your intelligence in service of the greater good, your love will never be boring.

GEMINI & CANCER

Loyal, contrasting, instructive

When the Mercury head and moon heart come together, miracles happen. You fell in love with your Cancer's beautiful expressions of emotionality, belonging, and empathy, initiated by their cardinal water bids for connection. Your moon baby loves the light in your eye, how it twinkles with joy, a bit of mischief, and a whole lot of intelligence. An inconjunct match between two neighbor signs, you'll have to accept each other's differences first, agree to willingly find the tender spot between you and call it home. This match can handle the paradox of desire and love because it is itself a paradox. You're forever learning new dimensions of each other, so it'll never be boring and the chemistry's sure to stay seductive.

As the cerebral one, you'll offer critical awareness to help your tender Cancer reality check their inner conspiracies. Especially while you're building the container of love, which should be held by Cancer, as they understand family and emotionality. Together you'll then develop trust, respect, and commitment for one another. Your eloquence will help you and your Cancer find the right intentions and values to keep your love safe. Your crab will expand your problem-solving repertoire by helping you wrap your head around your heart, a practice that makes them feel like they can love you more deeply. Something's in it for you, too, seeing as how emotional intelligence is a crucial skill for a meaningful life in today's culture. In this match between the moon and Mercury, water and air, you'll embody emotional intelligence and teach it to the zodiac in masterful ways, as you help us all find the right word for the right emotion. That way, we know we're not alone because you're in love.

GEMINI & LEO

Joyful, supportive, adventurous

Hey, jester! Like it or not, you're essentially your monarch's official entertainment. It's a good thing you don't take yourself too seriously, except about making sure you have a good sense of humor. You observed your royal Leo's worthiness and bravery, which made you breathe a bit faster. Sovereign Leo wholeheartedly admires the way your mutable air energy helps to uplift, inspire, entertain, and educate in every room. In return for your royal amusement, Leo offers you a castle of opportunities, excitement, loyalty, and empowerment from their fixed fire heart, helping you showcase your many talents not just to them, but to the world.

This sextile match inspires quick closeness, safety, and authenticity, which allows the love to survive and thrive for as long as you both decree. So long as you inspire your monarch to take themselves and their social conditioning a little less seriously, the desire between you burns very hot. Because in this space of contrast and friendly disagreement, you'll learn more about each other's different points of view and find inspiration. Your lighthearted approach helps the lion think differently about what it means to be the queen of the jungle, whereas the royal of the stars will help you contribute your work more bravely, with a beautiful blend of Leo-inspired openheartedness and the natural open-mindedness that springs forth from you. From this sextile space of reciprocated love between firepower and air intelligence, you're each other's biggest fans, and there's nothing your royal family cannot accomplish together.

GEMINI & VIRGO
Powerful, transformative, dynamic
Who's the valedictorian? When brainiac Mercury's only two signs align romantically, the sexy square battle of the know-it-alls begins, and only one will make the grade. You fell when you were inspired by the deep concentration behind your Virgo's glasses. You fell even harder when you witnessed their verbal communication skills, focus on interpersonal service, and hilarious wit. Virgo came around to appreciating how you're annoyingly both class clown and top of the class. They don't always admit it, but Virgo loves to laugh with and at you while learning which of your twins can partner with them on each. Dating you is truly two for the price of one!

Given your Mercury signs' insatiable curiosities, keep the chemistry and desire strong by not reaching for certainty, disclosure, and explanation—you'll be the dean of desire. The unknown, though annoying, keeps your square dynamic of mutable air and earth magnetized toward each other consistently. To secure the safety, trust, and reliability of love, follow your Virgo's education and encourage them to seek progress, not perfection, as the preferred outcome. They'll come to cherish your empowered authenticity, rather than worshipping what's unattainably perfect. You'll remind them to make boundaries instead of people pleasing. Virgo will help you find the divine in the details of organization, health, and finances, which admittedly aren't your strongest skills. When you take care of the micro, you can plan the macro by strategizing adventure, novelty, and intellectual activities during which you relearn each other. This will afford you both the companionship and fun you crave in love and life.

GEMINI & LIBRA
Harmonious, sensual, affectionate
Love is in the air! When you two air signs form this trine match, a calm, harmonizing, and romantic energy leaves the ethers and solidifies in the relationship between your cardinal air partner and your mutable air soul. You clung to every one of your Libra's poetic words, interpersonal graces, and romantic gestures throughout their day-to-day life. You couldn't help but marvel at their social popularity and magnetism, since the social domain is how you measure the romantic potential of your beloved. Assuredly Libra was impressed by your interpersonal thoughtfulness and diverse articulations. You're both relationally oriented, so when you find each other, it's a homecoming. This homecoming is the homeland for the

ease, closeness, trust, and harmony that trine love adores. While you join heart to heart and mind and mind, love is found.

Two social signs will have to willingly increase the distance, autonomy, and mystique that desire thrives on. You'll want to join less in the mind, but pursue more connection in the sensual, seductive bodies to keep the erotic space strong. Keeping you moving forward, Libra will teach you tact, forever reminding you how to get more with honey than you do with vinegar, you naughty one. You'll task Libra with courage over comfort. You'll have them personally question "What will people think?" less, and ask "What decision aligns with my values?" more. Between your Mercurial adaptability and their Venus-informed negotiation skills, you'll write your own script on love, declare the right expectations, and formulate the best contract, which helps you feel like it's forever a win–win deal in this trine dynamic.

GEMINI & SCORPIO
Surreal, mysterious, magnetic
"Odd couple"? Not so fast in this quincunx match, especially when you consider mythology. Scorpio's planetary ruler, Pluto, who governed the underworld in myth, allowed only Mercury, the ruler of Gemini, into his domain to move freely between heaven and hell. You were both intimidated and bewitched by Scorpio's mystique, wondering what magnetism and truths lay beneath their powerful exterior. Curiosity is one of your favorite values, and Scorpio leaves a lot of questions unanswered. Pointed Scorpio was initially unimpressed by you but soon discovered your psyche's depth

and then embraced your joy, humor, and vulnerability as wonderful values to incorporate in their own life. They realized you can fly between heaven and hell, which is why this quincunx match can handle the paradox of love and desire so effectively.

Your energies already reconcile two fundamental but opposite needs—freedom and commitment. So the desire between you is likely to stay strong, especially because the Scorpio will hardly reveal anything unless it's "need to know." But love needs the right agreements to afford you safety and trust, so you'll need to be the initiator of those tough conversations, be very clear about what emotional safety looks like for the both of you, and put in the effort to make it happen. You'll teach Scorpio how to keep assumptions, words, and behaviors in the highest energies toward love and compassion, instead of in the underworld's lowly, mean-spirited, and mistrusting energies, whereas your Scorpio will texture your vision with painful but necessary understandings of authenticity, intimacy, and belonging. So you'll see this isn't an odd couple at all, because both visions are necessary and that's your bind to each other: the mission of discovering and communicating the greatest truth.

GEMINI & SAGITTARIUS
Completion, romantic, compromise

Freedom fighters, unite! Under this polarity match of liberation, exploration, education, and expansion, you still have a beautiful basis of support and loyalty. Your one and only polarity sign, Jupiter-ruled Sagittarius picks up all of your Mercury-ruled research and data with a grateful heart and then shares its wisdom universally.

They fell head over hooves for you when you started talking. Verbal communication is Sagittarius's favorite pastime, and your words drip honey, a bit of salt, and just the right amount of humor to keep your centaur laughing and interested in everything you're saying. When your polarity sign took it upon themselves to challenge, complicate, and validate your beliefs, you fell, too. You love to square up in a debate as much as they do.

The thermonuclear chemistry and desire between you is effortless because, though you have a ton in common, you're still opposite signs. So this distance inspires more curiosity, seduction, and attraction. Then you'll want to identify which common points of trust, loyalty, and respect are defined by your shared values. Outside of love and desire, you'll inspire Sagittarius to narrow their visions a bit, so they don't get too scattered, whereas your centaur takes you out of the weeds of the micro and happily redirects you toward the sunrise of hope, adventure, and innovation instead. Combining your wealth of intellectual resources and Sagittarius's optimistic vision, this match is two halves of one beautiful whole. And when you merge together, you'll embody alternative possibilities and create conversations together that shift your personal and relational resonances in wonderful ways.

GEMINI & CAPRICORN
Surreal, mysterious, magnetic
You can fly to the heavens; they can climb to the mountaintop. Where the skies meet the peak is where this quincunx connection between cardinal earth and mutable air shines. Your seagoat's ambition, ethics, and self-mastery, instructed by their ruling planet, Saturn, might've scared

your sensibilities a bit, but you couldn't take your eyes off their dignity. The mountain climber loved your aviation senses, too. They're devilishly charmed by your Mercurial sense of humor, impeccable social skills, and intelligence, which disarmed them a bit too easily. This is a power-couple match of reliability and spontaneity.

The chemistry is electric because desire craves existential distance, which you'll ensure because you know when it's the right time to fly away. Since you're both so different, you'll stay unknown each other and the erotic longing will remain high. For love to continue thriving and surviving, you'll want to listen to the seagoat here and show integrity and consistency to your Capricorn—that is how they discern whether their love will be taken care of. Make sure you say what you mean, mean what you say, and do it because love is a practice, not a professing. You'll give your mountain climber a bit more self-compassion, which inspires them to be gentle on themselves during their climb. Your Capricorn will need to show you their lighter, more fun-loving dimensions, which will invite you to soften into joy and love with them. They'll need to learn not to take themselves too seriously, which will make you more comfortable. Especially since, when this match of air and earth is done well, there's no mountaintop or altitude your partnership can't climb to, and you'll bring out the masterpieces in each other.

GEMINI & AQUARIUS
Harmonious, sensual, affectionate

It's a firework show! Eccentric and flashy Aquarius explodes in Technicolor while in the perception of Gemini's keen mind. The minute you thought, "I never saw it like that," you fell in love with your genius, Uranus-ruled

Aquarius. Their intellectual prowess knows no limit, which is the energy behind this match between their fixed air and your mutable air love. Now every speaker needs a careful listener, so your Mercury-ruled willingness to take in Aquarius's information thoughtfully was when the water bearer took your name into their heart. A trine match, this is an amiable association—a harmonious, commonality-based synergy of mindful and romantic love. This is a magnificent foundation for love to soar from, because you feel safe, heard, understood, and cherished. As a trine match between two air signs, you have a freedom and mobility between you without effort.

You have the liberation down to a science, but the action and loyalty around partnership needs a bit more prioritizing. As two rather detached signs, you'll want to strategize physical and emotional intimacy through proximity, so you can show up for each other beautifully. Connections need to be tended to and hardly taken for granted. Talk specifically about attachment styles from your family of origin and explore the ways you bid for connection, so you can see love as language and listen carefully. In these interactions, you'll inspire the Aquarius to rationalize with less rigidity and gain more comfort with exploring the unknown, practicing curiosity, and accepting vulnerability, instead of being totally right all the time. Your Aquarius innovator will give you a strong repertoire of moral convictions to help you step up your research methods and verbal communication skills, so you don't back down on your pursuit for knowledge.

GEMINI & PISCES
Powerful, transformative, dynamic

The fairy and the mermaid. A passionate square dynamic between the winged air ones of Mercury and ocean-dwelling merpeople of Neptune, this love is fantastical, miraculous, and totally out of this world. You're both divine creatures, both mutable signs, different and yet similar. The premier wordsmith, you're forever curious to know all that's unspoken in life, and the Pisces heart lives where words can't dwell—on the ocean floor. Tender Pisces is completely charmed by your social graces, extroversion, critical intelligence, and effortless articulation of what you feel in the waters of your heart. In this square dynamic, the desire is often magnetic, because you're both very mystical and unknown to each other. A Pisces is probably the only sign you'll never completely figure out. Don't rush their disclosure or proximity, because Pisces is the leader of desire in this match. The mutable energy keeps you returning to each other sincerely and passionately until the lessons are learned.

Stability is helpful for love to bond you both—which is where you need to rise to on occasion, putting language to both of your needs, with clearly defined contexts for reliability, trust, and commitment. Integrity is the space that allows you to fly and swim beautifully together. Your creative Pisces will teach you one of the greatest lessons of all: that not every emotion needs to be said in order to earn validation. They'll encourage your fluency in nonverbal communication. Often your emotions can just be felt with the heart and acted upon. You'll invite Pisces to learn to identify, through the right language and word choice, what they need to feel safe and what they're feeling. If willing to learn, you can fly and swim together where the blue of the skies above meets the blue of the oceans below, and where your love is passionately one.

CANCER IN LOVE

Empathetic | Gentle | Attentive
Honor: Tenderness & Safety
Integrate: Boundaries & Discipline

When we fall in love, we come home. There are countless queer folks who feel abandoned by home and family, and Cancer meets them at the front door with open arms. In romance, Cancer invites their beloved into their heart as home, loves them like they're family, and builds a temple of belonging to honor romance.

Love needs to be tended to in order to survive safely, and safety is love's foundation. There can be no love without it. That's why home is a symbol, but no guarantee, for the ultimate security. Cancer, as the cardinal water sign, bids in attentive, gentle ways for relationships, to help keep romantic belonging safe.

For Cancer's connections to stay in integrity, Cancer has to honor their tenderness and desire for emotional safety, even prior to relationship commitment. Cancer has to initiate, embody, and demonstrate it without apology. They'll align with suitors who share the same romantic values, and they'll build a home together on mutuality.

To protect their sensitivities, Cancer would benefit from practicing proactive boundaries and emotional discipline. That way, Cancer stays safe, and others know what is or is not allowed. They'll need the discipline to transcend emotional self-indulgence, speak their boundaries, and then maintain them. When this is achieved, they can keep their heart open and maintain peace of mind. With that, Cancer is at home everywhere and treats everyone as family, with love in their heart.

CANCER & ARIES
Powerful, transformative, dynamic
Spring, meet summer! The confident ram and gentle crab were born after the solstices of spring and summer. So this square dynamic between your cardinal water personality and cardinal fire partner has both sexy tension and the right commonalities to secure trust. Your typically guarded heart fell swiftly for the zodiac's firstborn child, Aries, because you recognized another cardinal sign—a leader who passionately fights for their causes and goes out of their way to secure what they love. Their vigor is thrilling. Aries loves your summer magic. When you let partners in to experience your inner world, you're both gentle and uplifting, like a July breeze in a heat wave. You empower the Aries to let their dreams shine brighter in your perception, which radiates summer sunlight on your loved ones.

This square dynamic has an inconvenient but magnetic tension, which helps desire flourish. You know there's a common point between you as cardinal signs, though your Aries will stabilize the clashing elements and keep you mysterious to one another, and you'll want to trust their inspiration there. So you'll want to explore how to build trust and stability, because that's your homeland, so that desire has a place to prosper in the context of love. Identify and ask what affection and fondness mean to you both, based on your emotional dowries and attachment styles, then put it into practice. You'll learn how to incorporate more direct action and bravery in your life from your Martian's leadership. And your ram will study how you incorporate more interpersonal consideration and empathy in your daily life. This is a dynamic that is both mysterious and fairly consistent. Which gives you desire, joy, fun, and love.

CANCER & TAURUS
Joyful, supportive, adventurous

Creatures of comfort, unite! The tender crab and the steady bull like to live their lives as free from uncertainty, risk, and emotional exposure as possible, which is why this sextile match is centrally organized on ease and comfort. Your moonlit heart immediately felt the consistency, reliability, and strength from your Venus-ruled Taurus as the preferred container to hold your heart's ocean of love. The sensual bull felt your tide's gravity and was deeply impressed by your consideration, thoughtfulness, and gracious empathy. You felt called to show your identity's most authentic nature to one another because the safety between you is a sanctuary. Thus the loving contexts of trust and respect were given.

To hold the spark of desire that tethered you both to begin with, your task is to balance the natural comfort with a bit of edge. You'll want to implement privacy, boundaries, and personal space—hello, crab shell!— without letting the beautiful intimacy become intrusion. Because you're both so relational, it's hard to maintain distance. You'll inspire Taurus to indulge in excess a whole lot less and to share energy more freely—like conversation space, resources, and the room for others to disagree. Taurus will empower you to wrestle with any emotional discomfort and turbulence with practical values and their critical awareness. They'll help you stay skeptical of thoughts that give you stress and shame. Since you both love comfort, you'll want to strengthen your capacities to handle vulnerability and uncertainty in and out of the relationship. That way your love works as a beautiful protection agent, while you engage with risk and innovation outside your dynamic.

CANCER & GEMINI
Loyal, contrasting, instructive

Pass the torch! This spring-into-summer inconjunct match occurs when bordering signs romance. When you consider how the Mercury twins pass the torch to the moon-ruled crab, it lights up the journey from the head to the heart. At first laugh or aha moment, you fell slowly but surely for the Gemini's wit, humor, and problem-solving skills. Once the mutable air proved they could be reliable and consistent, you were all in. The twins were inspired by the depth of your cardinal water sign's emotions, your sharp sense of humor, and all the thoughtful words you use to tell your partner how loved they are.

When it comes to owning desire, let Gemini take the lead. This is an air sign who's often aloof, and this existential distance between you holds the possibility for the unknown and mystery to keep the chemistry burning. Of course on the safety, stability, and trust expressions that love needs to survive, that's all your domain. Outline the factors that help you feel safe without hampering desire. You know love's and desire's needs are different, so try to manage this anomaly as best you can. You'll inspire your Gemini to think critically still while expressing their emotional intelligence. The Gemini will offer you their thinking cap when you're drowning in emotional discomfort and give you the right thought, word, or idea to help reality check shame stories and conspiracies. This is the match that exemplifies emotional intelligence to the rest of the zodiac. Honor the differences, celebrate your strengths, and mission accomplished!

CANCER & CANCER
Safe, consistent, secure

Honey, I'm home! When two descendants of the moon romance, they move in together quickly. When something feels like home for you, you know it—and you both knew it. In this conjunction match between you two little homebodies and cardinal water signs, you find belonging, loyalty, and love with another who defines these values as specifically as you do. In your Cancer, you found someone whose heart sings the same melody for romance, family, and loyalty. In you, they found the place where this song originates, and this harmony of devotion fills every square inch of the home you've built. This match may be one of the few where desire and love sing the same song. You desire safety. You desire security. Your erotic side is highly emotionally invested. So this conjunction match may blend the best of both.

If not, that's quite all right! Consider which you need more of. Do you need more spark and longing? Or reliability and security? If it's the spark, then delicately introduce more space between you, or try new things together. If it's security, you'll want to negotiate the parameters of trust and reliability, then willingly implement them. Stay very clear, specific, and direct. On the growth front, you'll want to balance each other's emotional regulation tools with consistent and purposeful critical awareness and resilience. This will keep you from making up stories in your head or avoiding uncomfortable conversations for fear of conflict. If you've learned to use the right processing tools, this match is set to last. If love and desire are beautifully maintained, you'll build a haven where you can heal your internal worlds together, safe from the despairs of the external world.

CANCER & LEO
Loyal, contrasting, instructive
There are many poems and mythologies on the love between the sun and the moon. In some form, they all honor this match. When the moonlit Cancer stands in the grandeur of the Leo's sunshine, it's an inconjunct dynamic that inspires awe to both them and the world. In your fixed fire Leo, you've found a powerful emotional bodyguard, which honors your value of relationships as safety and as never-ending sources of fealty and affirmation. In your cardinal water love, the highly romantic Leo found an equally strong archetype, who waxes and wanes in partnership. Leo treasures connections from those who are all in and firmly engaged when it comes to love, which you are. You want quality connections and a person with whom you can share a life, family, and home.

For this moon/sun match, proactive disclosure on the exact and clear parameters for love, belonging, security, and trust would be the primary place for effort. Given Leo's fixed nature, they'll have a cat's paw up on you here. So consider their reliance, dependability, and tenacity. The moon and sun shine at different times, so find the full moon between you—the desire and attraction. As very different archetypes, modalities, and elements, you're unusual to each other, which, along with your natural mystique, keeps the dynamic passionate and erotic, so long as you accept each other's differences. You'll help the zodiac's royal exercise a greater concern for others and the relational good of all concerned, as opposed to their specific desires only, whereas your conflict-loving Leo will help you learn how to advocate for yourself, appreciate the value of straight talk for straight understanding, and teach you the strategies of filling up your own cup before filling up the cups of others. Your love lights up the sky.

CANCER & VIRGO
Joyful, supportive, adventurous
If love is a hospital for the soul, this match has the best emergency room in town. As two relational and highly interpersonally focused signs, you know the meaning of life is all about service. You didn't let Virgo's strong gaze of contemplation, tranquility, and focus distract you from feeling their emotional obligation to help others. As Mercury-ruled and mutable earth, Virgo loves to help their partners in all fashions—from the micro, like organizing spaces, to the macro, like business coaching. Astute Virgo saw that your moon-ruled, cardinal water heart is comfortable in similar practices: thoughtful caretaking and compassion. So when you align in this earth and water sextile dynamic, it's a union where you help each other handle the realities of the world with the healing effects of practical, thoughtful, and empathetic energy between you.

Of course the container of love and the trust-building behavior and conversations are organic in this match.

You'll have a wonderful structure to let love blossom if you see your natural affection, wonder, and loyalty as the key. The sextile spark of desire will take a bit more effort, so you'll want to delegate that to the Virgo, who can make it an intellectual challenge. Remember, pleasure and sexual preferences are undemocratic and self-preoccupied. So you'll have to temper your reflexes for interpersonal service with a little more self-concern and a willingness to receive, in order to keep the dance of desire in its wonderful choreography. You'll show Virgo how self-compassion and self-forgiveness are nonnegotiable for their mission to change the world. Then your Virgo will help you embrace emotional regulation tools like open sharing, mediation, and other resources that help you cultivate resilience while you teach belonging. With intellect and emotion, it's the hospital for the soul.

CANCER & LIBRA
Powerful, transformative, dynamic
When the solstice- and equinox-born align, it's a powerful, push-pull dynamic with both the necessary components of separation and the gifts of partnership. Venus-ruled Libra was born under the autumn equinox, so there's the cardinal air initiation of the balance between light and dark. Whereas you were born under the moon after the summer solstice, your cardinal water initiating safety and belonging without the balance totally fortified yet. As the cardinal square between water and air, the longing of desire often stays strong in the sweet spot between emotion and reason, closeness and distance, talking and feeling. Exploring this relationship as rich with chemistry, security, and mutual education will help you both realize that your singular

approaches to life don't hold all the answers, which is why collaboration is key. No one's inherently right. Or wrong. Only the harmony between you sings the sweetest song.

That's why exploring the vessel for love is helpful here. You'll want to initiate a thoughtful dialogue early, where you reveal just enough of what you both value so that safety, trust, and accountability can grow, allowing each other to feel cherished and respected. Your cerebral Libra will exercise a bit of emotional distance, so you'll learn how to objectively self-soothe using critical awareness, rather than with assistance or distraction. You'll empower relational Libra to hold space for their own and other people's discomfort, without rushing for a solution. You'll help Libra see their intellect as a powerful empathy tool, too. Since Cancer teaches us the value of family and belonging and Libra demonstrates how relationships make it happen, this is a match where we see the family more romantically between the solstice and equinox.

CANCER & SCORPIO
Harmonious, sensual, affectionate
Breathing underwater is totally underrated, isn't it? With this sensual and intimate trine match between Cancer and Scorpio, a beautiful arrangement of two water signs gives you both the ability to dwell in the oceans of creativity, compassion, affection, and love together. When fixed water Scorpio walked in, the 70 percent of cardinal water in your body was at a gloriously high tide, since that's what Pluto-influenced souls will do to you. And you knew you were in the resonance of someone who emotionally and intuitively understands your world, too. When Scorpio's inner eyes and senses felt your moon

power, they registered a like-minded soul who lives on a depth of emotionality, generosity, and devotion. As such, love as practice is easily made manifest here with your natural affection, kindness, and respect for one another, which are the favorite values of the water signs. You'll nurture the roots where love grows with these qualities, so prodigious within you both.

Trine water signs can't help but collude, so maintain the mystique without hurting each other's feelings, and carefully create the space for you both to continuously learn about each other by making the familiar novel again. You'll hold a high standard for Scorpio to rise to, where they can soften into emotional exposure with ease and make generous assumptions about the intent of others, as opposed to believing everyone is guilty. Scorpio will help you say no as a complete sentence to anyone—including yourself!—when something's out of alignment with your personal authenticity or the greater good. This trine match keeps you both feeling anchored in the water domain, since you're both wave and anchor. Happy sailing!

CANCER & SAGITTARIUS
Surreal, mysterious, magnetic
Contrast, anyone? This quincunx match between adventure-seeking Sagittarius and homebody Cancer is sure to make your own and others' heads spin with bewilderment and awe. As the cardinal water sign, you love to initiate emotional attachments to the places and people that help you feel comfortable and like you belong. Whereas Sagittarius's mutable fire personality likes to seek but not find. Their joy is in the wanting, exploring, and searching for

the unknown with optimism. That's why you were easily attracted to Sagittarius's essentially benevolent, honest, and altruistic nature. Like most of the zodiac, even you can't help but shine and smile around their energy, because their optimistic perception is one so many want to be seen and heard in. Wise ol' Sagittarius knows you're a professor of the heart, and they love listening to your stories, which are textured by the emotional intelligence you bring to relationships and belonging.

If you can find the same language to speak, you'll love to dialogue. So given your cardinal leadership, initiate a conversation on how you both learned affection, trust, stability, and commitment from your family of origin. Once you mutually agree to the terms and conditions, this quincunx match is safe. Since the desire won't have any issues—you're about as alien to one another as it gets, and Sagittarius will ensure existential distance because freedom is their value—your relationship will inspire thrill, longing, and seduction. You'll help your centaur find joy and belonging in the here and now, as opposed to constantly futurizing and seeking beyond. Your centaur will coach you to leave the confines of your comfort zone and the security of home in pursuit of adventure in the unknown. Bon voyage!

CANCER & CAPRICORN
Completion, romantic, compromise
The law of opposites strikes again! Your one and only polarity sign, diametrically across and opposed to you on the zodiac wheel, Saturn-born Capricorn picks up where you finish. In the responsible and ethically concerned seagoat, you've found Saturn's divine blend between

watery caretaker and earthy provider. As the seagoat, they're both mountain climber provider and sea-diving empathy giver. They reveal both sides at a glacial pace, so be patient if you're all in. In your moon-ruled soul, the seagoat carefully discerns a compassionate and devoted lover whose values on connection, like generosity, respect, and loyalty, are as timeless as theirs. This match is a blend of assertive meets receptive, forceful meets magnetic.

Polarity dynamics salute our best and reveal our worst. So I suspect the desire, seduction, and chemistry will maintain strength because there's often a tension that keeps you both wondering and trying to really get it right with each other. On the affection, respect, and trust qualities of love, this is a conversation you'll want to implore your Capricorn to engage in, because the earth element knows how to put love into practice. Find where you're both gifted and where you need improvement, then accept each other's contrasting styles so you can help sculpt each other on your way to greatness. Your waters will soften the edges of Capricorn and help them consider the possibility that everyone's doing the best they can with limited tools—increasing your seagoat's capacity for empathy. Strict Capricorn will help you place your compassionate energy in places where it's asked for and earned. Can't give away your energy for free! Together you're the container and the connection for love, home, and belonging.

CANCER & AQUARIUS
Surreal, mysterious, magnetic
"E.T., phone home?" This is quite an extraterrestrial pair between two quincunx signs. As a cardinal water sign governed by the comfortable moon, you love to under-

stand and practice true belonging, safety, and home. When you align with an Aquarius, you're face-to-face with the subversion of your nature. Their Uranus-ruled identity is rebellious, detached, and intellectually disruptive. Their nomadic lifestyle inspires you to consider alternative possibilities about laying roots in places you never gave a passing thought to. The Aquarius is curious to know more about the waters in your emotion ocean, and they're enthralled by your ability to tell the stories of love and connection. While you're in dialogue and mutually admitting emotional attachments to each other, be the Cancer captain of the conversation—outlining the expectations and contexts of respect, kindness, affection, and trust is so helpful. You're both benevolent beings, so it should be a wonderful talk.

As soon as that's defined, the sparks of desire start flying even more. You'll agree on what you need to agree on, and your extraterrestrial Aquarius will keep the detachment, wonder, longing, and seduction alive. If at the end of the story, you quincunx people define home and family the same way—you're golden. Especially since you'll teach Aquarius to consider not going it alone. The zodiac as a symbol of collective unity means we're not meant to do it alone. And your Aquarius will push you out of your comfort zones for a brave, daring, innovative ride into the wilderness. Enjoy the adventure!

CANCER & PISCES
Harmonious, sensual, affectionate
Love was found under the sea! You two water signs form a mighty match of supportive trines, and the dynamic is like a seaside cabana of harmony, calm, union, loyalty, and

creativity. The mutable water and Neptune-born Pisces sang the song of the sea, which matches the music in your heart. In their voice, you heard a lover who is searching for the same mystical home of safety and healing you are. When Pisces heard your song, they found the divine belonging only Cancer can give to their beloved. This trine match is like finding treasure in a shipwreck. The jewels of your love surround you with affection, devotion, kindness, and respect. It's really those little things and expressions that make the difference. These little things are your pearls of wisdom. So wrap language around attachment styles, family of origin, and love maps to show your Pisces how seriously you take relationship connection.

If you can pace yourself in the beginning and adjust to Pisces's naturally slower speed, it'll help keep the initial spark strong. Your Pisces may need a bit more time before revealing their unconditional love. So hold on to this trine's mystique and seduction without anxiety or apologies to each other, because it keeps you bonded, not bored. Don't rush it to avoid the initial vulnerabilities of relationship building. And remember, you can always make the familiar unfamiliar again by doing new things together. Your leadership skills will help your Pisces get started on their dreams, and together you'll make them a reality with your initiate empowerment and their prodigious skills. Your Pisces will inspire you to tap into your heart's intelligence through a spiritual practice, which will give you faith over fear and the experience to know the universe is working in favor of your love story's success, always.

LEO IN LOVE

Romantic | Generous | Devoted
Honor: Courage & Confidence
Integrate: Change & Deference

A Leo in love is a wonder of the world. When they're inspired to leave their throne because another sovereign captivates them, Leo will unveil such romantic grandeur, it's awe inspiring. When courage is in the air, it's contagious.

When Leo is in love, they show their heart with powerful bids for connection. When a Leo is all in for love, they're one of the most devoted partners you could find. They'd be wise to honor their capacity for courage by expressing the stories in their heart. It's vulnerable to demonstrate emotions, but it's necessary as a first step to earn connection with the monarch. Leo should also honor their confidence by never dimming their light or taking up less space to make others feel bigger.

Now integration is key! So Leo would benefit by embracing the wholeness of life's experiences and softening into change. Flexibility is a skill that's nonnegotiable for relationship health. So is deference. And Leo will shine when they humbly defer decision making and plans to their beloved when it matters most. That way, their beloved will feel a bit more supported while they corule the kingdom of their lives.

LEO & ARIES
Harmonious, sensual, affectionate
Burn, baby. Burn! You two fire signs set up a trine match

that's ablaze because Aries is the first spark to Leo's eternal flame. When you saw the Aries sparking, you rightfully intuited the ram could hold a candle to your tinderbox. Aries exhibits direct momentum, innovation, candor, and confidence as the cardinal fire champion. Whereas the zodiac's Martian knew you were no push-over, either, given your royal status. Aries loves strength matching strength. So you're a bona fide challenge and a powerful equal in your courage, passion, and skills. Aries can finally put down the boxing gloves in favor of romance. When fire joins, you both feel so joyful, empowered, and free. You're a trine match of fire signs, but one of your energies is better suited for love and the other for desire.

On love, this all Leo's kingdom. As a fixed sign, you are the royal of affection, consistency, and stability. So empower yourself and inspire your Aries to trust your lead on the contexts for respect. As the rapid cardinal fire sign, Aries knows desire's domain. As the first sign in the zodiac, they're often new to everything. So they'll inspire you to get out of your ruts and monotony with their erotic longing, adventure, surprise, and spontaneity. On the growth front, you'll inspire the ram to master their passions, not just dabble in them, whereas your leading lover will motivate you to begin ventures in uncharted territory. Aries will help you show up bravely in life arenas without guarantee. You're each other's biggest fans, and with this support system, there's hardly a milestone you can't accomplish together.

LEO & TAURUS

Powerful, transformative, dynamic

Where fire meets earth, this sunset match is a breath-taking sight to see. A square partnership between two dynamically strong characters is sure to sustain the chemistry. In your fixed earth Taurus, you've found a self-possessed Venus-born bull whose values, passions, and interests are entirely their own. This security attracts you because it's self-generated, just like your fixed energy. The sensual bull discerned your fixed fiery enthusiasm for romantic pursuits, embodied pleasure, joy, and all forms of the creative arts. If you can first celebrate each other's differences and accept them in order for the authenticity of the dynamic to unfold, love will be put into practice.

Between your heart-centered intelligence and Taurus's classic values, I suspect you'll have no issues building the container of love, which needs affection, dependability, and consistency. Because desire needs enough distance for each of you to stand down, that's where your unapologetic autonomy owns the throne. Protect the separation between your kingdom and Taurus's Eden ferociously. You can both be like dogs with bones when you're in love, so protect the romance by inhibiting the intrusion through the giving and receiving of space. You'll empower the bull to have more confidence in pursuing their life purpose with the bravery to lean in to risk without guarantees. Your bull will coach you toward taking the right practical steps to set up your inevitable success throughout the kingdom. Through a careful commitment to proactive discussions on the values that organize your love, this match will last as long as you want. Compromise and negotiation won't come easy for this pair, but it's necessary for the Leo sun to shine on the Taurus-ruled horizon.

LEO & GEMINI
Joyful, supportive, adventurous
You fell in love at first laughter. In this supportive sextile match between the kingdom's clown and you, its royal, the chemistry's rich with humor and joy. In your mutable air Gemini, you found a Mercurial storyteller whose communication skills enthrall you with information, anecdotes, and honey-loaded words of affirmation. In you, the fixed fire celebrity, the Gemini found an eternal flame of embodied inspiration, a passionate listener, and the courage to be all in to personal and relational experiences. Don't be afraid to trust your Gemini's strategies on desire sustaining. As Gemini is two in one, you'll have one twin fully in the relationship, but you won't be totally sure you have the other. This is a good thing! It keeps you enchanted by the unknown, and yet secure at the same time.

You'll have to instruct your Gemini on the efficacy of affection, proximity, affirmation, and kindness in love. They're not novices per se, but they may not know it's mandatory. That's where your royal education comes in, and Gemini's eternally a curious student. Additionally, you'll want to inspire your twins to theorize less with the research they've gathered as a defense mechanism and run right into the experience with a combination of head, heart, and worthiness. Your Gemini will give you the right words to understand dissent, listen effectively, and negotiate with others so they don't think you're a greedy queen. This match promises comfort, joy, and wonderful opportunities for growth, to help you become the sovereign you're capable of being.

LEO & CANCER
Loyal, contrasting, instructive

Truly, the sun's only heavenly match is the moon. When you met your inconjunct sign in the moon-ruled Cancer, you knew your sun soul was tethered for reasons beyond immediate understanding. When the sun shined on the cardinal water Cancer, you found a loving, compassionate, and nurturing partner who has the premier emotional and psychological skills to hold space for your devotion. In the kingdom of your heart, the safety-seeking Cancer found a protective, loyal, and fiery partner who was emotionally invested in making their relationship work. There aren't many signs you'll have to show deference to on the practice of desire, but Cancer is definitely one of them. As your crab is a cardinal water sign, you'll want to watch, listen, and follow their lead on all matters related to seduction and mystique. It's their kingdom.

When it comes to the affection, reliability, and strength of love, that's where you hold the crown. As a fixed sign, you're responsible for the little things that create a big container of love, and you'll think of ingenious ideas to make it happen for the sun and the moon. You'll gently coax the Cancer to seek less emotional safety in favor of experiences where they're seen and heard, because they're worthy. The Cancer will help you wrap your crown around the heart. So you'll develop the emotional lexicon that guides you to lead, innovate, and run in the direction of your dreams. The sovereigns of the stars, this match is the love that powers the sky.

LEO & LEO
Safe, consistent, secure

This castle won't be too crowded! Every Leo needs a partner who's their emotional, psychological, and behavioral equal. A tall order, I know. The essential law to make the royals of the zodiac happy is finding them a partner who won't back down. So welcome to this conjunct match between the fixed fire signs! In your fellow monarch, you've met a match who is your royal peer—another crowned one who's just as dramatically romantic, openhearted, powerful, and fearless in their pursuit of personal and relational well-being. You'll inspire each other to dare greatly, live a life that's larger than life, and love very loudly. Which is why I know you'll help each other keep the fires of love burning powerfully in emotional affirmation, consistency, affection, respect, and kindness.

You show how love is put into practice by tending to romance with elegance and majesty. As you fall into the comforts of love, don't forget to breathe the right amount of air into the desire between you, with just the right amount of healthy risk, intrigue, seduction, and sensuality. You'll also want to fan the flames of your own lives with passion and enthusiasm before cohabiting fully in the castle. It takes two before you can become one, after all. And to keep the castle from burning down with all your solar-powered passion, a quick but proactive outline of what values you share and what arenas you will or will not budge on will go a long way. And if you're on the same decree, then you'll rule the kingdom together with the highest of integrity, resilience, respect, and authority.

LEO & VIRGO
Loyal, contrasting, instructive

At your service! You two neighboring signs have more in common in this inconjunct match than just the physical proximity in the zodiac. In your mutable earth Virgo, you've found a partner who is deeply concerned and forever curious about ways to be of service to others, since they're ruled by strategist Mercury. Though you don't make it obvious, you're also concerned about others. Virgo's acumen, wit, and sense of responsibility unlocked your royal respect. When Virgo saw you, they detected a generous and openhearted leader who is trying their best to make a difference. Not so different after all. As an inconjunct match between two different archetypes, qualities, and elements, maintaining desire will be pretty easy. Provided your Virgo doesn't remove the uncertainty, mystery, or longing in the relationship with their hunger for knowledge and security, that is. Move at your Leo pace in the desire department, because your fixed fire knows when it's time to stoke the flames.

In matters of love and service, that's your Virgo's bailiwick. Pay close attention to their innate understanding of transparency, disclosure, generosity, affection, and compassion for those they love. As the royal of the zodiac, you'll give the more thoughtful, law-abiding Virgo permission to disrupt the status quo, break the rules, and be direct in their feedback while they act in service of others. Whereas the ever-so-healing Virgo will coach you on ways to invite others into your contagious confidence and empowerment and help you focus on the details required to run the kingdom together.

LEO & LIBRA
Joyful, supportive, adventurous

It's dawning! From an astronomical point of view: the sun rises in the Eastern Hemisphere, and the planet Venus—the planetary ruler of Libra—does, too, rising in the early hours before dawn, which is why Venus is known as the morning star. So this sextile match between the sun-ruled Leo and Venus-ruled Libra works like a heavenly charm on Earth. In cardinal air Libra, you've found a romantic partner who is interpersonally focused and who shines magnificently in social spaces, which helps you feel good. Elegant Libra finds your fixed fire charisma completely mesmerizing and appreciates you the most when you use your popularity and influence to empower or talk about topics that matter.

You're both so romantic and seductive, it's almost a tie for who's more qualified for love and who's better at maintaining desire. Even though Libra's ruled by the goddess of love herself, I think you take the crown, Leo. As the fixed fire sign, you know how to consistently, regularly, and loyally provide devotion, even when it's inconvenient. Don't hold back on love as a verb or love as a practice. And Libra won't hold back in showing you that Libra still belongs to Libra—their little secret garden of intrigue, detachment, and anticipation reminds us how seduction is done beautifully. Your divine worthiness will help inspire the more relational Libra to assert their desires, discomforts, and boundaries without apology. The balanced Libra will instruct you treat your pleasures as no or more less important than the greater good, because it's not always all about you. Then, you and the morning star will shine together!

LEO & SCORPIO
Powerful, transformative, dynamic

Long-distance lovers? The sun-ruled Leo and Pluto-ruled Scorpio are the beginning and end of the solar system. So when it comes to geographic space, this union is as long-distance as it gets. It's a square match between two fixed signs: you beaming with fire, and Scorpio born in water. In your Pluto-ruled Scorpio, you've discovered an equal strength of character, another assured alpha that doesn't have to brag—are you taking notes?—but lets their power, magnetism, and calm strength speak for itself. In your royal resonance, Scorpio quickly identified a titan whose energy is self-generated, which is how your fire attracts them, all the way out there in the cold, to warm up by the sun.

Scorpio doesn't struggle with desire, because they refuse to reveal all things too soon to a lover—their trust is slowly earned and given. Let their demonstration be contagious, and believe there's a reason for their mystique, because you'll never get bored. Of course you're the royal of romance, so you'll want to encourage your Scorpio to soften into affection, respect, and vulnerability without guarantees. If you win Scorpio's love, it's as close to permanent as it gets. So don't ask if you can handle its staying power. You'll inspire the skeptical Scorpio to lead and live with a more trusting and open heart, rather than imagining negative possibilities about the future. No relationship is risk-free. Intimate Scorpio will help you process discomfort happily within the relationship, as opposed to relying on denial, numbing, or avoidance. You don't have to pretend everything is fine when it's not! As the zodiac's bookends of daylight and nightfall, you embody the law of opposites the universe operates on, and the zodiac is grateful for you.

LEO & SAGITTARIUS
Harmonious, sensual, affectionate

It's a heat wave! In this passionate trine match between fire signs Sagittarius and Leo, the dynamic is sure to keep temperatures close to inferno status, so bust out the SPF 100+. Like many, you fell for Sagittarius's grand and contagious optimism. You love how the Jupiter-ruled sign longs for adventure, freedom, education, and expansion. It's a two-way street, because the Sagittarius was captivated by how your fixed fire soul can essentially stay put, but the light in your eye gives away how much you explore parallel universes internally. This trine match is sure to keep the desire context in midsummer temperatures, while Sagittarius teaches you through demonstration what curiosity, exploration, and adventurousness with each other does for desire's life span. Joy is your greatest aphrodisiac, so it'll bind you both pretty close.

You'll want to show your Sagittarius that relationships determine the quality of our lives by consistently responding with affection, trust, respect, and tenderness, which is the fire of love, and your legacy. Your centaur loves freedom, so you'll have to seduce them for commitment. If you help them see how much they gain from intimacy, you'll have a deeply devoted partner. Especially since you'll instruct your Sagittarius on your fixed methods for taking projects to their completion and accomplishing their extraordinary visions. Then your Sagittarius will summon the best of their mutable energy and show you the alternative possibilities they chase, providing inspiration and education to help you in your reign. So long as you pace yourselves, this supportive and harmonious match will provide power, loyalty, and wisdom to your lives in wonderful ways.

LEO & CAPRICORN
Surreal, mysterious, magnetic

The queen and the president. Two very different symbols of leadership, motivation, and power, but pretty equal in terms of the loyalty they can receive from others. In your quincunx match with Saturnian Capricorn, you've found your chief executive who can help you lead your kingdom. An ambitious, responsible, and cardinal earth–ruled worker, Capricorn inspires others to take personal responsibility and succeed in wonderful ways while they reclaim their power. In you, the seagoat finds a royal warmth that beams from the center of your fixed fire heart, which also motivates people to achieve personal development from a place of worthiness. This is a match where you'll want to step down on the practice of love and let the moral authority lead. Capricorn initiates structures like nobody's business, and they'll give your relationship the structure for affection, integrity, reliability, and trust.

As the fun-loving fire sign, you'll keep the dynamic as interesting and spontaneous as possible. While you fan the flames of desire through more adventure and surprise, you'll help the familiar feel new to the timeless Capricorn. What will mean the world to your partner is how you'll inspire your commander in chief to connect to others from a place of emotional exposure and vulnerability. And that's the best path for meaningful inspiration and leadership in today's culture. Then your Capricorn will help you develop the discipline and groundedness to leave the castle and mingle with the locals, so you'll have a greater wealth of experience in your platform. If you want a match that brings out the best of your possibilities, look no further than this quincunx. Now drop and give me twenty!

LEO & AQUARIUS
Completion, romantic, compromise
Us against the world! Even if the odds of two against billions are improbable, when Leo and Aquarius align in a romantic match, the world ought to be nervous. You felt a thermonuclear pull toward Uranus-ruled Aquarius, as their life demonstrates the best of fixed air energy, which is high-minded activism, community organizing, justice for all, and the glory of friendship. It takes two in this polarity match, so trust that the individualist rebel water bearer was suddenly feeling the urge to merge when they took in your magnetism, courage, and romantic nature. Polarity dynamics are peak-and-plummet experiences. So when it comes to the container of love and belonging, you'll want to showcase your natural abilities here and be egalitarian, transparent, and willing to negotiate the terms and conditions of trust, affection, and reliability every step of the way. Edit the contract often to keep up with how much you change together.

Your chemistry is highly unlikely to dissipate so long as you continuously maintain and celebrate this opposites-attract style, which comes like breathing for your airy Aquarius. Don't fall into gridlock, or holding on to pride instead of each other, because as soon as you emotionally lock each other out, you'll erode this beautiful connection. Your sunlit visions will uplift your Aquarius and help them see how capable they are of changing the world with their brilliance, activism, and vision for organizing society and culture in better ways. Your Aquarius will quickly help you change your kingdom by equally sharing resources and the opportunities given to you by the privileges of the spotlight. It's a polarity pair, so the paradox is strong, the desire's hot, and the love is given and received by all.

LEO & PISCES
Surreal, mysterious, magnetic
When the sun shines on the ocean, what's more beautiful than that? It's called sun glitter, and in this quincunx pair, you have to cherish the beauty you bring to each other's lives. Your fixed fire heart started to beat faster around the Pisces, whose oceanic creativity, compassion, empathy, and generosity toward all gave them that special something that caught your royal attention. Descendants of Neptune, the ruler of the oceans, Pisces finds you to be a teacher of valuable personal expressions, like grandeur, confidence, leadership, and fearlessness, which they're trying to reconcile within themselves. You'll help them integrate these Leo-ruled values while you take the lead on not just professing your love, but practicing it.

If you show up, completely engaged in the relationship, you'll affectionately, consistently, and lovingly give the Pisces the structure they need, which helps them feel fearless and confident. That's when their magnetic powers of seduction reveal themselves, and they'll give you the attention you crave, take it back, make you work for it—but you'll be so glad you did when they reveal their mysteries to you slowly, one by one, like pearls on the ocean floor. You'll empower your more relational Pisces to use their generous sensitivities in service of their personal well-being first, which will give them the resources to heal others, whereas Pisces will help you extend a bit more forgiveness and mercy to all, which is one of the most noble pursuits. The sunshine on water, this pair is an energy sure to enthrall you and all who witness you.

VIRGO IN LOVE

Considerate | Helpful | Reliable
Honor: Knowledge & Ritual
Integrate: Unknown & Mystique

Many of us get so enraptured with our beloved or the content of our desire that we overlook the fact that love is a skill. Love is a verb. It's a practice. A capacity. But Virgo knows. When they felt the spark, Virgo went to work putting their love to use and studying the skill of love.

Virgo's romantic competency—a skill-based model of relationship functioning, undergoing very Virgoan doctoral exploration—is informed by consideration and a willingness to help. In love, Virgos consider divinely detailed strategies to be of service to their lover, and they prove their reliability in romance time and time again.

Virgo in love will want to honor their natural intellect by demonstrating how interested they are in their partner's experiences and existential world. Driven by having knowledge about their lover, Virgo helps their partner feel understood, respected, and cherished. Virgo loves ritual and routine as a bid for reconnection, and such activities with shared meanings increase safety among the partners.

To grow, Virgo will want to increase their comfort level with the unknown by embracing mystique and spontaneity. That way, Virgo can strengthen their vulnerability muscles and wrap their head and heart around romance's surprises and novelties.

VIRGO & ARIES

Surreal, mysterious, magnetic

Don't dismiss this quincunx dynamic too quickly, know-it-all! Besides, most nerds like you have an unspoken sweet spot for the comedic relief in your Aries. Your mutable Mercury earth energy bent toward the more spontaneous and pleasure-seeking side when you were lit up by Aries's enthusiasm, comedy, and innovation. The ram as cardinal fire quickly registered your identity's intelligence and sensibility. Lovers of loyalty, Aries adores how you take responsible, detailed care of not only yourself, but the people on your team. Given this quincunx dynamic between fire and earth, it's a wonderful image of your earthly container of love and their fire-powered desire inside. You'll want to express your more receptive and curious dimensions to the Aries while they pursue you in bravery.

Your sensibilities are very different, which fortifies the strength of the chemistry, as long as you don't overspeak, overexplain, or numb the uncertainty of the delicate early stages. Take it slow! Over time, with the right tending to routine and ritual, the safety, affection, and trust of love between you will burst from the earth and bloom in the spring season of Aries. Your Aries will help you see farther than the facts and figures of the head, in favor of the experiences of the heart. You'll be inspired and a bit challenged by your Aries's autonomy and boundaries, which serve as the antidote for your chronic people pleasing. They'll strengthen your risk-taking talents. You'll inspire Aries to show more thoughtfulness, attention to detail, and strategy. This is a match with the best of your Mercury intelligence and their Mars action. With the right strategy and behavior, it's an undisputed championship.

VIRGO & TAURUS
Harmonious, sensual, affectionate

Meet me in the enchanted forest. You two earth signs embody the magic of the wilderness. A supportive trine match helps this dynamic feel romantic, sensual, and beautiful. As mutable earth governed by intelligent Mercury, your strategy on love is being both prepared and spontaneous, innovative and consistent, whereas your fixed earth Taurus is ruled by sensual Venus, so they're more sultry and romantic. Their values of affection, steadfast presence, and trustworthiness are exactly the ones you need to feel comfortable in love. You'll carefully, routinely, and happily build the right container of romantic experience between two earth signs that treasure commitment and that love to love.

Since you're both highly relational in different styles, you'll want to reveal yourselves to each other with careful timing. To prolong desire's life span, you'll want to trust your intuition on how to increase mystery, adventure, and curiosity between you, whereas your Taurus's domain is the foundation of love, so integrate their wisdom on companionship, safety, and trust into the relationship. You'll use your brilliance to help the Taurus take radical responsibility, stoking the passion to indulge in excess less and work harder at opening their life up more. Along the way, Taurus will tenderly and sensually pull you out of analysis paralysis and your sense of duty, in favor of feelings, joy, and even decadence, which will give your self-criticism an herbal remedy: self-compassion. You'll offer each other a forest of embodied sensuality, reliability, and love. This is a complementary and romantic match made in the universe's enchanted, romantic forest.

VIRGO & GEMINI
Powerful, transformative, dynamic

Love begins in the mind for this pair. When messenger Mercury's only two signs align romantically, the square partnership between your mutable earth follow-through and mutable air's impermanence takes to the skies! It took you a minute to wrap your head around Gemini as a gifted orator and speaker, comedian and connoisseur. You work so hard, but you love to laugh with your Gemini. In you, the twins found another renaissance soul who's deeply thoughtful, curious, analytical, and intelligent. It was a home run when relational Gemini saw your focus on interpersonal service.

To serve love, that's on you, Virgo! You'll want to own that lane quickly, so Gemini can understand how consistent, demonstrative practices of love like affection, disclosure, and trust are where love grows. Help them understand the why and the how—not because Gemini can't demonstrate these values, but because they love the education. When it comes to keeping that square spark of desire, you're the student in the Gemini's classroom. Avoid grasping for or demanding certainty and explanation. Desire's selfish, mysterious, and impermanent, so keep it that way, even if it's hard. You'll motivate the Gemini to appreciate personal administration—the little tasks, choices, and behaviors that improve everything from wellness to finances—thus improving the scope of Gemini's success. But helping you seek progress, not perfection, as the preferred outcome is Gemini's gift to you! They'll empower you to strive for authenticity—such a valuable skill in the queer community. You'll create a wonderful academy of love, desire, respect, intelligence, and joy together. Imagining yourself as both professor and teacher's assistant in this pair will help you both get the top grade!

VIRGO & CANCER
Joyful, supportive, adventurous

Call the love doctor! As a match of two relational, intelligent, and emotionally focused souls, you know the meaning of love is healing and service. In your moon-ruled lover, you found a cardinal water sign who is born to find belonging in the caretaking of others, through empathy, generosity, loyalty, and compassion. A sign of judicious tastes, you fell for Cancer's values, which are timeless and with universal appeal. Who doesn't love a thoughtful soul? They weren't fazed by the fact that your emotions were buried behind your mutable earth traits of contemplation, tranquility, and focus, but instead noticed your emotional obligation to help others. Which is why you two love doctors are at the top of this hospital for the soul. The practice of love through tenderness, compassion, and affection is given here beautifully because you're so considerate of each other.

The sextile spark of desire will take a bit more willingness. Erotic pleasure requires healthy distance, autonomy, and self-knowledge, so both of you giving souls will need to verbalize your own pleasures specifically and without apology. You have a wonderful ability to create structure where love can blossom, but desire can flourish, too, if the seeds are planted. You'll then inspire your Cancer to flex their emotional regulation muscles by teaching them to verbalize clear expectations, helping them remember that you are not responsible for their emotional health and sharing other life-management skills and resources that help Cancer cultivate resilience. Your thoughtful Cancer will preach the gospel of self-compassion as a nonnegotiable for your Mercury mission to heal the world. With this beautiful blend of emotion and reason, this match is the zodiac's hospital for the soul.

VIRGO & LEO

Loyal, contrasting, instructive

Recess is over! This inconjunct match between you two neighboring signs signifies the end of summer and the beginning of fall. So it's the classic inconjunct tension between duty and pleasure. In your royal Leo, you've found an emotionally generous, romantic, and open-hearted leader who is truly trying their best to make a difference on the world. Their sunlit grandeur and larger-than-life presentation might induce skepticism initially, but if you focus past Leo's glitz and glamour—which they can't help, by the way!—you'll see a person trying to hold space for the brilliance of others. In you, they've found a partner who is deeply concerned and forever curious about ways to be of service to others. Your acumen, wit, and charitableness earned their royal respect.

As inconjunct matches often go, the chemistry, passion, and desire will stay strong. That is, if you avoid your tendency to remove all uncertainty, mystery, or longing in your life. Have fun first! Follow your Leo's lead in desire, because their fixed fire and sense of self-worth gives them the autonomy they need to stoke erotic flames. In matters of love as a practice, that's your castle. Initiate transparency, disclosure, generosity, affection, and compassion gradually. Your monarch will give you more of the royal permission you need to disrupt conventions, be direct in your feedback, and avoid people pleasing, whereas you'll teach Leo about the right ways to invite others in—especially you!—to their shame-free domain and help them understand that ruling a kingdom includes serving its people.

VIRGO & VIRGO
Safe, consistent, secure

#FLAWLESS. This conjunction match between two especially precise mutable earth signs is very close to flawless! You don't always need to have your needs and values met exactly as you define them in romance, but when your eyes locked with another Mercury-born Virgo, you couldn't pass up the chance. In Virgo, you found another who defines these practices of love with the same language, so you were smart to run right toward the experience. With this conjunction match of two earth signs, your focus on the terra firma for love, with values like affection, emotional affirmation, loyalty, and stability, and the right disclosure is as natural as acorns to oak trees for you both. You maximize safety for each other with ease.

In order for the spark to remain, you'll want to explore the imagination of desire. It could be that you and your lover will only feel erotically invested where you're safe. Or you may need a bit of adventure, exploration, and curiosity, while reconciling how ritualistic, consistent, and stable you both are. These journeys can be taken through the right conversations proactively, and you'll want to have regular states of the union on it so you stay updated and willing with the most accurate emotional information. You'll help each other become as #FLAWLESS as possible in this dynamic through your acts of service in love and through your comfort with tough conversations on intimacy, transformation, accountability, and growth. When two mental masterminds join together for connection, that sole determiner of our quality of life, your relationship will texture your life with wisdom and meaning.

VIRGO & LIBRA
Loyal, contrasting, instructive
Ideally speaking...this is an inconjunct match between two neighboring signs and even planetary rulers. Mercury-ruled you and Venus-ruled Libra both speak to the ideal in the personal and relational. You were charmed by Libra's cardinal air style, which helps others feel connected, seen, heard, and understood. You have an unspoken tender spot for the kindness and decency that elegant Libra demonstrates. Your Libra was curious to know more about the ideas and analytics that are forever connecting dots in your head, and when you spoke about how that data applies to personal relationships, you had your interpersonal Libra's undivided attention. Given the differences between your elements, archetypes, and functions, the context for desire is sure to keep you both highly attracted to each other, and Libra's air nature sustains the space between you that keeps desire strong. Make sure you reveal your existential worlds mutually and slowly over small moments across time to keep the unfamiliarity working in your favor.

The context you'll have to work at only a bit is the terms and conditions for love, but your earthy ways will fortify the foundation. You're both highly affectionate, demonstrative, thoughtful, and respectful. But Virgo likes to prove love, and Libra prefers to discuss love. So long as you agree on the right values and practices that create the best connections, taking each other's preferences into account, you'll be a wonderful team. You'll inspire your Libra to focus more on their personal foundation of responsibility and autonomy so they don't extend themselves too far to rescue others. Your Libra will indulge you in their exceptional romantic skills and the sensuality you deserve, so you can have the experiences that remind you why you work so hard—because you love so deeply.

VIRGO & SCORPIO
Joyful, supportive, adventurous
Loyalty, thy name is Virgo and Scorpio! In this sextile match between you and the ruler of the underworld, a dynamic of radical intimacy, honesty, and commitment to each other is found. In your mutable earth romance style, you have just the right Mercury-ruled understanding of "both/and" concepts for loving other people when they're down and clapping for their success. In the fixed water heart of Scorpio, they hold the entire ocean's power in a single drop, which has the right emotional intensity to handle both the gifts and shame of their partner. Loyalty outs itself, and you recognized one of the finest practitioners of it in Scorpio, which is why this match began passionately and intensely and will stay in this form for so long as you two sophisticated signs feel it's right. When it comes to the dance of desire, let your Scorpio speak their native tongue in this dynamic. Nobody knows the balance between disclosure and mystique, closeness and distance, quite like this sign, whose primary function in astrology is the giving and receiving of intimacy.

Naturally your earth function is more qualified for the foundation of love. You're fluent in matters related to affection, consistency, accountability, and empathy, so here is where your gifts shine to illuminate your Scorpio. In this love and loyalty, you'll inspire the Scorpio to flex their adaptability, curiosity, and agility muscles a bit more, so they can keep up with the momentum and vulnerabilities of life, whereas your Scorpio will give you the right boundaries and authentic self-awareness so you're not placing your mind in service to inner conspiracy writing and/or saving people who don't want your help. Tough but real. This match will bring out the best of your mental and emotional skills.

VIRGO & SAGITTARIUS
Powerful, transformative, dynamic
Hot for teacher? It'll definitely sizzle in this classroom or campus. In this chemistry-packed square between your mutable earth intelligence and Sagittarius's mutable fire energy, it's a mentally active match between two teachers. You quickly observed Sagittarius's wisdom and how they philosophically approach their lives with a quest, always searching for meaning. Their naturally gregarious, optimistic, and joyful energy cracked a few smiles and laughter out of you, the tough audience. They probably showed up late to the party on this dynamic, but Sagittarius realized that your perception, analytical skills, and thoughtful concern for the micro is the reason they have the macro. The desire will stay hot, especially while you're in the friction of debates, dialogues, and joint quests to understand more around you. Sagittarius looks for alternative futures, whereas you're looking at the present's

reality. Honor this difference, because it keeps your chemistry active and your brainpower full.

You'll want to split the context for love down the middle, too, because you're more fluent in consistency, trust, and knowledge, whereas Sagittarius is qualified in affection, generosity, and warmth. Accept and celebrate they key differences to fortify both the scorching desire and comfortable love between you. You'll inspire Sagittarius to find the divine in the details and really appreciate the here and now, which gives them a stronger peace of mind and focus. Your Sagittarius will help you transcend perfectionism and control so your beautiful imperfections can reach the world, too. In this educational romantic experience, you'll learn the right tools to help each other grow.

VIRGO & CAPRICORN
Harmonious, sensual, affectionate
Ain't no mountain high enough! When you two earth signs find the trine love between you, there's no mountain high enough to keep you from getting to each other. In this trine match between your mutable earth energy and your Capricorn's cardinal earth structure, this is a bond that's built to weather the storms and survive the heat. The heart is hard to translate, but you knew it spoke the same language as your Capricorn when it beat around them. Their Saturn-ruled majesty, integrity, and ethical living was wildly seductive for the more practical nature in you. Your seagoat slowly emotionally revealed themself to you when they understood how you too are essentially trying to improve your own life and make a difference in the lives of the people you love. So the stability, comfort, affection, and respect that nurture the roots of love were

provided effortlessly in this match, and I suspect Virgo is the best teacher here. If love is a container of structure, it's invented between you, which gives you the right foundation for one half of the relationship paradox.

You two earth signs shy away from uncertainty, risk, emotional exposure, and mystery. But those are the roots of desire. So once you understand the efficiency—I'm looking at your Capricorn—of distance, seduction, and pleasure, you'll both work hard to maintain it. Capricorn is a blend of water and earth, so their invitation to the erotic is doubly qualified. In Capricorn, you'll have a provider and bodyguard. They'll teach you the right strategies to honor boundaries and discipline over people pleasing and enabling, whereas you'll soften Capricorn's structure and help them make time for joy, risk, and innovation.

VIRGO & AQUARIUS
Surreal, mysterious, magnetic

Mad science! It's alive! This is one beautifully bizarre quincunx match that has a sort of scientific laboratory feeling to it, with two intellectuals searching for radical and innovative thinkers. As a Mercurial erudite, you were drawn to but a bit repelled initially by Aquarius's intellectual repertoire, communication skills, and progressive thinking. You were inspired by their candor and creative consciousness. The Uranian-ruled water bearer needed to know you're not as rigid and uptight as others say you are, and once you showed them more disruption, adaptability, and a sense of humor, they were happy to shrink the distance between you. But not all the way, of course, because this is a quincunx match of your mutable earth, which is the saving grace here, and your fixed air Aquarius, who loves to uplift their convictions to the highest. These very different approaches, definitely led by your Aquarius, will inspire the seduction, curiosity, and the wild unknown to stay very much alive between you, so this serves the desire's life span magnificently.

Your impeccable consistency, affection, and techniques for trust will be the grounding through which love extends itself to you both. If you're the teacher here, the laboratory of love will stay operating at peak function, and the paradox of love and desire will come alive in this dynamic, given your intellectual and visionary skills. You'll inspire your Aquarius to be more tolerant of dissent, disagreement, and ideological contrast, which will help others listen to them more deeply, whereas your Aquarius will help you contribute your ideas and creativity to the world without worrying about critics or perfectionism. This is a showcase of genius!

VIRGO & PISCES
Completion, romantic, compromise
As above, so below. Or on earth as it is in heaven. This polarity dynamic is magnificent, as it represents the very middle and end of the zodiac. On earth, you have your Mercurial romantic strategies, finding acts of service, tenderness, and thoughtfulness as the best bids for connection. In heaven is your descendant of Neptune, Pisces—a potentially unconditionally loving soul who is in this world but not of it, and who loves so generously and divinely. You're of opposite ends of the veil. Yet, as with all polarity dynamics, you're both magnetically drawn to each other because your mutable earth

container is just the right vessel for their mutable water power.

So, given the floodgates are being opened, in the realm of desire you'll want to trust your Pisces partner, who will theoretically maintain relative existential separation, uncertainty, and novelty. It's inconvenient but necessary for this thermonuclear chemistry to stay electric. You won't blow it if you carefully pace yourself and soften into the Pisces mystery. Meanwhile, you're the Virgo genius who knows how to build the right vessel for this soulful love, with your thoughtful consideration, cognition, and the verbal communication skills that help you and your Pisces feel seen, heard, and understood. You'll inspire your Pisces the most here by demonstrating the right detailed actions of love, practicing love instead of professing it. This will transfer over to their personal evolution, too. And Pisces will give you the right enlightenment to see past the facts, figures, and data to a world beyond, and you may never want to come back.

LIBRA IN LOVE

Balanced | Seductive | Compassionate
Honor: Partnership & Negotiation
Integrate: Autonomy & Separation

When Libra enters the zodiac calendar, romance appears. At the moment of sunset, when the balanced sunlight and nightfall occur simultaneously, connection emerges in the calendar. Which is why this Venus-ruled sign can call love their homeland.

In love, Libra's skills of balancing their own needs with their partner's have earned them the symbol of scales—that's justice, and a requirement for romance. Radiating magnetism, Libra when ready is highly seductive, and they know how to invite pleasure. But they're not just looking for pleasure—Libra's compassion will be a soft spot that their partners fall for and use to heal and reemerge better than ever.

For Libras to stay authentic, they'll want to honor their reflex for partnership. Highly relational, romantic, and interpersonal, Libra believes "we" is much better than "me." When conflict arises, they'll want to take the lead with negotiation, because their skills here are supreme. They mustn't wait to honor their mediation magic.

Because the universe has a good sense of humor, it'll often attract the lovely Libra to a more independent soul. So, since integration is so natural for them, Libra will want to learn to incorporate more autonomy and distance. That way, they don't rob their partner of their own empowerment, and Libra learns to be "the one" for themselves first, before saying, "I do."

LIBRA & ARIES

Completion, romantic, compromise

On the run! Did you know Bonnie and Clyde were a Libra/ Aries couple? If you're the Bonnie in charge, I suspect you're a lot less "grand larceny" and more "authenticity." As I said in the Aries section, this polarity match is the very one that inspired this book and its methods. It's truly the epitome of the delicate balance between cardinal air Venus-ruled "we" (you) and cardinal fiery Mars-ruled "me" (your Aries!). As the more delicate, sensible sign, you were probably initially put off by your ram's brashness, direct action, and confidence, but you also saw how they light up all the rooms they charge through. Polarity is a mutual paradox. Your Martian was completely spellbound by your diplomacy, beauty, elegance, and popularity. Your polarity keeps the desire burning red-hot as long as you hold the Aries's interest, maintaining just enough breathing room and letting them be by themselves, because fire needs air.

You'll build the container for love, since you know exactly how to harmonize, negotiate, and balance personal needs with relationship needs. Aries will be your bodyguard and coach on authenticity, helping you overcome perfectionism and shame, whereas you will teach the Aries that everything isn't all about them. So you'll coach them on sensitivity and consideration. Your lovely self and Aries are the high teachers of love's paradox, and the zodiac is blessed beyond measure by your lead.

LIBRA & TAURUS
Surreal, mysterious, magnetic

"I love you so much. No, I love *you* so much!" When the only signs ruled by the romantic goddess of love join, it's a quincunx dynamic that still beams with romance, comfort, glamour, and loyalty, even though it's an odd couple match, given your cardinal air thought patterns above and Taurus's fixed earth sensibilities on the ground. With the right concentration on your behalf, and the right effort on the Taurus's, you'll easily find how Venus unites you. As two highly interpersonal signs, tending to the self-ishness, autonomy, and separation that desire needs will feel a bit awkward at first. But if you approach the space between you as the space of intimacy, you'll understand how effective and completely necessary it is.

In securing love, your natural focus on each other creates the right container of closeness, security, and trust for a deep Venusian love to emerge. Your justice-centered approach will help the more dogmatic Taurus expand their vision to allow people to disagree with them while they practice their resilience muscles. Taurus's earth-ruled perception will help Libra focus more deeply on function over form and values over appearance, helping them find more substantial arenas to consider over surface-level things. Together you both gravitate toward beauty, and you, Libra, are never in short supply of it. You'll make romance the crux of your relationship so you never lose the spark. Along the way, just remember that resilience, discomfort, and responsibility are necessary in life, too. So incorporate those qualities in the relationship as best you can, so you can handle both the comforts and pains together in good form and in the right style, always.

LIBRA & GEMINI
Harmonious, sensual, affectionate

Love looks with the mind and not the eyes, right? When you two air signs fly together in this trine match, a wonderfully harmonizing and romantic energy leaves the ethers and solidifies in the partnership between you and your mutable air partner. With smooth talker Gemini, ruled by the god of the persuasive tongue, you were impressed by their interpersonal thoughtfulness, diverse articulation of topics, and naughty sense of humor. They clung on every one of your poetic words, interpersonal graces, and romantic gestures, while marveling at your social popularity—the social domain is how Gemini understands the romantic potential of their beloveds. Since you're both so relationally oriented, when you find each other, it's like coming home to what you both have been searching for. This mind-meeting-mind match becomes the homeland for the ease, closeness, trust, and affection that trine loves cherish.

You two social butterflies will have to willingly increase the distance, autonomy, and mystique that desire needs. You'll also want to join less cerebrally but pursue more in the sensual, seductive, and physical dimensions to keep the erotic space breathing beautifully. Gemini will coach you to embrace more courage over comfort. They'll be taking you to the witness stand, while helping you ask yourself, "Instead of what people think, does this decision align with my values here?" Whereas your Gemini will learn how to elevate their skills beyond the intellectual to the relational by watching you negotiate with ease. When you fly together, mind to heart, your love is found and here to stay.

LIBRA & CANCER
Powerful, transformative, dynamic

Summer and autumn. This erotic tension creates a strong power dynamic, which embodies both of the necessary components of a relationship, but in different styles. Venus-ruled you were born in the autumn equinox, when the daylight diminishes and nightfall reigns supreme on the Earth. Whereas Cancer was born under the moon after the summer solstice, so their cardinal water initiates safety and belonging. In the square match between cardinal water and air signs, the passion and desire often stays strong while you two fight to find the sweet spot between Cancer's sensitivities and Libra's objectivity, between feeling and talking. Exploring this tension beyond the difficulty, as a relationship packed with chemistry and mutual instruction, will help you leaders realize your specific approaches to life don't have a monopoly on the truth. No one's inherently right or wrong.

That's why exploring the container and practice for love is crucial for this square match. Let your Cancer initiate a dialogue as proactively as possible, where you agree to support each other's needs around safety, trust, and accountability to help keep the container of this relationship intact. They'll help you see their intellect as a powerful empathy tool, too. Since Cancer teaches us the value of family and belonging, you'll want to help the Cancer impose an emotional distance, so they'll learn how to individually self-soothe with critical awareness, rather than with your unlimited assistance or distraction. They'll empower you to hold space for your own and other people's discomfort without rushing for a solution. Libra begins romance. Cancer begins family. You two are the best of both seasons.

LIBRA & LEO
Joyful, supportive, adventurous

Meet me at sunrise. Because the astronomical point of where the Sun—the luminary ruler of Leo—rises in the Eastern Hemisphere and the Planet Venus—the planetary ruler of Libra—is the same meet cue and that's why Venus is known as the morning star. That's why this sextile match between Venus-ruled Libra you and the sun-ruled Leo works like a heavenly charm on Earth. You're totally smitten by Leo's fixed fire charisma because it's rightfully mesmerizing, and you search for how Leo uses their popularity and influence to empower or talk about topics that matter. In your cardinal air heart, the sovereign's found a romantic partner who loves to make them feel good because you're so interpersonally romantic, and they shine magnificently in social spaces, which helps you feel good.

You're both so charming and romantic, it's definitely a tie for who's more skilled around the practice of love and who's more qualified at maintaining desire. Though Libra's ruled by the goddess of love herself, I think the crown belongs to Leo when it comes to taking the lead on love. As the consistent fixed fire sign, Leo knows how to passionately, regularly, and loyally provide devotion, even when it's inconvenient. Libra won't hold back showing you that Libra still belongs to themselves, and while they maintain their autonomy, they maintain their mystique, detachment, and longing, which reminds Leo why seduction is Venus's domain. Leo's divine worthiness will help inspire your more relational self to assert desires, discomfort, and boundaries without apology, whereas you'll carefully instruct the queen to carefully to broker their pleasures as no or more less important than the greater good, because it's not always all about them. This is why you're the morning star—because this astronomical duo has to radiate in the sky together!

LIBRA & VIRGO
Loyal, contrasting, instructive

Best-case scenario? Venus-ruled Libra and Mercury-born Virgo both know how to speak to the ideal in personal and relational matters in this inconjunct match, since they're both intellectually and romantically concerned. You were curious to know more about the unspoken ideas and wisdom that seemed to be spinning around in your Virgo's concentrated glare. If they were outspoken enough to share how their intelligence applies to personal relationships, Virgo had your undivided attention. Virgo's cognition is a gift, and they were charmed by your cardinal air style, which helps others feel connected, seen, heard, and understood. Given the differences between your air and earth, and your functions within the zodiac, the foundation for desire and its mystique is sure to keep you both highly attached to each other. Make sure you're in charge of setting the pace on disclosing your existential worlds mutually and slowly over small, meaningful moments across time to keep the unfamiliarity working in your favor, as you have the right sense of timing here.

The arena you'll have to dare greatly in is the arena of love. You're both compassionate, engaged, considerate, and respectful, though Virgo takes the prize on love as practice. Virgo likes to prove love, and you're more comfortable theorizing about it. So long as you align on the appropriate convictions and practices that create the best connections, you'll be an unbeatable team. Please indulge your hardworking Virgo with your exceptional romantic skills and the sensuality you both deserve, so they can earn the rewards of their work. Virgo will inspire you to focus more on your personal foundation of responsibility and autonomy, so you don't extend yourself too far to rescue others, forever reminding you that you can't give from nothing. So just give to each other, and you'll never run out.

LIBRA & LIBRA
Safe, consistent, secure

I love you; I love you not? When these two lovebirds join, you're both in and not sure, because you're both the balanced scales. Since the both of you are exceptionally romantic, sensual, and loving, when you found each other, you found another who cherishes love as deeply as you. That's why this cardinal air conjunction between you two Venus signs is a solid match, so long as you're both agreeing on the right values. Shared values are what'll keep your forward-thinking signs more tethered together. This could be the match of all matches when it comes to teaching the zodiac how to balance the paradox between love and desire. In love, you're both naturally very thoughtful, consistent, compassionate, and you pay attention to each other. So often we forget that love is a mental practice, and you two air signs know how to offer each other the gift of awareness.

It's possible, too, for desire to come naturally, so long as you remember to maintain the seduction, allure, and magnetism. You both love relationships, so you may move very fast in an effort to secure what you want the most. Try to discipline this impulse, so you're gradually revealing yourselves and allowing this Venus-ruled chemistry to blossom beautifully. You'll salute the best Libran qualities, like proactive anticipation of desires, negotiation, harmony, and peace. But you'll want to integrate more resilience, boundaries, and an autonomy strategy in an effort to remain as holistic as possible in this romantic connection. Life is hard, and you'll want to nourish each other with the joys of this connection.

LIBRA & SCORPIO
Loyal, contrasting, instructive

You're going to hell! But not the way you think, Libra. In Pluto-ruled Scorpio, you're connecting to a lover whose emotional and psychological depths are ruled by the underworld. So your more light-filled, romantic, and uplifted personality won't serve you where you're going. This inconjunct match between your cardinal air and their fixed water has a focus on intimacy and commitment. As a child of Venus, you're relationally oriented, with a skill for compromise, understanding, and balance between both partners' needs—which your Scorpio loves. It helps them, too. You were attracted to their soft charisma, magnetic personality, and soulful intensity, whereas Scorpio was drawn to your light and glamour so much, they rose out of the darkness where they love to dwell. This mixture of Venus lighting and Scorpio intrigue is a strong match for desire to emerge because you're both so unknown and contrasting to each other. Lean on your Scorpio's skills with seduction and intimacy, and you'll feel like nothing can keep you apart.

Maintain that chemistry outside the bedroom, because it stays stronger on top of the practice of love.

That's all your lead! Demonstrate, discuss, and review what the practice of love means to you both, as it's related to affection, service, touch, trust, and mutuality. Since you're a natural conversationalist, focus topics on attachment styles, the ways love was expressed at home, and other specific origins that influenced your love styles. That way, both preferences are valid and implemented. You'll teach your Scorpio to consider the possibility that others are trying their best. You'll help them see the other side of arguments. And your Scorpio will help you know when it's time to let go of the benefit of the doubt. Their radical honesty will protect you and keep your generosity safe and appreciated. So enjoy the Addams Family–style dynamic!

LIBRA & SAGITTARIUS
Joyful, supportive, adventurous
This match reminds us that the architect of desire is our imagination. Given your cardinal air soul, you know exactly how to talk, listen, and consider imaginative possibilities. The Venus in you shines when you're imagining your lover's life. So when Sagittarius, as the mutable fire, let your cognition shine, this sextile match was off to the horse races. In Sagittarius, you have a Jupiter-ruled visionary artist who never makes you bored, because they're so dynamic, in motion, and excited. In you, the optimistic Sagittarius has a lover who believes in them and holds space for their dreams to come. So the practice of love, as it's built through affection, empowerment, gratitude, and loyalty, will secure this match of free spirits joining together—and you're the leader of love. Help the Sagittarius connect the dots between what they learned in

childhood to how they bid for connection, which creates their container for adult relationships.

Between your thoughtful words and Sagittarius's action, you'll each know you are cherished. Since sextile dynamics are often comfortable, you'll want to imagine how to stay on your toes. When you fall into the practices of love, don't forget to keep imagining your Sagittarius as a new person. Always make them unfamiliar to you, and you'll keep the magnetism between you strong. This is the couple that should always be traveling together to secure the sextile spark. You'll motivate your Sagittarius to develop more tact and emotional impulse control so they don't destroy or abandon their projects and relationships. Your more candor-loving Sagittarius will help you develop the quality of decisiveness and direct speech. Sometimes the truth needs no sugar or chaser. Between your elegance and Sagittarius's optimism, this is a match that is sure to bring out the best personal, relational, and international experiences.

LIBRA & CAPRICORN
Powerful, transformative, dynamic
Law and order! Not just a bingeworthy show, but the right theme for this relationship. Don't let the severity fool you—it's an extremely sensual and chemistry-packed match. As the Venus scales, you're focused on what's righteous, fair, and equal for all. That's why your seagoat noticed you from their mountaintop. Those qualities usually out themselves, and they're very attractive to all. When you dynamically squared with the cardinal earth Capricorn, you found a Saturn-ruled mastermind who wants to build the order, the space for you to put all your

ideas on law, righteousness, and equality. The magnetism in this match is extremely powerful because you're both so similar, with just the right amount of contrast. Your approach to desire is very mental, curious, and imaginative. Capricorn's is nonverbal, embodied, and hands-on. With these complementary, not competitive, styles, you should be working on the right framework for this very charged law and order–themed intimacy.

On the practice of love, you'll want to approach this conversation like you're running a business. So unromantic, I know, but I think you'll learn more about what behaviors on love mean to you, and that will allow you to develop the affection, consistency, structure, and reliability that makes both of your hearts sing. Your solid seagoat will help you with the right discipline to take steps on self-improvement, because they don't indulge any laziness—not from themselves or their partners. On the other hand, you'll be the player of the self-care song, where you'll inspire your Capricorn to make joy and self-care a nonnegotiable part of life, so they don't burn out from all the work they do. With you two on the same team, you're undefeated.

LIBRA & AQUARIUS
Harmonious, sensual, affectionate

Take to the skies, you lovebirds! As two air signs, this trine connection is ethereal, mental, dynamic, and committed. Both lovers who treasure verbal communication and language, you fell quickly for each other because of the way you speak to one another. In Aquarius, you found a match who was giving you Uranian "aha!" moments one after the other. They kept your notoriously indecisive attention completely undivided on them. In you, Aquarius found a Venus light worker who was an instrument of peace, joy, and love, which means more to the zodiac's humanitarian than you could possibly know.

Which is why the practice of love and understanding is given here pretty well. It's the ground beneath the fly zone. As two emotionally regulated signs, make sure you prioritize quality time and define physical touch, reliability, and consistency as necessary in the relationship. Once it's negotiated, you can put it into practice and give each other the right amount of stability. On desire and maintaining seduction, it takes mystery. So as air signs, you'll want to move slowly as you open up to each other, which your Aquarius will know how to do naturally. You'll want to carefully and deliberately reveal your existential worlds to each other because, to protect the distance, desire needs room. Aquarius will help you formulate ideological autonomy. You'll be less concerned with what others think of you or how they critique your work and more focused on staying true to yourself. You'll help your passionate activist Aquarius consider other people's platforms instead of building an ideological echo chamber and show them how to be less offended over people who disagree with them.

LIBRA & PISCES
Surreal, mysterious, magnetic
Comes in colors, everywhere! They're like a rainbow. This quincunx match is where two seemingly different natures can be reconciled in Technicolor. Your cardinal air heart was captivated by the way Pisces brings their color to not just the creative arts but to their universal compassion for

everyone around them, which means the world to you. In your Venus-ruled demeanor, Pisces found their muse—the one who inspires their art, loving, and tenderness to masterpiece levels, because you modeled the way. This is a match where desire and love can be easily explored. In the practice of love, you're the most qualified. You'll demonstrate what it means to show up to the party and tend to connections through attention, affection, awareness, and reliability. You'll carefully inspire the Pisces to build the vessel of love.

For desire, water wins. Mutable water Pisces can't help but demonstrate the push and pull, closeness and separation, mystique and disclosure, as they're two fish in one. You're the scales, so you can balance their opposing natures, knowing there's much strength if you accept each other's differences and let the rainbow be. You'll help Pisces wrap their hearts around the right words for their experiences. They're allowed to be appropriately nonverbal, but you'll help them improve their emotional lexicon so that you can feel safe, because you understand what they're feeling, whereas Pisces will remind you that not everything needs an explanation, reason, or word to exist. Their transcendental attitude will help you see beyond the logic of air in favor of the mysteries of the spiritual waters. You'd be wise to combine your creative capabilities and do something wonderful for the world with your love.

SCORPIO IN LOVE

Intimate | Committed | Vigilant
Honor: Eroticism & Seduction
Integrate: Generosity & Tenderness

After the relationship agreement is made, the power of Scorpio reveals itself. Once expectations and negotiations are understood, the opportunities for intimacy, the erotic, and transformation are boundless.

A Scorpio in love shows how to honor intimacy through meaningful commitment to all people involved. Once they finally consider one ultimately worthy of their loyalty and affection, Scorpio is vigilant about doing the work to honor their lovers and the space they make together.

Since authenticity is Scorpio's modus operandi, two qualities they'll want to honor within themselves truthfully in relationships are their eroticism and skills of seduction. By eroticism, I mean honor your mystery. Honor the imaginative distance between you and your love. You can operate at a need-to-know disclosure level.

Since the primary outcome of intimacy and commitment is always growth through contrast, please try to practice more generosity and tenderness. Extend the same expectations you have for yourself to others, so you're not so emotionally guarded. Tenderness will help you forgive and release, so you're not stuck in the past but loving deeply in the present. Make sure you're willing to hear and offer apologies.

SCORPIO & ARIES
Surreal, mysterious, magnetic

All is fair in love and war, right? This match is a bizarre quincunx between your fixed water soul and cardinal fire Aries. Many astrologers consider both Scorpio and Aries to be coruled by the planet Mars. So with willingness, flexibility, and negotiation, you can see what you have in common with your Martian comrade. You're completely turned on by your Aries's bravery, confidence, and passion to seize the best of life. It's brand-new to you. Supported by this action-oriented Martian energy, your love is given and received when you both discern that your partner is strong. You know you're not matching with a pushover or doormat. That's why you desire each other—because you admire each other's valor. That's about it for what you have in common, though, which is why the desire context ought to stay undefeated. You're a great mystery, and Aries loves the thrill of existential discovery.

The biggest battle will be agreeing on how to mutually practice love in a way that suits you both. You'll want to be very clear, direct, and transparent (so painful, I know), so that straight talk gives you the straight understanding of how you define affection, consistency, safety, and trust. From your fearless partner, you'll learn how to soften into the risks of vulnerability and trust. Tenderness gives you the assumption of kindness from others, and you'll want to search for innocence over guilt. Your methodical focus will help Aries find more meaning in the mundane, and your concentration will help them finish the ideas they start. Aligning your ideas on intimacy and commitment, this match is an enormously dynamically powerful match to be reckoned with. Maybe it takes two children of Mars to win when love is a battlefield?

SCORPIO & TAURUS
Completion, romantic, compromise

I hope you liked *Beauty and the Beast*, because this dynamic has that symbolism all over it. It's an oppositional energy between your Scorpio's fixed water authenticity, handling discomfort and beastly things with ease, and the Taurus's fixed earth Venus sensibilities, which love aesthetics and peace. You recognize that the bull's pleasure pursuits, sensuality, and comfort-loving consistency are only earned so they can share with others. That's why you revealed your ideas of profound intimacy and depth, because you're two sides of the same coin. Both ways of living are valuable and necessary for each other. As always, the polarity dynamic is at peak desire status, as you're both constantly exploring, understanding, repelling, and attracting each other. So the desire, chemistry, and magnetism are likely to stay alive in this match.

But you both appreciate the familiarity and comfort of consistency, so in order for the longevity to maintain itself, you'll have to name the exact parameters you expect regarding security, loyalty, and transparency. You'll achieve this so long as you follow the bull's lead and soften into joy and emotional exposure, without dress rehearsing tragedy. You'll do intimacy imperfectly, but do it anyway. From your underworld, you'll help material Taurus cherish things they can't see, touch, eat, drink, or hear—you'll turn their focus to their heart instead, to guide them to deeper dimensions of intimacy, which makes you the caretaker of desire. Your efforts will allow you to come together beautifully in the paradox of love and desire. When you cohabitate and extend your resources to each other, this match offers transformation, security, novelty, and joy. You'll chart new territories and return to the heart's home together.

SCORPIO & GEMINI
Surreal, mysterious, magnetic

You're coming out of the closet for loving an extrovert, even though you're so deeply introverted. This match has ancient ties, as its mythology shows us. Your planetary ruler, Pluto, governs the underworld, and Pluto allowed only Mercury, the ruler of your Gemini, into his kingdom to move without barriers between heaven and hell. Admittedly, you were initially not hot or bothered by Gemini. But you soon discovered what your ruling planet, Pluto, did: Gemini's capacity for depth, and then their happiness, sense of humor, and comfort with risk. You're truthful enough to recognize these are wonderful values to incorporate in your round-trip journeys between heaven and hell. That's why the desire is twice as strong—because Gemini's spellbound by Scorpio's mystique, wondering what magnetism and truths lie beneath your powerful exterior. Don't ever tell them!

Your dynamic houses many paradoxes, like Gemini's lightness versus Scorpio's darkness, along with two fundamental but opposite needs, like freedom and commitment. Love needs the right agreements to afford you safety, trust, and reliability. So you'll need to be very clear about what emotional safety looks like for the both of you, and put in the effort to make it happen. Since it's a negotiation, trust your Gemini's counsel, because they're the messenger between opposing forces. You will elucidate the Gemini's vision with painful but necessary understandings on authenticity, intimacy, and belonging. Your extrovert will teach you how to keep your assumptions, words, and behaviors in the highest energies toward love and compassion. In this match is found both shadow and sunlight, hell and heaven. I believe both visions are necessary to understand truth, and that's what tethers you to each other.

SCORPIO & CANCER

Harmonious, sensual, affectionate

Shape of water, much? With this passionate and beautiful trine pairing, a gorgeous arrangement of two water signs invites you to stay home together in your native oceans of fantasy, generosity, loyalty, and trust. You trusted your inner authority, and your observation was accurate when it registered a water-dwelling soul in the moon-ruled Cancer, who radiates devotion, compassion, and tenderness. When Cancer saw you, the 70 percent of cardinal water in their body was at a high tide. With this trine, love as practice is easily made manifest through your predisposition for affection, altruism, and compassion—all favorite qualities of the merpeople. You'll easily water the roots where love grows with these practices, which come so naturally to you both.

Trine water signs run the risk of colluding, so you'll want to separate the seas a bit from time to time, without taking it too personally. And that's on you, Scorpio. You'll create the opportunity to continuously learn about each other by making the comfortable and familiar more novel and unknown. You don't want intimacy to become more like intrusion, do you? Your Plutonian power will help your sensitive Cancer with boundaries—including with themselves!—when something's out of alignment with their personal integrity. Your moon lover will help you soften into emotional exposure with ease, so you can practice being more vulnerable around others. This trine match keeps you both reveling in the mystique of longing and anticipation, while totally anchored in the water domain for love and safety. It's the ship and high tide. Enjoy the sailing!

SCORPIO & LEO
Powerful, transformative, dynamic
Devotion is this match's middle name. Even though your Pluto-ruled soul and the sun-ruled Leo are the beginning and end of the solar system, you're tirelessly devoted to each other. It's a square between two fixed signs: you born in water and Leo coronated in solar fire. In your monarch, you've identified a titan whose energy is self-generated, and you only want to be connected to others who don't need you, but who desire you. Their fire attracted you to come out of the cold and cozy up by the sun. In you, the royal discovered an equal, a strong character who has quiet confidence and who lets their sense of security magnetize you toward them. Fixed signs shouldn't struggle with desire, because they refuse to reveal all things too soon. For them, trust and disclosure are slowly earned and given.

You should take the lead on disclosure in this match. Of course, your partner is the royal of romance, so you'll want to let their courage and vulnerability feel contagious. You'll need to lean into affection, respect, and vulnerability without guarantees. Your Leo will inspire you to lead and love with a more trusting and open heart. Because no relationship is without risk or vulnerability, you'll have to toughen up with resilience around both, whereas your intimacy will help Leo process discomfort happily within the relationship, as opposed to denying, numbing, or avoiding it. As the zodiac's bookends of where our solar system begins and ends, you embody the law of opposites the universe operates on. With devotion as the harmonizing impulse for these contrasting energies, you do it so well, you'll prove that anyone else can, too.

SCORPIO & VIRGO
Joyful, supportive, adventurous
This pair puts the *sex* in sextile, okay? In this match, between you as the ruler of the underworld and Virgo as the "virgin," a powerful dynamic of intimacy, authenticity, and loyalty to each other is found. You fell unusually quickly for Virgo's mutable earth romance because they practice just the right Mercury-ruled ideas for both holding space for the healing of others and cheerleading them on their path to success. In your fixed water heart, you carry the entire ocean's power, which is the perfect container to hold the entire multidimensionality of a partner like Virgo. Loyalty outs itself, and you recognized Virgo as one of its greatest extenders. Which is precisely why this match began.

When it comes to dancing in desire, this is your move. Nobody knows how to remain above analysis and prediction like you, the most mysterious sign of them all. And whose primary function in astrology is the giving and receiving of intimacy? That's right, you again. If desire is your box step on the dance floor, love is Virgo's waltz. Virgo's earth function is a bit more qualified for tending to the roots of love. Given their intellect, Virgo is fluent in practices of affection, consistency, and accountability. So here is where the sextile match shines. In this relationship, Virgo will inspire you to exercise your attitudinal muscles for flexibility and detachment, so you can wrestle with the momentum and vulnerabilities of life, which offer no guarantees or returns on investment. You'll give your service-oriented Virgo the right parameters to give only to others who ask for help, earn it, and/or want it. They think they're the world's hero, but they need a hero, too. That's where you come in! This sextile match will bring out the best of your mental and emotional skills, so show us what you've got after you get down where it matters.

SCORPIO & LIBRA
Loyal, contrasting, instructive

If you're the broody Plutonian type, you can't neglect the more delicate side of your personality now (which we all have). In this inconjunct match, you're captivated by the more ethereal, Venus-beautified, romantic, and elegant personality of Libra. This neighboring assignment between your fixed water and their cardinal air has a twofold approach to intimacy and commitment. That's why you were bewitched by the Libran skill for compromise, beauty, and balance. It was a two-way street, because Libra loves a challenge—and your privacy and nondisclosure agreements weren't a walk in the park for the Libra to understand, because you hardly reveal anything too soon. This bond between Venus's light and Scorpio's brooding is a strong context for desire to emerge, since you're both so contrasting to each other. And even while your personality contrasts seem to keep you apart, the intimacy between you allows you to be both autonomous and one.

You'll want to maintain this natural chemistry outside the bedroom, so it stays even stronger while resting on the foundation of love. That's all your Libra's genius, so you'll want to follow their natural inclination toward the giving and receiving of love. When they demonstrate, discuss, and review what the practice of love means to you both—related to affection, service, touch, trust, and mutuality—you better listen! That way, both preferences are validated and implemented. Your Libra will also teach you a thing or two about how to imagine that everyone is doing the best they can. You'll help them see the other side of arguments, and you'll want to teach Libra that it's time for the guilty verdict where they're struggling with the benefit of the doubt. Your radical honesty will protect their light, and they'll keep you cherished and joyful through commitment and intimacy.

SCORPIO & SCORPIO
Safe, consistent, secure

You'll be the death of me! Well, not quite. You two signs are ruled by Pluto, which is the archetype of death and transformation. So you'll never be who you were prior to meeting in this conjunction collision of the most transformative planetary power in astrology. I don't know how or when you two finally ceased the standoff gridlock, but once you did, you were so relieved. In each other, you've found the fixed specificity you crave on values and practices related to love, desire, trust, and commitment. If I even thought about what you do in the desire domain, you'd kill me. So I'll just gently suggest moving slowly with the Plutonian atomic power you have, and mutually honoring slow disclosure, seduction, and magnetism, so you have the right container to handle this dynamic.

That right container will be based on a very proactively vulnerable negotiation on what affection, trust, loyalty, accountability, and responsibility mean to you. You have to talk about what you learned about attachment styles, love languages, and family if you want to turn on the light into love. Otherwise, not talking is a communication failure that keeps you two totally in the dark. Given your sensitivities to discomfort, this conversation is the right flashlight to navigate the subterranean depths you'll take together. For each other, you'll provide refuge, transformation, and unending support. This will salute the best of those Scorpio qualities, like emotional commitment, both relational and personal authenticity, and loyalty. But be careful, as it could also indulge the not-so-light-filled qualities of Scorpio. You'll want to reality check each other's conspiracies, fact-check suspicions, and put a cancel on the searches for guilt with friendly doses of optimism. That brings about the death of the former selves and the resurrection of you two as a couple.

SCORPIO & SAGITTARIUS
Loyal, contrasting, instructive
Can you handle the truth? I don't know which one can better. But you're both bound to discover more of it, which is why I love the sound of this inconjunct match. In Sagittarius, you've found the mutable fire soul who really does say what they mean and means what they say. So you know you can trust them because they're so honest. In you, the

Jupiter-ruled soul found a person who's also searching for more meaning, authenticity, and wisdom. So your common values are on truth discovery, sharing, and authenticity as a practice. So much similarity could get in the way of the desire domain just a bit, unless you identify your intimacy as the only place where complete transparency isn't necessary. Don't let it kill you! Let your Sagittarius encourage privacy of thoughts and desires. It's their divine freedom that helps you maintain the autonomy and magnetism between you, by showing you how to accept that you'll never completely know each other—which is a wonderful aphrodisiac.

The only certainty you'll want to establish is on how you both put love into practice. Does love mean brutal honesty? Not always. So define your expectations regarding trust building, affection, respect, accountability, and forgiveness by analyzing each other's love maps. That way, you'll have the careful parameters that protect you both around the loaded topics of truth, honesty, and authenticity. Your Plutonian power will help Sagittarius take their expansive visions and focus them. Their vision is panoramic, whereas you like your perspective a bit more zoomed in and specialized. That doesn't always serve your agility skills, so your liberated Sagittarius will help you know when it's time to release attachment to results and move on to the exploration of the unknown.

SCORPIO & CAPRICORN
Joyful, supportive, adventurous
With this sextile match between deliberately chronological Capricorn and your more discerningly cautious, soulful approach to love, it's all in the divine timing. This pair is cardinal earth and fixed water, which is why

you realized that the Plutonian depth of your emotionality, vulnerabilities, and loyalty could pour itself into the Saturn-ruled structure, boundaries, and ethics of your seagoat. You're both very strategic, responsible, and disciplined, so it might've taken a bit longer than usual, but nothing worthwhile should be too easy and fast, right? With sextile matches, the practice of love expresses itself very naturally. So an exploratory dialogue, led by your Capricorn, on the values and behaviors that inform your ideas of respect, trust, affection, accountability, and forgiveness will certainly fortify your practices.

When it comes to seduction, who's in charge? Both! Remember, the seagoat is still half water sign. So Capricorn, too, knows how to magnetically draw you in. They'll make you work and wait for it, which'll drive you nuts in the best way. And you'll obliterate their sense of separation with the intimacy practices uniquely given to Scorpio, so you'll teach them a thing or two, too. When it comes to personal development and self-mastery, consider Capricorn's feedback as the way they show love to you. Try not to take their delivery too personally, unless it totally warrants it. At the same time, you'll show your Capricorn that not everything needs to be completely mastered to have worth, and that there's beauty in imperfections, too. Only timing will give you the right outcomes here, so stay patient and present for the rewards.

SCORPIO & AQUARIUS
Powerful, transformative, dynamic
You're a real glutton for punishment, you know that? Between the already tough but oh so sexy squares, these two fixed signs make the rest look as loose as Sunday

spaghetti. Which is exactly why you're drawn to each other. Strong characters appreciate other strong characters—there's no doubt about that—which is why you loved the self-composure of the Uranian-ruled Aquarius. You sense an innovative thinker who remains completely untouched or unfazed by meaningless stimuli, in favor of convictions that would turn the whole world upside down or right side up. It takes a titan to know one, so your Aquarius loved your Plutonian stature, loyalty, and willingness to invest in your passions. So long as you're both passionate for the exploration of each other, the desire index will be Armageddon. You'll love the thrill, chase, pleasure, push, pull, and battle for power here, without democratic principles but with pure fantasy and eroticism.

To practice love, you'll want to thoroughly negotiate what closeness and separation means to you both. Look no further than childhood, relationship history, and self-diagnosing your attachment styles. If you agree and they're compatible, awesome. If not, there will likely be no bending or compromising. So you'll want to really ensure that you're on the same page about values and behaviors that support affection, trust, consistency, accountability, and forgiveness to keep this dynamic safe and secure against self-sabotaging. Your Aquarius will strengthen your verbal repertoire so you can explain the inner mysteries of the world in very powerful ways, and will give you the awareness to wrap language around emotion. You'll be the emotional intelligence teacher for the Aquarius, who wants to find their way to their heart more than their head.

SCORPIO & PISCES

Harmonious, sensual, affectionate

I've talked about "intimacy" rephrased as "into-me-see," and if there's a trine match that accomplishes this, you're in it. As the fixed water sign, you're longing for the right spaces of meaningful bonding with another, where you can place all your powerful intimacy into the heart of another. In Pisces, you've found a mutable water sign who will grow stronger through your influence, and who will empower you to see yourself as beautifully as they see you. This is easily a trine match that could also explore desire and love in similar styles, with a slightly higher sea level for Pisces on desire, and for you on love, which is a wonderful complementary union. So I suspect your desire realms could be in the same dimension, because you know how to magnetize, seduce, indulge imaginations, and let fantasy run wild. Keep in mind, you'll want to honor a bit of a barrier, because waters can easily collude.

On sustaining the values and behaviors of love, you'll want to find the right words—a challenge for water signs, but totally necessary for the conversation on trust, affection, loyalty, respect, accountability, and forgiveness. Discuss specific actions you'll want taken, and what bids for connection with these outcomes mean for you both. If you work to find the words, you can uplift the best of your intimacy practices and help each other see the existential oceans within you. You'll lead your Pisces to finish what they start, because your concentration exemplifies the right focus they need. And you'll show them the authentic boundaries to protect their tenderness. They'll have the opposite effect on you, showing your fixed waters how to share and uplift others, especially when it's not convenient. So you'll want to expand your emotional repertoire to include more vulnerable places.

SAGITTARIUS IN LOVE

Adventurous | Visionary | Optimistic
Honor: Wanderlust & Freedom
Integrate: Focus & Attention

As the grand finale of the fire signs, when Sagittarius is in love, it's like the sun never sets on their heart. They turn on every light, every source of power, every everything when they're in love. The universe wouldn't have it any other way.

Sagittarius is an adventurous lover who makes the known unknown again with their visionary thinking. This way, they'll keep their lovers on their intellectual toes. With the right blend of optimism and intellectual gravitas, Sagittarius has major romantic skills. Love is risky, and their optimism gives them strength to do it.

Hardly struggling with authenticity as a practice, Sagittarius will want to vocalize and demonstrate their essential passion for wanderlust. Love's an adventure, and Sagittarius wants to experience every moment fully alive and freely. Love is not ownership, so Sagittarius needs to request breathing room so they can be in love.

Thankfully Sagittarius's comfort with contrast is Olympic level, but they'll want to integrate the skills of focus and attention. Romance needs to be carefully observed, so Sagittarius will have to see it with a narrower lens than usual, and focus more specifically so their lovers feel valued. Paying attention is mandatory, and Sagittarius will need to integrate this ability in order for romance to flourish.

SAGITTARIUS & ARIES
Harmonious, sensual, affectionate

The UX index on this match is not healthy! When you two fellow fire signs align in this inferno of a trine match, you'll raise the temperature to scorching levels. Since you both crave adventure, independence, freedom, and joy, as the cardinal and mutable fire signs join together, you'll stop at nothing to keep each other autonomous. When you were together for the first time, your fire burned hot thanks to the Aries's beginner's luck, Martian leadership potential, and supreme confidence. You love that they love themselves. Fire grows in proximity, and Aries loves your Jupiter-ruled intelligence, your comfort level with your freedom, and your zeal for making the best of life.

Make sure you take your natural enthusiasm and wrap it around loving the mystery. Fire energy is in your face, which is beautiful in the right places, but desire needs mystique and seduction, which you know how to protect. So be enthusiastically up front about your existential freedom without demanding disclosure and up-front candor, if you want to let this fire stay burning. On honoring the love between you, you'll understand the right behaviors to support accountability, forgiveness, affection, safety, and trust by following your Aries's lead. You'll just want to understand the values that *inform* the behaviors. You both sometimes struggle to finish what you start and embrace meaning over impulse in life, but you have a better handle on these skills than Aries, so try to serve as a guide for your impulsive Aries, and show them how to solidify their plans. Whereas your Aries will keep you from getting accidentally lost in your wandering—in a relationship, you may need to pick a path and walk it.

That's where Aries comes in! You'll be walking the path of joy, security, love, and passion for as long as you freedom lovers want it.

SAGITTARIUS & TAURUS
Surreal, mysterious, magnetic
It's no animal house here! Sure, you're the centaur and Taurus is the great bull, but there's a deeper connection in this animalistic match. As the Jupiter-ruled, philosophy-loving sign, you know that in Taurus you have another person who lives their life in accordance with their wisdom and values. In your freedom-loving soul, you'll be blessed and inspired by their consistent Venus-valued integrity. Who are we if we don't keep our values alive in our hearts? Taurus fell in love with your contagiously positive thinking, passionate exploration, and curiosity. Your adaptability and enthusiasm invites glorious personal and relational expansion for you both in this quincunx match. Between your mutable fire and their fixed earth, the energy of desire rages like a forest fire. You'll both be quick to explore each other's perceptions, experiences, and stories because you'll be curious to know the exotic history of your lover.

In order for love to coexist with this desire, you'll want to ask for just a bit of breathing room, coaching your Taurus on resilience while experiencing risk and vulnerability. Then you'll need to be very specific—no Sagittarius armchair philosophy here!—around what affection, loyalty, consistency, accountability, and forgiveness look like to you. Because in this dynamic, you're both inclined to seek meaning and philosophical value over demonstrative practice. You'll help the Taurus explore the unknown with a gumption they never knew they wanted or needed—even if it takes a while for them to realize it—whereas your Taurus will help you sit still, stay tranquil, focus, and finish what you start. This blend of powerful fire and earth energies is both exciting and stable, which will allow both love and desire to burn on your fire and Taurus's wood beautifully.

SAGITTARIUS & GEMINI
Completion, romantic, compromise

Talk love to me! Under this polarity match where communication, exploration, education, and expansion bind you together, you have a beautiful foundation of support for your mutable fire and mutable air. Your one and only polarity sign, Gemini, collected the microfocused Mercury research and data, and you love to use that material in order to educate the masses of people who learn from you. You fell head over horse feet for your Gemini as soon as their words started flowing, like rainbow satin ribbons. Verbal communication is their favorite hobby and skill. The twins' words are twofold, of course, with a flavor that's both sweet and just the right amount of sour, with a little bit of milk and honey to keep you laughing and loving. The thermonuclear chemistry and desire will last between you because the hunger for each other's wisdom keeps it burning. Your polarity distance inspires curiosity, and with freedom as a primary value for Sagittarius, you'll keep the seduction, a bit of sexy conflict, and powerful attraction alive.

Good thing you two love to talk, because you'll want to communicate about your common points of affection, loyalty, and trust. Beyond the contexts of love and desire,

Gemini will inspire you to zoom in on your visions so you don't get too scattered or lose the credibility of your words. As their opposite sign, you'll happily motivate the Gemini to zoom out and redirect their focus to the widest symbol we have on Earth—the sunrise of hope, adventure, and innovation. When your Sagittarius wisdom combines with the Gemini's wealth of intellectual resources, you'll create a relationship of infinite possibilities, fulfilling conversations, vitality, and love.

SAGITTARIUS & CANCER
Surreal, mysterious, magnetic

Difference of opinion? This quincunx match between world traveler Sagittarius and home-loving Cancer is sure to keep you both curious and inspired. As the mutable fire sign, you love to explore, finding more joy in the journey than in the destination. Your heart searches always for the unknown. But as the cardinal water sign, Cancer is the master of creating a sense of home and belonging, seeking comfortable emotional attachments to both people and places. That's why you're drawn to Cancer—you're in awe of their ability to texture everything in their life with sage emotional intelligence, building connection wherever they land. Cancer was attracted to your energetic, honest, and altruistic nature. Your wisdom and optimism called to them from across the globe, and they shine in your presence.

You're both master storytellers and conversationalists, so if you can find the common ground in the stories of your lives, you'll love to share everything with each other. Given that Cancer is the cardinal leader of belonging and connection, let them take the lead on initiating conversations about how you both give and demonstrate love. Talk about how you learned affection, stability, and commitment from your family of origin and past experiences. Once you agree to the language of love that works for you, this quincunx match is safe. Your shared desire won't diminish—you're about as different from each other as it gets. As the fire sign who loves freedom, you will ensure that your relationship has plenty of mystery, longing, and seduction. Cancer will help you look for happiness and belonging in the here and now, as opposed to constantly looking to the next adventure. And you will inspire your crab to leave their comfort zone and dive into new experiences. Together you'll enjoy the best of both worlds!

SAGITTARIUS & LEO
Harmonious, sensual, affectionate
Burn, baby, burn! This trine match between two fire signs, Sagittarius and Leo, is a glorious conflagration to behold. When the royal took you to their throne room, you were captivated by how their fixed fire soul radiates effortlessly from their heart space. The queen fell for your enthusiasm and contagious optimism. They love how you were itching to leave the palace for adventure. This trine match is sure to keep the desire context like a disco inferno, because you two fire signs are naturally passionate—that is, so long as you both maintain mutual mindfulness toward each other, adventure, and a sense of wonder about the other. With that interpersonal reaching, often led by you—which you'll want to name and identify to the sometimes self-preoccupied Leo—the fire won't go out.

Romantic and relational Leo will teach you that relationships determine the quality of our lives if they consistently demonstrate how deeply you matter to them. And you'll want to learn from Leo's royal lead here because, without this center of meaning, there will be little relationship success. As the freedom seeker, you're more qualified for autonomy, so you'll have to be properly seduced for the right commitment structure. If Leo helps you see the crown jewels of intimacy, you'll express your more devotional side. Leo will coach you on how to take your vision to manifestation and will help you follow through on your dreams. Then you'll shoot the centaur's bow and arrow and summon the very best of the alternative possibilities you chase, like adventure, joy, and wisdom. So long as you both pace yourselves in passion—which is a hard feat for fire signs—this trine match will provide strength, power, and loyalty for the kingdom you'll rule together.

SAGITTARIUS & VIRGO
Powerful, transformative, dynamic
Class couple! Sparks will definitely fly on campus—and wherever you two curious signs are might as well be a university, you both so love education. In this passionate and chemistry-charged square between your Sagittarius mutable fire energy and your Virgo's mutable earth intelligence, it's a quicksilver match between two brainiacs who are both teacher and student. You probably showed up tardy to the seminar, which lost you brownie points in the eyes of the Virgo. But once you realized that Virgo's analytical skills and thoughtful concern for the detailed things in life give you the foundation to explore your macro wisdom, you wanted to know everything the Virgo knew. When Mercury Virgo saw your naturally gregarious, optimistic, and joyful energy, they finally cracked a

few smiles. Square dynamics usually keep the desire hot, especially yours, since you'll likely be in the friction of debate during your joint quests to understand more about the worlds you inhabit. You search for alternative curricula always, whereas Virgo is top of the class wherever they're enrolled. Remember to respect this difference, because it's the life force of desire, and it keeps your minds on full speed.

Speaking of differences, you'll want to understand the differences you have on the context for love. As it turns out, Virgo is more fluent in consistency, trust, and knowledge, which is the container for love, whereas you're more skilled in the arts of demonstrative affection, generosity, and warmth. With your mutable adaptability, you can readily celebrate and adapt to the key differences between you, which fortifies both the square's scorching desire power and the safety of love between you. Your Virgo will help you inhabit the here and now and teach you to stay impeccable with your word. You talk a big talk, and Virgo will help you deliver. This will give you peace of mind and focus. What's better? And you'll teach the teacher on how to manage the grip of perfectionism, people pleasing, and control, so even their beautiful imperfections reach the dynamic. In this collegiate love story, you'll educate each other on the right personal and relational skills that are needed to succeed and triumph off campus. And with each other as allies and colleagues, there's little you cannot accomplish.

SAGITTARIUS & LIBRA
Joyful, supportive, adventurous
The philosopher and the artist. Your Jupiter-ruled percep-

tion registered Venus-born Libra as one who creates new imaginative possibilities. So when you, as the mutable fire, let your fire join with the cardinal air Libra, this sextile match was off to the equestrian races. In Libra, you have your partner as your biggest fan—a lover who believes in you and holds space for your dreams to come true. In you, Libra has a visionary thinker who's never boring because you're so entertaining, in motion, and alive. The practice of love, as it's made manifest through affection, empowerment, gratitude, and loyalty, will secure the bonds of this match, where two free spirits can join together to live a meaningful life. Between Libra's thoughtful cognition and Sagittarius's action, you'll know what the other needs to help them feel loved.

Since sextile dynamics are often very comfortable, you'll want to imagine how to make the familiar unfamiliar again in this dynamic. When you fall into the practices of love, you have to remember that your Libra is still a new person, no matter how long you've been together. Plan activities where they have to reintroduce themselves to you in a sense. This is sure to keep the longing, seduction, and magnetism scorching between you. This couple is the one that should try traveling, taking classes, and exploring their neighborhood to secure the sextile spark. Your Libra will motivate you to develop more diplomacy and impulse control, because reactivity gets you into trouble. Your frankness will help Libra recognize the power of straight talk and how it leads to straight understanding. Between your proactive optimism and Libra's glamour, this is a match that is sure to bring out the richest dialogues and aesthetics whenever the world finds you two bohemians falling in love.

SAGITTARIUS & SCORPIO
Loyal, contrasting, instructive

The truth will set you free! This inconjunct match pairs the zodiac's two signs that are most obligated to inquire about the most truthful experiences of life, which is why it's sacred. When the light of day caught Scorpio, you found another detective who's also searching for what lies behind the veil, beyond illusions and distractions. So although this a different match, you have a great tether connecting you, because you're committed to the discovery, communication, and teaching of truth. In you, Scorpio Sherlock's found the mutable fire soul who really does say the first thing that's on their mind, and so they can respect your candor. This comfortable connection that always wants to make the uncertain certain could numb the power of desire in the match. So a word of caution: Perhaps you'll want to listen to the Scorpio when they identify the bedroom as the only place where complete disclosure isn't totally necessary? You'll want to respect each other's privacies and fantasies by honoring the separation. Acknowledge and celebrate that you'll never completely know or have each other. Which is an elixir of an aphrodisiac that actually keeps you together; counterintuitive logic and all!

The only certainty you'll want to establish is how you both practice the behavior of love, which is your challenge to rise to. Does love require brutal honesty? I don't think so. So name your expectations and behaviors around trust building, affection, respect, accountability, and forgiveness before the conflicts occur, in order to have a first aid kit handy that can heal future wounds. Your Scorpio will encourage you to narrow in on your dreams and focus on them one by one, so you achieve little by little. Your vision is 360 degrees, whereas Scorpio's is 0.01. Their intense focus doesn't always serve their agility skills, so you can help your precise lover know when it's time to release attachment to results and move on to the exploration of the horizons.

SAGITTARIUS & SAGITTARIUS
Safe, consistent, secure

The herd is coming! Why not run brave and wild with another half human, half horse in love? This conjunction match between you two mutable fire signs is sure to set the world on fire, while you gallop in a herd together. You finally found another who knows how to hold space, show enthusiasm, and extend curiosity just as well as you. Both of you are Jupiter-ruled academics and students. You're happy to alternate roles, because adaptability is your modus operandi. With the rarity of strong intellectual stimulation, it's too good to pass up! Given how much you both treasure your freedom and separation, the desire index will stay high. But you'll want to temper the disclosure a bit, because you need mystery for magnetism, so don't reflexively blurt it out, you two! Make each other work hard, then harder for it.

The area where you may need to strategize is in the values and practices related to love. So spend time in your own Sagittarius seminar exploring what accountability, forgiveness, affection, and trust mean, leaning on research from the relational experts listed in the beginning of this chapter and on insights from each other's childhoods, parents, and romantic histories. Then you'll both need to collaborate together on how to implement what you learned—this match brings out the best and worst of the sign, and concentration isn't one of your fortes. So remember, maintain, and commit! Also help each other work on that famously rough delivery of yours. Practice tender compassion, not brutal. The good news is this will be one of the most joyful, adventurous, and contagiously loving dynamics the world has seen. You'll share your mutual happiness, laughter, and support, not just with each other, but with the world at large.

SAGITTARIUS & CAPRICORN
Loyal, contrasting, instructive
Pull up your sleeves, Sag! The work begins. Hopefully the days of your thrills and Jupiter escapades are behind you, because if you want to partner with a Capricorn, they mean business . . . and there's no such thing as ruled horseplay. Maybe you're ready for that stability now more than ever, after the mutable fire fun you've had, which is why you're pulled into this inconjunct's orbit to the cardinal earth mountain climber. Capricorn secretly wants to play as hard as they work, so that's why they're all in with you. Your wonderful resonance gives these Saturn souls the ability to clock out of work early and run wild with you. Once these key differences are established and accepted, you'll then have a powerful pull toward the erotic and intimacy. Your differences, once overcome, are what make this chemistry as explosive as it is, so ensure that you keep the freedom alive to always feel like you've never quite acquired each other. You're both signs who like to explain or get the answers you need, so you'll want to take the lead on tempering this tendency to just let your bodies, fantasies, and sensuality do all the talking.

But do all the talking verbally when it comes to the practice of love! This is where you'll want to encourage your Capricorn to model the negotiation around the values, choices, and behaviors that form the constellation of love between you. You're a straight talker and so is Capricorn, both on the speaking and listening front. So draw your love maps and name your love languages early. Your Capricorn will help you follow through on your visions with the right plans and structures to support your success. You'll counsel your wise old Capricorn on not getting stuck in circumstances, but remembering to live out of a greater vision so they can have the ideologies that promote their changes. Now get to work!

SAGITTARIUS & AQUARIUS
Joyful, supportive, adventurous
Rebels love their freedom! Freedom loves rebels. So this sextile match between your mutable fire freedom and Aquarius's fixed air rebellion is sure to make the front-page news. In your Jupiter-ruled soul, you love to explore new books, countries, and conversations. Which is why you loved exploring the Uranian-ruled lectures, because once this fixed air sign starts giving you the shifts in perceptions and eureka moments, there's no stopping them. They appreciate curiosity, so when you questioned their dialogue with the right resource, book, or academic support, you had their undivided attention. That's where the spark of desire was lit: from your wise words. You two never run out of things to say to each other, so I suspect this intrigue, dialogue, and mystery will wrap you both in compatibility for as long as you keep paying attention to each other.

Of course, for love to sustain itself between a rebel and a freedom seeker, you cannot operate in a definitional void. So you'll want to explain the values and behaviors that align with love, by your demonstrations. What does integrity, reliability, trust, affection, forgiveness, and accountability look like in the three-dimensional world? You're both so future focused, you'll want to look to the here and now for these answers. While you're there, you'll inspire your Aquarius to have less contempt for concepts they don't understand and more enthusiasm to explore the unknown. They're fixed air, so they're rigid! Whereas they'll centralize you a bit more, so you don't waste precious energy in unbecoming places. Use their rebellion to find your freedom, and let this match be a little sanctuary for you.

SAGITTARIUS & PISCES
Powerful, transformative, dynamic

Dream come true? Perhaps! You two mutable signs are forever in la-la land and fantasy futures. So when you join, you take each other out of the worldly circumstances into a metaphysical plane, with the help of your ruling planet, Jupiter, and theirs, Neptune. This is a square between your mutable fire and Pisces's mutable water. A notoriously clashing energy, your tie to romance is the mutable energy you share. That's what you recognize in the Pisces's eyes: the "both/and" or "not only but also" ideology, which you have, too. Pisces adores your mastery of many topics and your flexibility with the material and spiritual worlds. They love a light-on-their-feet thinker, and you're galloping quick. Their emotional fluency and your expansive mental visions make this strong clash charged for desire. Square dynamics are constantly repelled and drawn toward each other. It's frustrating, but it makes for wonderful experiences in intimacy. Intimacy is born in Pisces waters, so see them as the shaman here, and you'll use this space to connect on the erotic level more deeply.

To protect this fantasy, this dream-come-true energy between you, the right conversation on the philosophies and choices that sustain affection, accountability, trust, and integrity for love will prove mandatory. That's all you! Make storytelling a favorite activity on date night and tell each other your stories about your emotional dowries from parents and former lovers. Along the way, you'll help your nonverbal Pisces choose the right words here and evermore. Your communication skills will help them wrap their heads around the right language to support emotional exposure. They'll help you develop your fluency with the invisible ethers and nonverbal cues, like body language and other energies. You're both in this world, but not of it, and that's why this match has the potential to make your life more of a dream than you ever thought.

CAPRICORN IN LOVE

Disciplined | Providing | Dynamic
Honor: Boundaries & Responsibility
Integrate: Empathy & Risk

A Capricorn in love is a miracle. The seagoat falls rarely and very slowly. These mountain climbers look at love like the peak experience it is. Since top-of-the-mountain experiences are serious business, it takes time. When it occurs, it's worth the wait.

When Capricorn falls in love, they're uncommonly disciplined in making sure they don't give in to the appetite for connection, but wait for the heartfelt desire of it. Once they've found a partner who's a partner in every sense, Capricorn will provide both resources and energy to their lover, with dynamic approaches to keep their relationship thriving. Since it happens so infrequently, Capricorn will want to trust me when I say this (even if they don't have experiences to confirm): they need to honor their reflex for boundaries. Boundaries protect desire in the long term, empower their partners, and secure mutuality. Also, they'll want to take the more responsible path often, because relationships are work, and Capricorn knows how to do it.

To integrate values that help them reach the mountaintop sooner, they'll want to remember that empathy is defined as "feeling with." Capricorn can feel deeply with another, even if they haven't personally experienced it. Capricorn should remember: it's emotion, not experience, that matters. And they'll want to practice their comfort level with risk, since there's no risk-free relationship.

CAPRICORN & ARIES
Powerful, transformative, dynamic
Who's the boss? We may never know! With your disciplined management style and Aries's leadership qualifications, you two alphas can run this relationship like an empire. You're almost embarrassed to admit how moved you are by Aries's power, assertiveness, and cavalier approach to rules. You love how Aries disrupts the norm, even if it's an inconvenience. Disruption is the birthplace of creativity and change, which inspires you to read a page from their leadership manual. Aries might've acted like the babies they are around your cardinal-earthy ethics, outstanding discipline, and willingness to work at making the relationship work. But your no-nonsense approach proves to them that it's actually that easy! Looks like you're both the boss! This dynamic is a clash of the cardinal titans embodying the best of productive earth and powerful fire. The clash keeps the desire pulsating, because you're both unknown and yet highly consistent with each other. You can't predict Aries's next move, which keeps you longing and reaching.

It you want to run the relationship like the corporation it's meant to be, make sure you're proactive about declaring what you'd like executive leadership on, and ask your Aries what they're more passionate about taking charge of. If the outline of your core values and actions related to love are agreed upon, you'll prove to be lifesaving support systems of accountability, chemistry, adventure, and safety with each other. Nuance and specificity will help your cause while you draw your love maps. You'll want to humbly listen to your Aries, too, as they explain all the ways in which they can feel safe, trusted, respected, and adored. Mutuality guarantees they'll return the courtesy. When you find your common-alities—as you're both born to the goat family—your rela-tionship is sure to ascend to peak experiences while you step up, and step back, in leadership.

CAPRICORN & TAURUS
Harmonious, sensual, affectionate
This love is like a protected park, as the trine between you two earth signs. Remember, triangles are the strongest geometric shape because they won't collapse. Neither do you, as paragons of the earth element! Trines are supportive dynamics that aren't as susceptible to societal pressures. As the fixed earth forest and cardinal earth mountain, no sign combination honors this protection and strength quite like you two pillars. Once you've discerned the Venus-ruled Taurus as unsuperficial, you're emotionally moved by their unbridled devotion to their life's passions and relationships. In their Saturn-ruled heart, Taurus is taken by your majesty, all the ways you exalt your life and connections with impeccability. In trine matches, especially ones with earth signs, the stability and close-ness that allows love to have a home builds itself beauti-fully. Safe to say, earth signs need this level of security for connection before revealing their love, and fortunately you are both experts at safety and support.

With that taken care of, make sure you see one of your primary responsibilities as exchanging the need for security with a bit of risk, by strategizing more ways to allow desire to grow through distance and mystery. That's on you! Organize your relationship with some space for autonomy built in, so you can help each other become the people you're capable of, while maintaining enough distance to keep you both in curiosity toward of the experiences of each other. To aid in this process, Taurus will balance your workload by helping you pause and take in the joys of life, in an effort to remember why you work so hard. You'll help your Taurus lean in to vulnerability so their energy can take it over from there and finish what they start. Your combined love, built on the trine's mountaintop, will give you the rock-solid foundation you need to succeed.

CAPRICORN & GEMINI
Surreal, mysterious, magnetic

Going up? You climb to the mountaintop, and Gemini flies to the skies. Both signs meet at nature's peak, and that's where this quincunx match between cardinal earth and mutable air finds its strength. Somehow this cheeky Gemini devilishly charmed you with their Mercurial sense of humor, gracious social skills, and intelligence. They disarmed your armor a bit too easily. Whereas your long-term ambition, ethics, and self-mastery, instructed by your ruling planet Saturn, might've made the twins a bit nervous at first, but they kept all four eyes of theirs on your stature and dignity. This match is a power couple where both your tie to tradition and Gemini's penchant for progress find their sweet spot. This keeps the gravity between you inescapable and electric—desire breathes the air of Gemini, which is existential distance, mystery, and the unknown. Since you're both so different, you'll stay unknown to each other, and that's why the emotional and/or erotic longing remains strong.

For love to secure itself in the dynamic, Gemini will

want to show their practicality, reliability, and consistency to you. You will need Gemini to prove they have these qualities before you discern whether or not your love will be taken care of, because that's your price of admission. Ask the Gemini to say what they mean and commit to it. Then Gemini's love will show you how to cultivate more self-compassion. Their example inspires you to be just as light on your feet as the twins, and gentle on yourself while you climb to the mountaintop. Show your lighter, more fun-loving dimensions, and this will invite Gemini to soften into joy and safety in their love for you. They'll need you to not take yourself too seriously, or they'll have trouble creating intimacy with you. But it's worth it, especially since, when this match of air and earth is done well, there's no height your partnership can't climb or soar to, and you'll bring out the best of each other.

CAPRICORN & CANCER
Completion, romantic, compromise
Home is where this love is. As the only polarity sign that stands diametrically opposite to you on the zodiac wheel, moon-ruled Cancer picks up where you leave off. Your Saturn sensibilities carefully found a highly empathic and devotional lover in Cancer, whose bids for connection, textured by compassion, sensitivity, and loyalty, are as classic as yours. In the responsibly and ethically considered you, your Cancer found a divine blend of heart healer and life builder. As the seagoat, you're master of both the earth and sea. So you're materially generous and emotionally responsive. This polarity match is a blend of direct meets receptive, assertive meets magnetic.

Polarity dynamics tend to bring out our glory and highlight our shadow. So assuming you're both comfortable with the gravity of this assignment, polarity relationships sustain desire, because there's often a healthy erotic tension that keeps you two striving to manage yourselves and the potential of the relationship. On the unpacking of the affection, respect, and trust qualities of love, this is a dialogue you'll want to have sooner than later. Courageously share where you're both skilled in the foundation for love, and honestly admit where you may need improvement. Along the way, you'll have to pay close attention to the integrity of the conversation, because you'll want to accept each other's contrasting styles as best you can. Your strict values will help Cancer place their benevolence only in places where it's earned and requested, so they don't give away their love too easily, whereas your Cancer's waters will wear down your boundaries and barriers while they help you demonstrate the values of empathy, compassion, and kindness. In this passionate opposites-attract dynamic between winter and summer, earth and water, home is where your love and loyalty are found.

CAPRICORN & LEO
Surreal, mysterious, magnetic

This love is like a constitutional monarchy, where you have Capricorn's parliament and Leo's royal family. They are two very different symbols of power, dignity, and leadership. But both are equal in terms of the formidable devotion they can receive from their constituents. In Leo, the seagoat understands and reveres the charisma that radiates beautifully from the center of their fixed fire heart.

When Leo awakens to their divine potential, they invite others to awaken to their power, glory, and worthiness. This is a value that your ruling planet, Saturn, is initially skeptical of but comes to value for its efficient effects. In you, Leo finds their chief executive or central government agency who can help them consider all the ways to lead a kingdom, since Capricorn initiates structures like it's an executive order. You'll give this relationship just that: the structure any dynamic needs to sustain affection, integrity, reliability, and trust—and this is a match where Leo will want to show deference on the practice of love and let you be the moral authority on how love is made into action.

As the happy-go-lucky fire sign, Leo will have no issue keeping the chemistry dynamic as interesting and spontaneous as possible. The sovereign wants to fan the flames of desire through more adventure and surprise, so you'll have to go along for the ride. Your values, on the other hand, will help the sovereign develop more interpersonal consideration and tranquility. You'll urge them to leave the castle confines and mingle with others so they'll develop the capacity to listen and honor a wealth of experiences from stories of others who confide in them. You'll want to let the Leo teach you how to connect to others from a place of vulnerability and comfort with risk, which is the only door for thoughtful inspiration and meaningful leadership in today's culture. If you want a match that brings out the best of your possibilities in the government of relationships, look no further than this quincunx. Now long live the queen and country!

CAPRICORN & VIRGO
Harmonious, sensual, affectionate

This love is like the Grand Canyon. When you two earth signs find the trine love between you, there's no natural beauty on earth like it. In this trine match between your Capricorn cardinal earth structure and Virgo's mutable earth energy, together you've found a sanctuary that protects you from the environmental hazards of life. You only emotionally revealed yourself to the service-compelled Virgo after your wisdom understood how diligently they're working to improve their own life, so that they have the foundation and moral authority to make a Mercurial difference in the lives of the people they love. The heart speaks many languages, but you knew it spoke the same earth language as your Virgo when yours beat next to them. So the stability, affection, and wonder that water the roots by which love must grow was provided—thanks to your Virgo's education here. Their mutability is more engineered toward interpersonal matters of the heart.

You two earth signs feel like an earthquake is shaking the ground whenever you're confronted with uncertainty, risk, emotional exposure, and mystery. But you cannot have the chemistry and spark of desire without risk. So once you two fully embrace the purpose of mystery in seduction and pleasure, you'll work hard to maintain it for the health of the relationship. Since Capricorn as seagoat is both water and earth, your educational qualifications around the erotic are dually drawn from earth and water. You'll coach your helpful Virgo on the right strategies to implement mutuality, discipline, and tough love over people pleasing and conflict avoidance, whereas Virgo will excavate the weeds from your Capricorn garden and help you soften into the purpose of joy, risk, and innovation. So together you too can continue attracting nature-loving crowds who want to witness the majesty of earth.

CAPRICORN & LIBRA
Powerful, transformative, dynamic
Justice and liberty! Despite the severity of these two values, this pair is a sensual and chemistry-packed match. You were enchanted a bit too quickly by the Venus-ruled Libra and how their balanced scales help inform them on what's righteous, beautiful, and possible for all. When Libra dynamically squared with your cardinal earth heart, they found a Saturn-ruled mastermind who wants to construct the new order—which could become the space for Libra to apply all their just ideas on diplomacy, beauty, and activism. So the magnetism in this match is extremely powerful because you're both so concerned with meaningful life concepts, with just the right amount of contrast between you. As an earth sign, you approach the sexy space of desire as a bit more nonverbal, sensual, and embodied, whereas airy Libra is of course more mental, verbal, and lighthearted. If you see these styles as highly complementary, with a bit of a competitive streak, you two should be working in the right jurisdiction for intimacy, loyalty, and commitment.

On the practice of love, you'll want to explore these conversations like the opening statement of a trial. It'll be completely unromantic for the Venus descendant Libra, but I think it's vital to prove and testify to what love means to you both. Love needs affection, consistency, forgiveness, and reliability. Your authority will help Libra with the right discipline to take steps on self-improvement, because you won't enable any laziness or self-indulgence from them, whereas Libra will be the player of the self-care song, and you'll be inspired by them to make joy and self-care a nonnegotiable for your own life. Exhaustion shouldn't be a status symbol, and hyperfunctioning is not a healthy lifestyle. Thanks to comfort and competence, and justice and liberty, you two on the same team make this relationship undefeated.

CAPRICORN & SCORPIO
Joyful, supportive, adventurous
Divine timing is the name of this relationship's game! With a sextile match between your Scorpio's more intuitive approach to love and your methodical and chronological approach to connection, you two know when it's the perfect time to bond. This pair is fixed water Scorpio and cardinal earth you. Your Saturn rings could feel the power from Scorpio's Plutonian depths, which beam with loyalty, intimacy, and honesty. Like water, Scorpio's power then poured itself into your Saturn-governed boundaries and structure. When it's the right time to align, you both become stronger together than apart. As signs that are strategic and disciplined when it comes to pursuing pleasure, it might've taken a bit longer than usual to connect, but nothing worthwhile should be too easy, right? With sextile matches, love as practice reveals itself very naturally in the dynamic because you're both so complementary to each other. A never-ending series of conversations that explore not only the values but behaviors around trust (especially for the Scorpio), affection (especially for the Capricorn), and accountability and forgiveness (for you both) will certainly fortify your practices.

So when it comes to the master of seduction, who's in charge? As sextiles, it's up to you both! Remember, you as the seagoat still possess the magnetism of the water signs. So you know how to magnetically draw the Scorpio in and then make Scorpio long for and reach for you. Once you do, they'll dissolve the sense of separation with the intimacy practices uniquely given to Scorpio, and you'll feel as one with them as two people could ever be. You love to show love through ideas on personal development and by coaching partners on self-mastery, so deliver your feedback gently and with gratitude as the way you show love to Scorpio. Wouldn't you know that Scorpio will show you that there's beauty in imperfections, too— not everything needs to be completely mastered to have worth. Of course, only divine timing will give you the right perceptions here, so you'll want to lean on your best practices for patience, perseverance, and loyalty to find the rewards of this fated connection.

CAPRICORN & SAGITTARIUS
Loyal, contrasting, instructive
Welcome to the one, the only Sagittarius freak show! You're ready to play as hard as you work, so that's why you're all in to this match with Jupiter's larger-than-life resonance. Sagittarius clocks you out of work early so you can run wild on adventures with them. Hopefully, though, the Sagittarius's wildest days of thrill seeking and escapades are in the past, because you mean business when it comes to relationships and you won't put up with horseplay, even the mythological variety. When you align, it's because you're both ready for something different from the past, which is why your cardinal earth was

pulled into this inconjunct's mutable fire orbit. Once your key differences are accepted, you'll then have a powerful pull toward eroticism, desire, and intimacy, because your differences outweigh the commonalities. The chemistry here is as thermonuclear as it gets. Take the lead on eroticism because, while you're both outspoken signs, I think your inspiration on fantasy, sensuality, and the unknown keeps the gravity between you strong.

But make sure you're articulate, exploratory, and thoughtful about the practices of love as soon possible! This is where you'll want to understand the values and behaviors that form the emotional genealogy of affection, trust, and consistency between you. I'd venture to say Sagittarius has the wisdom needed for the foundation of love in this particular match. Listen to their suggestions that are textured by feelings of warmth and wonder. You'll then help your sometimes distracted Sagittarius follow through on their ideas, with the right plans and structures. They'll teach your old soul to not stay stuck—to simply lighten up a bit and not take trivial circumstances too seriously. Along the way, think of Sagittarius as the ideologies, and you're the container to hold them. Dare I say you'll hold the key to changing the world, because the world changes when conversations change. So show us all how it's done at this circus show but hardworking love affair.

CAPRICORN & CAPRICORN
Safe, consistent, secure

Hey, power couple! When two Capricorns form a conjunction connection, these two seagoats put the power in partnership. In this match between two born under the only sign ruled by ambitious Saturn, it's sensual, deliberate, visionary, and responsible in romance. In each other, you've found another skilled technician of love. You're both unafraid of the work required to earn the rewards of love, desire, and intimacy. And you're excited to roll up your goat sleeves and get to work on the connection. In every Capricorn as Seagoat is a paradox between worldly, practical, seeking goat and empathetic, sensitive fish. So I suspect you two can navigate the complexities of love and desire well, as soon as you identify it as the paradox and you two as symbols of it.

In love, you'll want to explore the specificities of what trust, commitment, follow-through, forgiveness, and accountability mean to you both. Discuss each other's family of origin and how relationships were explored there, and then you'll start drawing out each other's definitions of romance. Then you'll easily get to work on it! Remember together that desire is nonverbal, imaginative, seductive, and magnetic. So be deliberate with implementing mystery, play, and creativity in the connection. Let certainty and control go, and you'll have each other to fall back on. With you two seagoats together, you'll inevitably accomplish triumph after triumph. So in each other, honor the seagoat's balance by also making sure you're giving each other the permission to rest, recharge, and fuel up with joy. Only love—not work!—is life sustaining, seagoats!

CAPRICORN & AQUARIUS
Loyal, contrasting, instructive
Learn the rules, break the rules. Meet the Buddha, kill him. Think of Capricorn as the Buddha and Aquarius as Buddha killer. This match has the inconjunct proximity astrologically, and is linked to the inconjunct theme

above. Once Capricorn learns the law, Aquarius breaks it. When your strict Saturn soul registered a Uranian rebel who loves to break rules, you were a bit turned off, but inspired. Your cardinal earth perspective identified how their fixed air convictions are unattached to hierarchy, tradition, and structure, yet somehow their life still works. Aquarius was curious about Capricorn. Even though you may ideologically disagree, Aquarius respects you as a person of virtue, ethics, discipline, and responsibility. That's why the desire between you, sparked by the Aquarius, could move the mountains you love to climb. It's an undemocratic clash of titans, and the longing, anticipation, seduction, and mystery stay in the air because of your air partner.

It's the practice and structure of love that may need some extra effort. Given how principled you both are, you'll want to discuss what needs fundamental agreement for love to grow. Are your expressions of trust, accountability, affection, respect, and forgiveness closely aligned? Of course, you're the leader of this in practice. So you'll want to have tough conversations around family of origin and attachment styles to understand the structures you need to feel that love is safe. If the expressions are similar, wonderful. If not, break the rules. You'll have to chart new relationship territory together if you want to sustain the romance between you. Luckily, once you get to work on the construction of this chart, you'll be working with the right convictions and plans to make your love thrive. You'll learn to innovate, question, and disagree more firmly from your radical water bearer, whereas you'll keep your Aquarius focused, pointed, and more grounded, so their brilliance has application where it's called.

CAPRICORN & PISCES
Joyful, supportive, adventurous

"Beyond right and wrong, there is a field—I'll meet you there."[27] Sufi poet Rumi found the field for Pisces and Capricorn in this sextile match. Beyond your cardinal earth soul and Pisces's mutable water one, there is a place where many miracles can emerge. You're both committed to service, meaning, and depth. The union between your Saturn-ruled soul and their Neptunian spirit is the space where the physical and metaphysical is one. You were widely magnetized to the Pisces because you knew they're trying to make a difference in the world, too, just with a different form. They too were helpless against your dependability, thoughtfulness, gravitas, and rare but beautiful moments of emotional disclosure. This is why this match has the context for both effortless desire and love. Since you both slowly reveal and get close—which is a good thing!—desire's life span is sure to be long. Honor the chemistry, but don't consume it all at once. Gently, deliberately, and thoughtfully let its power be.

For the container of love, you're both negotiators. So make your own constitution of connection in an effort to see what affection, compassion, trust, accountability, and forgiveness mean for you both. This is the Capricorn mountain that looks upon the sea of Pisces. From Pisces, you'll learn how to be more proactively compassionate, empathetic, and merciful. Their generous assumptions help you unlearn the knee-jerk judgment. You'll contain

---

27   ala l-ad-Di n Ru mi and Coleman Barks, *The Essential Rumi* (San Francisco: Harper, 2010) 35.

your Pisces with the right structure, critical awareness, boundaries, and values so they place their power in that field beyond right and wrong, where you're both safe.

AQUARIUS IN LOVE

Innovative | Accepting | Altruistic
Honor: Rebellion & Friendship
Integrate: Proactivity & Vulnerability

Whoever said the best romantic relationships start as friendships was probably an Aquarius. How easily would our romances unfold if we approached potential suitors like friends? With Aquarius agility, companionship, and loyalty? In love, Aquarius takes this timeless friendship turned love and textures the connection with innovation. Aquarius loves to disrupt constrictive relationship norms, expectations, and structures.

When nothing outdated is bogging down the relationship, Aquarius loves with wonderful acceptance of who their partner is—flaws, glories, dreams, fears, and all. In order for Aquarius to receive the acceptance they give, they'll want to honor their penchant for rebellion. That way, their partners know Aquarius is not one for authority, control, or status quo. More gently, Aquarius would wisely begin their romances with a friendly demeanor and activity, to build the base.

For wholeness, Aquarius can demonstrate more proactivity. They're magnetic and receptive, but sometimes direct, dynamic energy around discomfort is helpful. They'll also need to integrate vulnerability into their relationship repertoire through direct movement toward risk, uncertainty, and emotional exposure.

AQUARIUS & ARIES
Joyful, supportive, adventurous

Follow the leader! Which one? Both of these individualist signs are focused on the fullest, most embodied expression of the self and on ways to extend that outward in the world. So the questions that need answers early are "Who's leading who, and when? Both? And who's building the relationship context, and when? Both?" Don't let my sense of urgency distract you from the fact that there is still a harmonious, supportive sextile match between you, the fixed air rebel, and your cardinal fire individualist. You probably belly laughed loudly at Aries's candor and fearlessness, and were admiring of their passionate movement toward self-exploration. It was a two-way spark, because the Martian was probably both intrigued and a little intimidated (though they'll never admit it!) by your detached demeanor. This keeps the desire wattage running high because you're both strong individualists, and thus the intimacy won't involve collusion or intrusion. The contrast in your fire/air natures lets the spark of desire electrify you both into exploring new conversations and horizons together.

In this sextile space of rich conversation and dynamic action, you'll have an easy time practicing the kindness, comfort, and trust for love's foundation. Try to explore what these values mean and how they're expressed. Since you're both individualists, it's important to define the systems and languages you have for connection. Aries's bravery will inspire you to put the pedal to the metal every day, show more proactivity around discomfort, and soften into vulnerability. You often disassociate from other people, preferring your intellectual world, which prevents you from showing up to the party when you have to, but Aries will help draw you out. You'll help your Aries concentrate on the right intellectual and communication practices that sustain the initial spark of their dreams, so their dreams can come true. So long as you have the proactive conversations that help you pick your beats, lanes, and arenas early in the relationship, then you'll follow the right leader at the right time, and switch it up when you're called to. Along the way, this supportive sextile match will help you both find the right balance of freedom and commitment wherever it serves you.

AQUARIUS & TAURUS
Powerful, transformative, dynamic
Lao Tzu said, "The hard and stiff will be broken. The soft and supple will prevail."[28] Keep it soft and supple to prevail, you two! This fixed square match can work wonders as long as you both go out of your way to release inflexibility and dogma—which isn't always easy for these rigid signs. In Taurus, you found a solid partner who says what they mean and means what they say in a very beautiful Venusian fixed earth style. Their convictions inspire you to learn more about their specialties and respect them as masters of their craft. The bull's fascinated by your Uranian self-possession, how you embody the best of the fixed air principles with tranquil detachment. This clash in personalities is the erotic homeland of desire. It loves to explore the power play and search for the tender sweet spot between two fixed, hard forces. You'll sustain the

---

28 Laozi, Yi-Ping Ong, Charles Müller, and George Stade, *Tao Te Ching* (New York: Barnes & Noble Classics, 2005) 76.

chemistry and intimacy for as long as you recognize its value in helping this relationship succeed.

It's the practice of love that will definitely require more effort, since it asks for a relational nature that upholds fondness, compromise, and forgiveness. Luckily Taurus has Venus's help. Together you'll achieve the practice of love when Taurus inspires you to consider negotiation and harmony very carefully, whereas you'll help Taurus rise above cozying up with the devils they know and find a greater passion for inviting joy through uncertainty, risk, and exposure. This clash of fixed earth and air signs gives you both the context for desire and love. Together with Taurus, you can emerge with relational skills that make you competent in handing all the Uranian changes and Venus-ruled consistencies of life with elegance and intelligence.

AQUARIUS & GEMINI
Harmonious, sensual, affectionate

Hey, airheads! This trine match between fixed air Aquarius and mutable air Gemini has an ethereal energy that beams bright and beautiful between your minds. When your Mercury-ruled Gemini started thinking out loud, you knew you were in the presence of another whose heart speaks the same language you do. When they realized, "I never would've considered that before," your Gemini fell in love with your genius Uranian intelligence. It's not just a highly intellectual and stimulating match, but it's an amiable one—a harmonizing, commonality-based space for thoughtful, romantic love. This is the premier foundation for love to take flight, because in communication you two feel adored, valued, and understood.

You have the need for freedom and liberation down to a science, but the skill of partnership needs a bit more practicing than professing. As two detached and very verbal signs, you'll want to talk less and do more around physical and emotional intimacy, and texture it with closeness so you can show up for each other with the right behavior that the other needs to feel loved. Talk about what affection, trust, and forgiveness look like for you, then apply it. Relationships need to be tended to and never taken for granted. In these interactions, you'll give the Gemini a clarity of values—they can deepen their research and pursuit of knowledge when they know what values and convictions to cherish. Whereas Gemini will let you borrow their winged sandals so you can stay light on your feet. You can get yourself into trouble when you're weighed down by control or fear of risk. So the Gemini will inspire you to engage in life with more comfort around vulnerability. In the skies that rule you, you fly together toward loyalty, friendship, and love.

AQUARIUS & CANCER
Surreal, mysterious, magnetic
Earth to Aquarius, come in! Of all the zodiac's matches, this is the most extraterrestrial one. You might as well be aliens to each other. Your Cancer is the cardinal water sign and governed by the cozy, emotionally charged, sentimental moon. Cancer is obligated to understand and practice true belonging, safety, and home. You're Cancer's complete contrast, since the Uranian identity has to stay detached, roaming, and intellectually disruptive. Ever the altruist, you're still very curious about the waters in Cancer's emotion ocean, especially when they share

stories of love, kindness, and connection. You're a disciple of people, and Cancer is the priestess of family. Your rebellious mind inspires the more law-abiding Cancer to consider rule breaking and revolution as regards the meaning of home and family. When you're in shared dialogue and exploring emotional interests with each other, a mandatory conversation on the expectations and behaviors that build fondness, trust, and forgiveness is so helpful—especially around what you learned from your family's attachment styles, as this can help you better gauge each other's relational languages.

As soon as that rocket ship transports you to each other's moon and Uranus (winky!), then the sparks of desire start circulating in the universe between you. You'll agree on what needs to be negotiated, while your extraterrestrial dynamic keeps the wonder, longing, anticipating, and seduction thriving. If, in your galactic travels, you two define the values and practices of home and family in complementary ways—you're totally in the clear! Cancer will teach Aquarius to consider the interrelatedness of us all, especially chosen family and friends. These two signs connect the most in their social bonds, whereas you'll inspire the crab to move out of their shell and out of their comfort zones, for life-defining experiences of bravery and integrity. To infinity and beyond!

AQUARIUS & LEO
Completion, romantic, compromise
The prince(x) and the pauper? These two opposite signs are from drastically different social standings, but the magnetism is enough to make you two consider the transformation possible here. Your heart was knighted quickly

by the royal and romantic Leo; you loved how their fixed fire self-possession brings out the best of people, both personally and relationally, under the sun that rules them. The royal felt a thermonuclear pull toward your Uranian soul, as you demonstrate the best of fixed air high-minded activism, justice for all, and the glory of friendship. Polarity dynamics are opposite extremes together. So when it comes to finding the container of love, which is all Leo's domain, and desire, taught most effectively by Aquarius, you'll want to feel as equal as possible with each other, transparent when necessary, and willing to negotiate the terms and conditions of trust, affection, forgiveness, and accountability every step of the way to handle the depth of this connection.

Edit the contracts often to keep the transformational goal alive. Your chemistry is unlikely to lose its grip on the connection so long as you celebrate this opposites-attract dynamic. Avoid engaging in gridlock or holding on to pride instead of each other when conflict strikes. You'll help the Leo step into more grandeur by helping them expand and share the opportunities given to them by the privileges of their cosmic spotlight. Your Leo will empower you to see how capable you are to change the world with your disruption and strategies for access for all. With this polarity pair, the desire's hot and the love is loyal.

AQUARIUS & VIRGO
Surreal, mysterious, magnetic
World domination! You two intellectuals are on the passionate search for radical and innovative ways to make a big difference on the personal and collective levels. Given your combined mental powers, I suspect

global domination is likely if you embrace each other's differences and commit to learning from one another. In your mutable earth Virgo, you've found a partner who's deeply concerned with the divinity in the details and the Mercury-ruled practicality and reason that makes the world go round. Totally necessary, but not your beat. So with mutual respect for each other's different talents, Virgo can extend appreciation for your expansive, progressive vision of the future as a descendant of Uranus. Again, totally necessary for the world to change! Just not Virgo's function.

These different approaches to life and world domination will also serve as the context for seduction, curiosity, and the wild unknown to stay very much alive in this quincunx dynamic, which lengthens desire's life span magnificently. Analytical and verbal signs, your discussions on the philosophies and practices of love will help you two unpack what loyalty, mutuality, trust, and consistency look like in meaning and practice. Then you'll want to get to it! You'll motivate your astute Virgo to contribute their quicksilver ideas and messy creativity without fear of criticism, rejection, or failure, because they trust your intelligence so deeply. Your flexible Virgo will inspire you with communication practices that reconcile ideas without as much dissent, disagreement, and ideological contrast. This will help others listen to your revolutionary ideas with readiness, because they feel there's no contempt when you disagree with them. A meeting of the minds, revolutionaries, and skills, this match can rule the world!

AQUARIUS & LIBRA
Harmonious, sensual, affectionate

World peace! As two intellectual air signs, this trine connection between you is very ethereal, curious, and dynamic. Both lovers who esteem verbal communication in relationship virtually above all else, you fell for each other because of the word choices and the styles of speaking. It was that simple. In your Libra partner, you've found an altruistic Venus light worker who only wants to extend more peace, joy, glamour, and love in the world. As the zodiac's Uranian-ruled humanitarian, a person who's trying to make a positive impact on the world means more to you than any other value. In you, Libra has found another brilliant social strategist who's trying to actualize access to justice and equality for all, which leaves their notoriously indecisive attention completely undivided on you. That's why the practice of love and respect is given here pretty effortlessly. Now, as emotionally aloof air signs, prioritize quality time, physical touch, reliability, and consistency for each other so you're practicing love and professing it with equal measure.

When it comes to seduction and desire, work on being embodied and pacing yourselves. You'll want to deliberately reveal your existential worlds slowly and with the intention to protect the distance desire needs. Libra will help you consider the validity of other people's disagreements, as opposed to building an ideological echo chamber around only those who agree with you. You'll help the relational Libra formulate more autonomy and comfort with conflict management so they can bring about justice with assertiveness. Between Libra's diplomacy and your strategy, this is a trine match that could bring about world peace for times that desperately need it.

AQUARIUS & SCORPIO
Powerful, transformative, dynamic

Pain and pleasure! If there's a reason they're so tethered while exploring eroticism, you two fixed signs may know why. Which is exactly why you're spellbound by each other. I think strong personalities really do appreciate other strong personalities in relationships. In your Pluto-ruled partner, you found that Scorpio intensity, emotional power, and a willingness to search for the most authentic experiences of life. On the other side of this strong personality spectrum, the Scorpio loved your Uranian self-composure. The Scorpio sensed you as not only an innovative thinker whose values could turn the world in a different direction altogether, but one who would hardly follow the mob mentality or abandon themselves to fit in. So long as you're both passionate about the exploration of each other, the desire index will be at peak ecstasy, with just the right amount of pain. You'll love the longing, anticipation, and battle for dominance in this match that subverts politeness and pleasing.

With desire locked down, thanks to your water bearer, you'll want to honor your gifts by exploring the practice of love together. Verbally negotiate what closeness and separation mean to you both. Consider which partner has a greater fear of abandonment and which one has a greater fear of freedom loss. If you agree, fantastic. If not, there's likely to be little compromising between this fixed square of alphas. So you'll want to really ensure that you're on the same page about values and behaviors that support affection, trust, consistency, accountability, and forgiveness from the beginning, especially if you want to keep this dynamic safe and secure over self-sabotaging.

Scorpio will be your emotionality and flexibility coach, while they help you develop the right words for the lexicon of sensitivities that keep your heart beating. You'll get your Scorpio out of the dark with the light of critical awareness, so they're not just experiencing pain, but pleasure, too. This match stands to be undefeated while they navigate the pain and pleasures of life.

AQUARIUS & SAGITTARIUS
Joyful, supportive, adventurous
A date with destiny. This sextile match between your fixed air rebellion and Sagittarius's mutable fire freedom is sure to have a fated feel to it. In your Jupiter-ruled Sagittarius partner, you're in the arms of another who loves to wrap their arms around thoughtful conversations. Your Uranian dialogue proved rich with the right insight and academic support to catch the Sagittarius's undivided attention. That's where the spark of desire was lit. They're always willing to hear you. And since you two never run out of important things to say to each other, I suspect this intrigue and mystery will wrap you both in desire for as long as you keep each other in a state of mindfulness and wonder.

For the practice of love to sustain itself between a freedom-loving Sagittarius and a rebellious Aquarius, you'll want to define the behaviors surrounding love. Explore each other's relationship histories and philosophies. Learn about relational proficiency together, because you're both so curious, you'd love to educate yourselves on meaningful connection. Hopefully you'll have the answers on what integrity, reliability, trust, affection, forgiveness, and accountability look like in practice. You're both so future focused that it's important to stay present in the here and now for these answers. While you're there in the present moment, you'll totally centralize your Sagittarius's perceptions with the right focus and concentration, so their expansive soul doesn't waste precious energy in unbecoming or irrelevant places. Sagittarius will help you develop more broad interests, rather than feeling contempt for the unknown. Between your genius and Sagittarius's action, you'll learn why destiny brought you together in this love.

AQUARIUS & CAPRICORN
Loyal, contrasting, instructive

Do you like to move in counterclockwise directions? I hope so! This reverse-order match has a strong pull because, although inconjunct matches are very contrasting, this one's at least on the same clock. Even in the heat of ideological debates and disagreement, you deeply respect Capricorn as a beacon of timeless wisdom, a statue of virtue, ethics, service, and righteousness. When their strict Saturn soul registered you as the Uranian rebel you are, you demonstrated how your fixed air convictions are healthily unattached to anything that limits progress. That's why the desire between you, and largely initiated by you, could move the mountains Capricorn has to climb. It's an undemocratic clash of time titans. You act for the future, and Capricorn preserves what's eternally true. So the dynamic holds the right space for longing, anticipation, seduction, and mystery.

It's the architecture of love in practice that may need some extra consideration, but Capricorn is happy to do it. Given how principled you both are, you'll want to agree on what you have to agree on. Are your expressions of trust, accountability, affection, respect, and forgiveness closely aligned in time, or too far removed from each other? If aligned, wonderful. If not, teach your Capricorn how to break the rules. You can always create new relationship time travel if you want to sustain the romance between you. You'll help your Capricorn break control and rise above the rut of routine and monotony with innovation when needed. Your seagoat will help you apply the right urgency and direction when you need to get out of your own way and take responsibility for your own life. Theirs is a problem-solving tool that never goes out of style, just like your innovation. To infinity and beyond!

AQUARIUS & AQUARIUS
Safe, consistent, secure

A match made in the Milky Way galaxy! When you two intergalactic travelers align in this romantic conjunction match on earth, it's a vision. Both ruled by disruptive and progressive Uranus, you'll join in love with extraterrestrial ideas on connection. Since you're fixed air signs, it makes intellectual sense for you two specific specialists to join with another who aligns with you body, mind, and spirit. That's why you're both attracted to each other—because you recognize the nuance and focus in each other that helps your energy keep its momentum. Feeling the natural push-pull paradox between engagement and separation, since you're ruled by Uranus, you'll have a strong basis for desire here, as you don't like to give too much away too soon. It's an imaginative, erotic space between you.

You can balance this outer-space energy with the right groundedness. As two loquacious aliens, a conversation on emotional attachment styles—trust, forgiveness, accountability, and affection—will help you hold the universe of love between you. Your explorations on these topics and the way you put them into practice will serve as the strength of this loyal match for eons and eons. Given the fixed conjunction, there's a possibility you'll want to remove the vulnerability, discomfort, and risk in the match. So the lesson here is making sure you two aliens help each other fortify your resilience and adaptability tools. This match made in a galaxy far, far away can help you both extend your extraterrestrial gifts out to the earth with brilliance, flexibility, and power.

AQUARIUS & PISCES
Loyal, contrasting, instructive
The grand finale! The final two signs in the zodiac, this match shows us the peak of personal and relational success. When your fixed air mind stood in the heart space of your mutable water Pisces, you knew it was an assignment of miraculous order. Neptune-ruled Pisces moves about the world with a certain otherworldly quality that captivates your attention because of its rarity and soulfulness. From their creativity to their gentleness, they leave you in awe. The Pisces was wrapped up in you when you spoke about your emotions more carefully and generously. They knew they could invite you into their waters when you demonstrated emotional intelligence. Inconjunct matches are strong in the desire index because your energies are contrasting, and given your natural need for detachment, you'll enforce mutual autonomy. So the mystery, longing,

seduction, and anticipation remain for as long as you enforce the distance.

But remember you're still neighbors! This match is secured carefully through the proper understanding and practice of love, affection, compassion, integrity, and forgiveness, which hopefully your Pisces can verbalize to you so that you're given the direction you need to keep their safety in mind. Once it's discussed and committed to in practice, the grand finale begins, so draw out your nonverbal Pisces and get them to explain their unique emotional styles. Pisces will teach you to spiritualize your mind and relationships. You're more literal and rational than you give yourself credit for, but you're also capable of metaphysical understanding, so let's balance both. You'll have the opposite effect on Pisces and prove a beacon of critical awareness and intellectual groundedness to guide the merperson as they navigate worldly structures. This is the grand finale: the peak of worldly intelligence in you and spiritual surrender in Pisces.

PISCES IN LOVE

Soulful | Healing | Creative
Honor: Devotion & Service
Integrate: Language & Detail

Pisces knows the only reason we're here, as spiritual beings having a human experience, is the giving and receiving of love. So a Pisces in love demonstrates the highest final expression of this energy.

In love, a Pisces partner is soulful, harnessing the power of the ocean and its depths toward the expression of romantic love. With these waters, Pisces is a healing space for their beloved, while they ameliorate the suffering of their lover. On land, they'll find creative, artistic expressions to demonstrate how deeply they love.

Since every language of love is different across the zodiac, Pisces will want to honor their essential values, like their devotional nature. It's cool to be unfeeling, but Pisces's devotion is highly emotionally invested. They'll also want to honor service as their natural reflex in love. Pisces loves to help, be of service, and take care of their love.

Integration is always vital in relationships. So in order for Pisces to integrate the right qualities to fortify their love, they'll want to study language. They're naturally nonverbal, but words in negotiation are a prerequisite for romance. Additionally, Pisces will want to focus on the details of life more, so their lovers feel like they're being paid attention to.

PISCES & ARIES
Loyal, contrasting, instructive

Spring is here! As the first and last signs, this inconjunct dynamic embodies truly the only two existential themes in all the great spiritual systems: the commencement of Aries and the conclusion of Pisces. So you're tethered to each other as the zodiac begins and ends. When your pioneering ram barged into your heart, they set several rooms on fire. Their cardinal fire heart woke you up to new ideas, conversations, and situations you never considered, since you're often so fascinated with how things end. Slowly but surely in this dynamic, the Martian Aries was enchanted by your Neptunian contemplation, sensitivity, and soulfulness. Given the existential distances between your conclusions and Aries's commencements, the mystical unknown that holds the entire zodiac also holds the powers of desire in your dynamic. It charges the space of intrigue and will force you to keep striving for meaningful practices on intimacy and personal transformation. Maintain the acceptance and celebration of each other's radical differences.

With magnetism as the natural dynamic between you both, you'll want to further explore the practices for love. Let your Aries's enthusiastic curiosity help you explore each other's relationship histories and attachment styles to complete the whole picture of each other. For getting your needs met, you'll want to get right to the point and be very specific. The ram can only hear straight talk. This integrity-driven foundation of open communication works as the powerful container to hold all the chemistry and power between your Neptune mystical waters and Aries's Mars fire. Then you'll want to partner on romance and personal success from the twofold question "What needs to start and what needs to surrender?" Let your Aries begin things, and you'll show them what needs to be released. From there you'll be working with the two greatest forces in the universe. Since you're the only bookends in the zodiac, this partnership can be a resonant field of possibility for you, and for us all.

PISCES & TAURUS
Joyful, supportive, adventurous

Welcome to the blue lagoon! This mystical match between your Pisces mutable water and your Taurus's fixed earth consistency gives rise to a romance that's a divine sanctuary. Your compassionate heart fell hard and fast for the Venus-ruled Taurus, whose consistency, loyalty, and strength beckoned like an island of Eden in the middle of the vast ocean. Your bull fell for your soulful nature and compassionate service as a love language. In water and earth matches, you create a gorgeous garden that grows out of the tender care you give to one another.

Since comfort is a shared value, you'll want to grip the idea that vulnerability and uncertainty is necessary for a meaningful life and for desire to spark. So stay healing toward each other, but not enabling. Stay close, but don't intrude. On love, you'll have shared if not identical understandings of affection, trust, accountability, and forgiveness, which holds the power between you beautifully. You'll help your Taurus embrace the beauty in not just what they can physically see and touch, but all the energies they cannot. You'll inspire the Taurus to love the unknown. Your bull will help you to commit and follow through on your words and will inspire you to concentrate on perspectives that matter. Your vision needs to be delivered, not just professed or imagined. You'll never stop showing up for each other, which will mean miracles in the blue lagoon of your love.

PISCES & GEMINI
Powerful, transformative, dynamic

The heart is hard to translate. A passionate square dynamic between your nonverbal, ocean-born merperson of Neptune and the winged wordy ones of the skies, this love tries to communicate love across languages. So in this dynamic, you're trying to wrap your heart and their head around love. Your thoughtful side was completely charmed by your Mercury-ruled Gemini's velvet tongue, extroversion, and intelligence. The premier wordsmith, Gemini is divinely curious to know all that's unspoken so they can write it down. Your Pisces heart lives there, where words can't swim but love must be experienced. In a square dynamic, the desire is magnetic, since you're similar but fundamentally contrasting to each other. You'll be called to retreat to the waters and the Gemini to the skies if the contrast is too strong, but it often keeps you returning to each other devotionally and humbly until the hard lessons on love are learned.

Stability is miraculously helpful for love to bond you both. So a careful negotiation of clear contexts for reliability, forgiveness, and commitment between you is the space that allows the Gemini to fly freely and you to swim creatively. Ask each other how you bid for connections, and then try your best to notice and accept the bid when it happens. Gemini's articulation skills will inspire you to rise to find the right language and word choices to feel safe. You'll teach Gemini the biggest lessons of all: that not every emotion needs to be said in order to earn validation. So watch for the place where the blue of the skies meets the blue of the oceans, and that's where your love is most colorful.

PISCES & CANCER
Harmonious, sensual, affectionate
Ahoy, mateys! You two seaside lovers form a marine match of water trines, and this dynamic is a treasure chest of harmony, passion, and loyalty. When you found Cancer's protected pearls, you found the divine belonging only Cancer can reveal to their beloved. In their heart space, you are nurtured, safe, protected, and understood. Ruled by the moon, Cancer gave you the home of the heart when they discovered you're searching for the same mystical home of safety and healing. So the ocean's vast treasures surround this pair with emotional and physical affection, devotion, kindness, and respect. So long as you can pace yourself in the beginning of this love-at-first-sight kind of match, it'll help keep the initial spark strong for as long you can handle it.

Try to keep this trine's mystique and seduction alive by being up front about your need for freedom, without anxiety or apologies to each other. Not everything needs to be revealed immediately. You can always do new things together, which will help keep you unfamiliar yet comfortable with one another. Since you're both water signs, the context of love, affection, trust, accountability, and forgiveness are similarly practiced. Your faith and convictions will inspire your Cancer to tap into their heart's intelligence through a spiritual practice, which will give the moon child more love and faith rather than fear and worry, whereas the Cancer's strong leadership skills will help you get started on your goals, projects, and dreams—the first step toward manifesting them outside your Neptunian la-la land. Anchors away!

PISCES & LEO
Surreal, mysterious, magnetic

This match sings *The Little Mermaid*. A beautiful sea-born soul falls in love with a royal? Absolutely. You wanted to leave Neptune to walk on land, because sun-ruled Leo is the monarch of valuable personal expressions like worthiness, security, and fearlessness. These are qualities you're always trying to reconcile within the two fish inside you, and Leo can help you here. Their fixed fire heart came ablaze while it was standing in the resonance of your compassion, soulfulness, and kindness. Leos could possibly outswim you in the pursuit of romance, but when they realized you too crave love, they were quick to get off the throne to understand you. Given the existential contrast between you, I'm sure you won't have too much trouble holding on to the flame of desire. With quincunx dynamics, timing and speed are crucial—especially in this match. So you'll want to be very thoughtful, and in charge, around expressions and behaviors that texture your intimacy, seduction, longing, and anticipation.

If you both remain all in to the relationship, you'll affectionately, consistently, and carefully provide the structure love needs, which is your Leo's castle. Explore your ideas and practices on accountability and forgiveness as early as possible, because hurt and imperfection are inevitable with relationships, so you'll need a strategy in place to avoid resentment. You'll help the Leo give others more generous assumptions and affirmations to those not born as confident as the sovereign. This inspires the royal to extend more forgiveness and mercy to all—one of the most noble pursuits in a Leo's life. The monarch will then empower you to focus your generous sensitivities in service to your betterment first. You can't heal others unless you're working on your own healing. With this integrity, you'll be a powerful resource to help on your mission to heal the world together.

PISCES & VIRGO

Completion, romantic, compromise

A match made in the heavens. Truly! This polarity dynamic is magnificent, as it represents the idea of "as above, so below." Below the spiritual plane, you were initially intimidated but admiring of your Virgo's Mercurial mental and romantic strategies. They go out of their way to be of service and thoughtfully bid for connection without mystery or subtlety, so you found their directness rather inspiring. No dummy, Virgo knew you were a descendant of Neptune. So your wonderful lineage offers you the possibility of unconditional love, given generously and divinely. Virgo wanted to be a part of you, the zodiac's grand finale. As with all polarity dynamics, you're both wildly drawn to each other, because your mutable water power is longing for their mutable earth container. So it is with this dynamic's desire. It'll be hard, but try to maintain relative autonomy, existential separation, uncertainty, and novelty—which is all on you, given your natural mystique. If you move too fast, it could complicate the nature of this heavenly union.

So consider temperance as a protective agent. In between the erotic moments and intimacy, have conversations about your emotional road maps and practices on love. Specifically, what does accountability, forgiveness, compassion, and reliability look like to each of you? Let your Virgo do some research in relational proficiency and apply what they learn to your relationship while you both glean the influences from your childhoods that still affect your love styles today. You're opposite signs, so you could have drastically different approaches, and finding the sweet spot between you is crucial here. You'll inspire your brainiac Virgo to measure life beyond the certainty of facts, figures, and data, finding the heavens beyond and in between. Your Virgo will help you carefully communicate and demonstrate detailed action with small, practical steps that help you follow through, execute, and build the life of your dreams, inspired by the heaven on the earth between you.

PISCES & LIBRA
Surreal, mysterious, magnetic

Dream on! This quincunx match is where an idealist and dreamer are reconciled in the Technicolor fantasy of romance. In the Venus-ruled grace and charm of Libra, you've found your muse, a wellspring of inspiration who motivates your best creativity and empathy to personal masterpiece levels, because Libra loves to inspire. Standing before your artist's gaze, Libra's cardinal air heart was captivated by the way you bring dreams to life, not just in the creative arts, but in the world around you, which means a great deal to the socially conscious and justice-oriented sign. In the practice of love, trust Libra's lead.

They'll demonstrate what it means to show up to the party with the right mentality to find communication strategies that facilitate forgiveness, affection, accountability, and reliability.

Desire's your domain! Your mutable water can manage the paradox between closeness and separation, mystique and disclosure, since you're already two fish swimming in opposite directions. You'll teach the ethereal Libra in creative ways that not every experience needs an explanation, reason, or word to be deemed valid. Your transcendental attitude will help your Libra look beyond the logic of right versus wrong, in favor of the spiritual experience. Less theory, more application. Of course your prudent Libra will help your heart wrap its arms around the right words for your life. You're obligated to be appropriately nonverbal, but Libra will help you improve your emotional vocabulary. With this match between Libra's ideals and your dreams, you'd be wise to combine your creative and intellectual skills to do something wonderful for the world.

PISCES & SCORPIO
Harmonious, sensual, affectionate
If intimacy is an ebb and flow, this trine match has the perfect rhythm for it. Your Pluto-ruled Scorpio is the fixed water sign—the flow—who searches passionately for the right spaces of meaningful intimacy with another. In you—the ebb—Scorpio's found a mutable water sign who grows twice as strong when you receive first. Scorpio's the yang flow and you're the yin ebb. So this trine match can also easily explore desire and love in similar styles, which is a wonderful outcome for intimacy.

I suspect your desire domains are in a similar dimension, because you know how to magnetize, create longing, indulge imaginations, and let fantasy run wild in the water. Though for desire's domain to stay safe, you'll want to enforce barriers, because the waters of intimacy can easily collude. On sustaining the context of love, you'll want to verbalize the right words, which is a typical challenge for water signs but totally necessary for the conversation on trust, affection, loyalty, respect, accountability, and forgiveness. As a focus point, make sure you explore your family of origin's practices on love and commit to implementing what you both need to feel safe and loved. You can uplift the best of your intimacy skills and help each other see the existential oceans within you. You'll inspire your Scorpio to release more into their vulnerability, especially when it's not convenient. You'll expand their emotional ability to handle risk and uncertainty. Scorpio will then lead you to finish what you start, with the right focus and the authentic boundaries to hold the power of this the ebb and flow intimacy magic between you.

PISCES & SAGITTARIUS:

Powerful, transformative, dynamic

A dream is a wish your heart makes! You two mutable signs are the patron saints of fantasy. So when you romance, you take each other out of worldly purviews into the metaphysical plane of wishes and fantasies, with the help of your ruling planet, Neptune, and theirs, Jupiter. This is a square between your mutable water and Sagittarius's mutable fire. A notoriously clashing but chemistry-filled energy, your tie to romance is the mutable energy of dreams and fantasy. You adore Sagittarius's mastery of many ideas and their adaptability within the material and spiritual worlds. Sagittarius loves a thinker and feeler who's light on their fish tails. Their expansive mental visions and your emotional fluency give you a strong context for desire.

Square dynamics are repelled and drawn toward each other. It's frustrating, but it makes for wonderful experiences in intimacy, strengthened by the Sagittarius's longing for the unknown, and you'll use this space to connect more deeply. To protect this fantasy and dream-come-true energy between you, the right conversation—led by you, because you're more specific than the centaur—on the philosophies and choices that sustain affection, accountability, trust, and integrity for love will prove mandatory. You'll teach your teacher Sagittarius more fluency in the invisible ethers, and help them develop nonverbal communication languages, like body language and other symbolic energies. Your straight-shooting Sagittarius will help you find the right words and optimism to get through life. This match has the potential to make your life a dream. More wishes come true than you ever thought possible.

PISCES & CAPRICORN
Joyful, supportive, adventurous
Take a deep breath and relax into each other. In this sextile match, you're both committed to service, meaning, and depth, which should inspire a certain level of comfort, because your values are so similar. The union between your Neptune spirit and their Saturn-ruled soul essentially is the space where the physical and metaphysical are one. That's why you were drawn to the Capricorn's cardinal earth dependability, thoughtfulness, gravitas,

and rare but beautiful moments of emotional disclosure. When they opened up to you, it was like every church bell rang. Capricorn was magnetized to your mutable water. You have a light in your eyes that informs the world of the difference you're trying to make and the healing you're trying to contribute. That's why this match has both the context for strong desire and secure love.

Since you both slowly reveal and get close, desire's lung capacity is sure to stay deep. You'll want to honor the chemistry, but don't let it explode all at once. Gently, deliberately, and thoughtfully let its power be. For the container of love, you're both wonderful negotiators. So make your own connection curriculum in an effort to see how your emotional backstories, attachments, and psychologies define affection, compassion, trust, accountability, and forgiveness. That's where the sea of Pisces breaks on the mountain of Capricorn. You'll teach the stodgy seagoat more compassion, empathy, and mercy. They'll contain you with the right structure, critical awareness, boundaries, and values, so you place your power in service of your relationship health.

PISCES & AQUARIUS
Loyal, contrasting, instructive
Closing time! With the final signs in the zodiac, this grand finale match shows us the peak of personal and spiritual success. You know you pick up where Aquarius left off, so you're fascinated by their Uranian brilliance, education, humanitarian values, and social skills. When the water bearer stood near your mutable waters, their fixed air mind knew it was an assignment of miraculous order. From your tenderness to your creativity, you leave them

in awe. Inconjunct matches tend to be strong in the desire ratings because your energies are so diametric, and your caution around revealing yourself makes the distance between you attractive and exciting. This fortifies the mystery, longing, seduction, and anticipation for as long as you two are smart enough to enforce the distance between two neighboring signs that don't have too much distance to start with.

This match is secured carefully through the proper understanding and practice of love, if you're open to being taught by your Aquarius about their ways of implementing affection, compassion, integrity, and forgiveness. Once your values on love are discussed and committed to in practice, the grand finale of the zodiac starts to play. You'll use your divinity to help the more skeptical, rationally leaning Aquarius to spiritualize their consciousness and relationships. They're a bit more literal and fixed than they let on, but they're capable of metaphysical understanding. Whereas Aquarius will have the opposite effect on your spiritual soul and prove a beacon of helpful critical awareness and intellectual skills for you on your marathon swim through worldly structures. That's why it's the grand finale. Through the zodiac's peak of worldly intelligence, evidenced in Aquarius, and spiritual surrender, embodied in Pisces, our greatest lessons are learned.

PISCES & PISCES
Safe, consistent, secure
Soul to soul mate. When you two Neptune-born fishes join together in love, it's profoundly soulful, spiritual, creative, empathetic, and a conjunction dynamic completely out of this world. In each other, you found the

person who speaks the same language of the sea in their heart. You two mutable water signs want to swim in love together because this match is a homecoming to the ocean floor. You'll reinforce and salute the best of each other's natural and shared qualities—like compassion, generosity, empathy, and spiritual seeking. The values of love given and received should be almost identical. Of course, you'll want to explore each other's emotion ocean history and ask the right questions on what security, love, affection, accountability, and trust mean to you both. Then you'll want to let the water meet earth and give it some structure to contain the dynamic in integrity.

To keep the desire deep, you'll have to be comfortable with each other's natural push-pull dynamic. Don't take distance, space, or silence personally, since those unknown moments work like a high tide, pulling you closer to each other right when the moon is full. In this conjunction match, you'll want to collaborate on ways to increase each other's resilience, discipline, and focus, so that you can keep one fish of each of you on earth long enough. Discuss how you can strengthen each other's boundaries, concentration, follow-through, and verbal communication so you can be the best of both fishes. Where the magical and practical align, that's the peak of this transcendent match.

INTERVIEWS

As a white, cisgendered, able-bodied gay man, I do not speak for the entire queer continuum. Within a community that tries to incorporate inclusivity, visibility, and representation for all, I felt it was crucial to have a range of intersectional voices share how astrology helps them with self-identification, acceptance, and relational success.

Christina X. Mui
Pisces Rising | Sagittarius Sun | Aries Moon
Brooklyn, New York

1. How do you self-identify?

I identify as a spirit living in a queer cisgendered female Asian American body.

2. How did astrology find you?

My childhood was marked with symbols of the Chinese zodiac, and I've always felt lucky to be born in the Year of the Dragon. My mother kept a jewelry drawer that housed each family member's animal, made of jades, silvers, and golds. It felt really auspicious to me. Western astrology found me during my studies in college at the School of the Art Institute of Chicago. Freshman year brought *The Secret Language of Birthdays* into my life, and I became fascinated with how time of birth denotes personal characteristics. By the time I graduated college, western astrology had become a part of my everyday life.

3. How and why do you use astrology?

In addition to using the cosmic calendar and its transits as times to honor various themes in relation to my birth chart, I love using astrology as a tool to identify patterns on both an individual and a collective scale. Some patterns are harder to decode than others, but the ones I find are most prevalent relate to the idea of "sister signs." Sister signs symbolize the merging of transformative energies between two polarities in the zodiac. As astrology scholar Astrolo-Cherry writes, "The twelve zodiac signs represent six pair polarities, which esoterically indicate our soul journey...

your sister sign is the duality of you, often subconsciously repressed."[29] I came to understand more deeply my Pisces mother and Virgo father's forty-year marriage, and why I've had so many soul bonds between myself, a Sagittarius, and my opposite-sign Geminis. Synergizing with one's polarity can teach powerful lessons, for better or for worse. I see it time and again throughout media, history, and everyday life.

4. Has astrology helped you understand yourself? If so, how? If not, why?

Astrology has indeed provided insights into self—particularly my passionate nature and the way I hold energy. As a child, at about seven or eight years old, my older brother and I would have playdates with our upstairs neighbor. One day, they built a fort out of bedsheets and clothes hangers. I was so excited to crawl in and experience the magic with them—until my brother enforced a (highly bullshit) "boys only" rule. I was cast out alone. Instead of crying in despair, I was overcome with a rage fueled by feelings of injustice and confusion. I felt inside me a heat powerful enough to burn their fort and the entire house down. I found a pair of scissors that my tiny self planned to murder them both with. I don't remember much else from that night, but I know it ended with both boys in tears, and my neighbor's mother having "a talk" with my mother.

So, I carry some natal don't-fuck-with-me energy that I attribute to the abundance of Aries energy lighting up

---

29 AstroloCherry, "Sister Signs," *AstroloCherry*, September 16, 2012, astrolocherry.com/post/31617300346/sister-signs.

my first house of self-identity. In fact, there I have a natal Aries, Mars and Aries moon conjunction. I've learned that I need to sit still with my emotions and feel them through in order to unlock the high-minded answers. This is especially true in difficult situations like a breakup or a loss of a job. While patience is not an attribute most associated with Aries, I draw from its polarity, Libra, the lessons of grace, balance, and diplomacy.

5. Has astrology helped you strengthen your relationships? If so, how? If not, why?

I've been with my partner for over three years, and the connection—a Jupiter/sun conjunction in Taurus—is undeniable. I have learned that the more I surrender into the relationship—embracing the love and intimacy as much as the quarrels and disagreements—the more I find my own voice. Mutual concentration on positivity and opportunities for growth. We always trust that things will work themselves out, no matter how bleak a situation seems.

6. How and when do you feel loneliness? In times of loneliness, how do you find resilience?

Feelings of loneliness have nothing to do with relationship status or where you live (whether NYC or Arkansas)—you can be a high-profile celebrity and still feel entirely alone. To me, loneliness stems from the belief that we are all separate entities and not inextricably connected to one another by an invisible web—as wide as the world—the *true* World Wide Web. Eckhart Tolle says that enlightenment "is simply your natural state of felt oneness with Being . . . essentially you and yet is much greater than you."[30] I find resilience from practicing meditation, which combines present-moment awareness with faith that I am beyond my thoughts and connected to a source. Basic things like exercise, talking to close friends, or therapy help, too.

7. How and when do you feel belonging? In times of belonging, what does it feel like?

My partner and I just moved in together. She and I are the only openly queer women in our respective families, so it means a lot to be able to create and define a space together as a team. We're both interested in spaces that empower women (of color)—conferences, parties, screenings, etc. At times, these safe spaces can feel like church, where there is a spirit of oneness with others. As a kid, I often felt a sense of not belonging based on my Asianness, gender, sexual orientation, or even height (I'm five feet tall). But I'm in the throes of my Saturn return, where the time to shed past identification and trauma makes room for reinvention and higher ground.

8. Where do you see astrology in queer culture?

Astrology by nature is a queer subject, and this has been made so by modern culture, where rational and scientific thought prevail. That sounds weird when you think about ancient civilizations in Babylon, Egypt, and other places using planetary alignments and astrology as a way of life. I use the term *queer* in both its primary and secondary definition, which is both "unconventional," and "homo-

---

30 Eckhart Tolle, *The Power of Now: A Guide to Spiritual Enlightenment* (Novato, CA: New World Library, 1999).

sexual." The LGBTQIA community celebrates the feminine, embraces otherness and an openness to spiritual ways of thinking. To me, queer people (whether gay or unconventional) are in a perfect position to make astrology in vogue again. This is what we're seeing in places like NYC's Mood Ring—a queer-friendly bar with a rotating menu of astrological-inspired cocktails. It has been penetrating both popular culture and our everyday vernacular.

9. Has astrology helped, complicated, or empowered you to navigate capitalism, patriarchy, heteronormativity, oppressive structures, and/or white supremacy?

With Jupiter transiting Libra and then Scorpio from September 2016 to 2018, we saw calls for justice in democracy, human rights, and gender equality. At the same time, we shed light on the unspoken truth about sexual harassment and toxic masculinity across nearly every industry. While astrology has helped contextualize some things, the question for me is "How can I be the most high-minded embodiment of change?" This I think relates equally to radical self-transformation and practicing spirituality, as much as it does to voting, community service, and kindness—things that are antithetical to patriarchy and white supremacy.

10. How can astrologers provide helpful resources to queer consumers?

Simply providing a safe space for exploration and curiosity. Astrology can be a powerful tool for self-knowledge and healing, so inviting queer voices into the conversation and making diversity and inclusion the bottom line is important.

11. Do you connect with other metaphysical and/or spiritual resources?

I've been devouring Eckhart Tolle's teachings. The way he speaks about present-moment awareness is so simple yet powerful, and it is the only point of access to the realm beyond the mind. He says, "Enlightenment is not only the end of suffering and of continuous conflict within and without, but also the end of the dreadful enslavement to incessant thinking."[31]

I used to feel paralyzing fear and indecision about what happened in the past and what might happen in the future, but as soon as I come back into feeling my inner body, it's like I'm free. Why is this important? Most people think, "I am my mind and my thoughts," but as a society, our best thinking got us to two minutes to midnight as of 2018. There has to be another way.

---

31   Tolle, *The Power of Now.*

Laurence J. Jones
Virgo Rising | Gemini Sun | Sagittarius Moon
Oakland, California

Hi, I'm Laurence Jones.

I was born on a Saturday in early June, just after high noon. My mother's ob-gyn miscalculated—I was supposed to be born in early April. My maternal grandmother, having a Gemini ex-husband and a Gemini daughter (my mom) openly hoped I'd be born a Taurus, or a Cancer like herself. I was born into astrology. I really had no choice in the matter.

Naptime stories from my grandma Anne included *Linda Goodman's Sun Signs* alongside *Goodnight Moon*. In her peculiar way, I feel that she wanted to hand down an alternate practice of understanding. She never seemed to get this from the spiritual practices of her youth. She knew such a practice would have a profound effect on her grandchild with the Sagittarius moon.

I look at astrology first as a tool in grounding my ancestral practices. There's a strong thread of mutable planetary energy from my direct ancestors. I see myself as a culmination of that energy. In the understanding of queerness to disrupt and question narratives, I'm able to understand via astrology that my queerness is a pause in generational trauma, because it's disrupting what's come before.

I'm *lucky* to get to question what it really means to be a Black cis male person that forms their most intimate bonds with other cis male individuals. I'm *also lucky* that I was given a tool for understanding my innate character, plus a study guide for creating space for empathy and compassion for individuals I encounter. I get to see people more clearly where they are.

I can understand someone might show me their rising sign first. I understand how our societal past and present affect how that might show up in harmony or conflict with other factors of their being. Astrology informs my communal present, whether that's someone I'm undressing literally and figuratively in front of, or someone I'm just friends with.

At the same time, looking to past astrological cycles for lessons, while grounding ourselves in ritualized practice in the present, opens the door for us to create futures that will celebrate and cherish the diversity of our lives. "This too shall pass" is an oft-overused phrase, yet astrology reminds me that energy and environment does often prompt short- and long-term life rhythms.

After all, this whole solar system we live in is bound by gravitational pulls from our neighboring celestial bodies. What we have in modern mainstream astrology doesn't include every culture's wisdom. It often sets things into rote, easy-to-digest binaries. Realistically, all of those that came before us looked up to the heavens in moments of joy and pain. They noticed repeating patterns in the tapestry above. They all weren't heterosexuals looking for marriage and money.

Luckily, our digital universe has started to draw us closer together and out of isolation, to share and compare notes under these skies. With my slightly Jovian character, I say once again: I'm lucky to get to share in this moment.

mizChartreuse
Leo Rising | Gemini Sun | Capricorn Moon
Chicago, New York

I'm mizChartreuse and I'm a first generation, Zambian American, cisgendered femme woman and mother, who has partnered with people of myriad ages, ethnicities, and identities. "Bisexual" works, since I've loved both men and women, and I love the inclusive umbrella of "queer," since my overall perception of relating is 180 degrees away from the world's thinking when it comes to relationships.

I discovered astrology when I was eight and my adoptive grandparents from our Baptist church refused to gift me a Talkback "My Dear Diary" console for Christmas because it featured horoscopes. I was just a young girl who was constantly writing and who loved the idea of an electronic device on which to journal, but since astrology was so taboo, naturally I dived in to learn more about these forbidden horoscopes. Astrology affirmed the truth of who I am from jump! Learning I was a Gemini and that writing and communication were fitting for me helped me feel seen.

Although I've been a stargazer for decades, the cosmos continues to reveal itself. In 2016, Colin, who is my astro-twin, asked me, "How do you experience your twelfth house Cancer Venus?" I sincerely could not answer. Yet I'd been married for four years and had myriad loving relationships with a host of friends, none of whom I necessarily ranked above another, or even above my husband or nuclear family members.

Colin's question sparked my journey of concertedly examining my Venusian love function, complete with leaving my husband at my Saturn return and dating a Capricorn woman (how fitting, since Saturn rules Capricorn), and completing that relationship at the end of that transit.

It took me blowing up my love life to see how I was responsible for every relationship drama I'd experienced. Seeing how parts of my natal chart reflected my history of codependency and my inability to be alone for longer than a few months in between years-long relationships (hello, Libra south node!) was also reassuring.

In the aftermath, I learned how to love being alone with myself, reliant solely on God and not looking to a partner for salvation through an illusion of security or even just hot sex. My solo journey unearthed a productive way of sharing the twelfth house gold of unconditional love and oneness, and astrology showed me how to value myself and show up in partnership the way my chart had been screaming for me to do my whole life.

After a year of discovering what holy relating looked like, while on a journey of authentic sacred union with a man who is my actual mirror of Venus, I knew I had more than enough market research and life experience to support others through every type of relationship challenge.

Since Venus is the key player in the ways we love and had shown me so much that I couldn't see until I turned thirty, I expanded my astrological offerings to go beyond just chart readings. I created the Venus Academy of signature services, courses, and programs to empower others to transform all of their relationships from special (exclusive) and codependent to holy (inclusive) and righteous.

Astrology is only useful if we are actively applying

our universal planetary support on the court of our daily lives. My relationship transformation discovery sessions continue to yield remarkable results in causing people around the world to create breakthroughs in their own connections, and astrology is simply the launchpad.

All of life is relationship. How we are in one area of life is how we are everywhere, since there is no separation—and the 360-degree astrology wheel demonstrates our wholeness impeccably.

Above all else, I am spirit-identified. I'm not overly concerned with the temporal matters of the flesh, and sexuality is no longer my driving force when it comes to intimacy. Friendship is the highest form of relating, and connecting to "the One" is rather about a state of wholeness found in connection to a source. As such, everybody can embody the beloved, my friends are the great loves of my life, and my masculine divine partner opens me up to God and activates the highest expression of my essence, which is how I know the union is righteous. Astrology has shown me that all is one, and I'm grateful to live as such and empower others to do the same.

Liam Mugavin
Sagittarius Rising | Gemini Sun | Gemini Moon
Brooklyn, New York

1. How do you self-identify?
I am a gay, transgender male.

2. How did astrology find you?"
During my senior year at the New School, I became very close with my Brazilian roommates, who were avid astrologists. Before developing my relationship with them, I didn't really believe in astrology . . . but it grew on me.

3. How and why do you use astrology?
Fast-forward almost four years later—astrology is like a religion to me. The more I study, the more I realize just how complex we are as human beings and how the human experience is very nonlinear. It's ironic, because when most people hear about one's belief in the cosmos, they're apt to believe that we as astrologers base human understanding on newspaper astrology, when actually it's quite the contrary.

4. Has astrology helped you understand yourself? If so, how? If not, why?
In terms of understanding the self, astrology has helped me grow as an individual. Everyone's experience on this earth is unique, and astrology gives us a lens through which we come to understand ourselves by deepening our knowledge of the collective. I think the most important thing to take home about astrology, and the self in general, is that we are always learning. To say we know it all is to express that we are at our most ignorant.

5. Has astrology helped you strengthen your relationships? If so, how? If not, why?
I think astrology has made me more empathetic toward others. I have found that since beginning my studies, I am less inclined to condemn others' behaviors and more inclined to figure out why they behave as such.

6. How and when do you feel loneliness? In times of loneliness, how do you find resilience?
The most difficult times for me personally are when I am not immersed in the queer community. I have lived quite a few places in my life, and although I have been blessed to have spent the bulk of it in New York City, the queer "Mecca," some of the places I have lived have been rather conservative. I think technology has really helped with bridging that gap. If I can't find community in the day to day, I can build its foundation by connecting with others technologically.

When I think of astrology and loneliness, I am apt to think of where Pluto is positioned. For example, with Pluto in Scorpio, I think our generation imbues itself with a pervasive sense of loneliness. But at the same time, I applaud our efforts for overcoming this loneliness. Particularly with this sense of Dada-nihilist humor we have adopted to cope with a nation in the throes of existential crises. Instead of trapping our loneliness in four square walls, we have exposed it. Building a culture that screams, "You are lonely, but you are not alone!"

7. How and when do you find belonging?
In times of belonging, what does it feel like? I find my deepest sense of belonging in the queer community. When

I say "queer," I do not just mean sexuality. Rather, I find myself at home with the oddballs and the outcasts. The more strange someone is, the more likely I am to connect with them. I guess you can blame this on carrying a multitude of intersectional identities my entire life, ha.

8. Where do you see astrology in queer culture?

Astrology is everywhere in queer culture. I don't think it's possible for the two to be mutually exclusive. Astrology, like queerness, highlights and celebrates the weirdest intricacies of the self.

9. Has astrology helped, complicated, or empowered you to navigate capitalism, patriarchy, heteronormativity, oppressive structures, and/or white supremacy?

Oh god, definitely empowered. It creates so much community and provides some light of purpose in all of this mess.

10. How can astrologers provide helpful resources to queer consumers?

Really the best way to be a helpful resource for queer consumers is to keep everything gender neutral. No more of this male sign versus female sign. More about who you are as a human being with an astrological identity.

11. Do you connect with other metaphysical and/or spiritual resources?

I love tarot and oracle cards. I connect with the dead through these mediums. Not in a Poltergeist-y way, but definitely for guidance from those who are no longer with us in the corporeal realm.

12. How can queer astrology improve, and what's next for this conversation?
I think astrology will really help us to regain purpose in a somewhat bleak, capitalist era. Bringing astrology to the mainstream is helping to explain just how multilayered it is. I think we are beginning to show the masses that we are all predisposed and interconnected to some degree.

Amal Amer
Sagittarius Rising | Taurus Sun | Leo Moon
Paris, France

Nonbinary, bisexual Arab art witch. Both queer and Muslim, I am on a journey to build imagery, stories, and power. In the face of oppressive structures that call for deconstruction, I call on the tools of astrology, art, and magic to dismantle patriarchy, racism, and colonial modes of seeing.

A child of diaspora, my family and I are uprooted from our homelands. Unmoored, I ground myself both in my queer brown community and in the stars. Through astrology, I choose wholeness. Integration. Collective. Interdependence. Following the moon and its cycles allows me to both measure the spiralic passage of time and align my body and schedule more with the universe's natural rhythms, instead of with capitalist production. After leaving behind the semester system that disciplined my body and mind in school, I felt lost and broken. Realizing the moon was above my head felt both beautiful and decolonial, especially since Islam also uses the lunar calendar. Though the moon moves quickest, the other heavenly bodies cycle as well. The promise of patriarchal, linear time is foreign to those of us who work with trauma. Astrology positions time as inverted on itself, always circling back to familiar territory, spiraling indefinitely.

Through astrology, I learn to encompass contradictions—both in myself and others. The dance of planets whispers that complexity and wholeness are possible to us all, despite the paradoxes contained in our bodies, identities, and experiences. Personally, this has involved naming and embracing my nonbinary gender identity. My Venus in Aries and Mars in Leo connect me to traditionally masculine archetypes and energies. Along with my Leo moon and sun in the fifth house, I feel most at home in the feminine masculinity typified by Prince and David Bowie. Though how I dress swivels between decadent diva aesthetic and soft masculinity, my nonbinary gender is the constant earth underneath shifting light. Similarly, each planet remains themselves even as their expression assumes the roles and energy of separate signs. Astrology gives us the gift of distinction within wholeness: despite capitalist, heteronormative monoculture, people express themselves differently, value different things, and emerge from different backgrounds.

Embodied by myself and other QPOC, astrology becomes a system devoted to liberation and justice. Astrologers like Colin, Naimonu James, Jessica Lanyadoo, and Alice Sparkly Kat create the container for us to do the necessary work of healing, individually and in collective. The imperative we queers have of finding safe community in a violent world conforms with astrological tools. We embrace this system to understand ourselves and relate to others. Lovers and friends enter and leave our lives in sync with transits. The moon controls the waves of the ocean, and I am part of a sea of queers doing liberation work together, armed with the knowledge of our interconnectedness and our place in the wheel of the heavens. For this I thank my goddess Allah, beneficent, merciful, loving, guiding.

Amal Amer is on Instagram at @youcandoithabibi. Their podcast *Diaspora Babes* explores maintaining one's creative practice under capitalism as a queer of color. Website: amalamer.myportfolio.com.

Brielle Williams
Gemini Rising | Capricorn Sun | Pisces Moon
Queens, New York

1. How do you self-identify?
I identify as a Black queer woman of the trans experience.

2. How did astrology find you?
Astrology found me via Tumblr. I had already been somewhat into it, but AstroloCherry completely opened the
door for me, and I found so much information. During
my last semester at Parsons, I fell into a group of friends
who were also really into it. I got my birth chart read for
me, and that was also a really eye-opening experience.

3. How and why do you use astrology?
I use as astrology as a means to understand the world
around me. Because of it, I am able to empathize with
others, and I use this information to create peace around
me. There can't be any drama in a place where everybody's
strengths, weaknesses, turn-ons/turnoffs are known from
jump. It creates sensitivity. I use astrology to figure out what
it requires of me to create the most healing, safe, inclusive
spaces for the people who are around me on a daily basis.

4. Has astrology helped you understand yourself? If so, how? If not, why?
Astrology gave context to my complicated, rigid, dogmatic,
very little room for self-interpretation childhood. I understood on a serious level the work that I had to do in order
to live the life I wanted to live. In real life, I am a shark.
My tongue is sharp, and I'm as quick witted as they come.

I dreamed of hardwood floors and floor-to-ceiling windows since I was a little girl. It gave context to my ambition. The audaciousness of my dreams. It gave me permission to own that I didn't want a regular life and that I didn't have to settle for living outside of my purpose and my potential. The Capricorn story is one of triumph—it tells the tale of the goat overcoming adversity through the sweat of its own brow to ascend to the top of the proverbial mountain. My story is about a young Black girl succeeding despite all odds in a world that would sooner tell her to shut up and die than live in truth. How this little Black girl grows up to be a beautiful, driven, shit-talking woman. It's the same thing.

5. How and when do you feel loneliness? In times of loneliness, how do you find resilience?
I feel loneliness when I see the relationships that others have with their parents. I had to come to terms with mourning the loss of the childhood that I felt like I never had, the loss of a girlhood. I often times feel like even though I was my mother's daughter, I was never treated like my mother's daughter, and for me that was a huge point of contention in our relationship, and still is, even now. When Mother's Day comes around and I see people making all of these posts on social media about how their mom is their best friend, it's very alienating. I find resilience in knowing that I have a community of older queer femme women who uplift me in love and compassionate maternal energy. Some of the wrongs have been righted in my life. I find resilience from the divine mother, and ultimately from the divine one in myself.

6. How and when do you feel belonging? In times of belonging, what does it feel like?

I found belonging in the ballroom scene. As someone who has been a lover and spectator of this art form for ten-plus years, I saw myself in so many Black trans girls who throughout the years started in one category and reinvented themselves over and over again. Black girls who stood in the gap for me and through proxy gave me permission to be myself. To be as beautiful and as devastating and as sickening as I want to be. Ballroom is all about creativity. Showing up and showing out in a crowd that lives for you, affirms you, and embraces you. These are the girls that gave me my swag, and gave me my language. The embodiment of Black trans brilliance... Black trans opulence, the heart of that is in the scene. I carry that in me every day.

7. Does astrology contextualize loneliness and belonging in any way?

Astrology contextualizes loneliness and belonging by being an alternative to what is already out there. Astrology is more inclusive, and now more than ever millennials are denying church on Sundays in favor of astrology because it no longer serves them. Millennials want something that is real, that feels tangible. As a former church kid, I can say that there are parts of modern Christianity that feel somewhat performative and fake. I personally felt pushed out because I did not fit the ideal mold of what a "Christian" was supposed to be. Astrology is an individual road map on how to navigate life tailored specifically for you. It doesn't require anything of you. It doesn't ask you to give up parts of yourself, which is why it is so popular among queer people, who have routinely been abused and pushed out of religious spaces based on sexual identity and gender identity.

8. How can astrologers provide helpful resources to queer consumers?

Astrologers can provide helpful resources for queer people by providing astrology through a lens of intersectionality. Also in focusing on the things that bring us together, as opposed to what brings us apart. It's bigger than what sign doesn't get along with another sign—more what sign you are more compatible with. And the memes are funny and relatable, but on a grander scale: What do all of us bring to the table? What are we going to do to change the world that we live in for the next generation?

Jessica Lanyadoo
Capricorn Rising | Capricorn Sun | Capricorn Moon
Oakland, California

1. How do you self-identify?
I'm a beige, queer high femme, professional people helper.

2. How did astrology find you?
The first thing I remember is when I was six years old, telling the kids on my block about how, since I was a Capricorn, I was going to keep my wisdom teeth, because Capricorn ruled teeth. I don't know how I knew that bit of astrology, but my interest never left me. Eventually I took my first formal astrology classes in Cégep, and I was hooked. I moved to San Francisco to become a professional astrologer within two years of that first class and have never looked back.

3. How and why do you use astrology?
I use astrology as a tool for understanding people, events, and trends. I counsel people with it in efforts to help them use their nature to overcome the parts of their nature that trouble them, and to empower them to make the most of their circumstances. Supporting people to achieve self-acceptance and live their best life is my aim in each consultation I give.

4. Has astrology helped you understand yourself?
Yes! Astrology is math and patterns, and I find that so reassuring.

5. Has astrology helped you strengthen your relationships?

In that it's helped me to be a healthier, more self-reliant, and self-accepting person, yes. I don't use astrology in my personal relationships. Instead I use the insight and tools that I have garnered for myself to have healthy boundaries, and to love in the best ways I can in a given moment.

6. How and when do you feel loneliness? In times of loneliness, how do you find resilience?

In my view, loneliness is a part of the human experience that is netted in the illusion of duality. We are not separate or alone; we are vast organisms that are interconnected with all things and beings. That said, I feel lonely often. It happens like clockwork right before I get my period. It happens when I am going through major shifts and am scared to be in the feelings of it. Loneliness is a gateway that yearns for gentleness from those who cross through it.

7. Does astrology contextualize loneliness and belonging in any way?

Yes! There is no better system for understanding the roots, triggers, and remediation for loneliness than the birth chart, IMO.

8. Has astrology helped, complicated, or empowered you to navigate capitalism, patriarchy, heteronormativity, oppressive structures, and/or white supremacy?

Astrology hasn't helped or hurt my relationship to those things, but I use my work as an astrologer as a tool for affirming and upholding the dignity in all peoples.

9. Do you connect with other metaphysical and/or spiritual resources?

I am a psychic medium, and my spirituality is a huge part of my life. Though I don't do energy work professionally.

10. How can queer astrology improve, and what's next for this conversation?

There are plenty of queer astrologers that are expert on heterosexual issues; we need more straight astrologers that prioritize queering their use of astrology.

11. Where can readers find your work? Social media handles and sites?

Site: https://www.Lovelanyadoo.com

Podcast: https://itunes.apple.com/us/podcast/ghost-of-a-podcast/id1422483488

Social: https://www.instagram.com/jessica_lanyadoo/https://twitter.com/jessicalanyadoo

CONCLUSION

The LGBTQ+ pride flag was designed by the San Francisco artist and Gemini Sun Gilbert Baker in 1978. Baker's original design had eight colors—hot pink, red, orange, yellow, green, turquoise, indigo, and violet. Within each color is a symbol inspired by Buddhist teachings from another gay Gemini Sun, Allen Ginsberg. So you see, queer issues and spirituality are deeply embedded in our culture. Although the pride flag usually signifies a welcoming in queer spaces, I want to explore its themes here as a grateful benediction from me to you.

Hot Pink: Sex
May Mars blaze your sexuality and erotic intelligence to levels that transform you and your partners. Let intimacy guide you to the fascinating mystical spaces between you and your lovers. Let sex be a safe haven, a pleasure chest of excitement and adventure, and a temple of healing.

Red: Life
Look up to the sun that shines behind your constellation, and you'll find your template for life. In every myth and archetype, the sun bestows upon you the direction you need to find your power and glory. You deserve to feel wholehearted and completely worthy in your self-actualization.

Orange: Healing
Living a life of courage, authenticity, and worthiness guarantees you will experience failure and despair. To live and

love is to lose. So let us intend for the power of Saturn's resilience and Neptune's compassion to work its healing miracles in our hearts when we need it. For the bravest have broken hearts, since they have the strength to love.

Yellow: Sunlight

When I think of sunlight, of course I think of our sun sign in astrology, but I also think of power. To know these principles of spirituality returns power to you. To be in power is to express it responsibly, ethically, and inclusively. So I invite you to harness the sunlight and power to heal, to be of service, and to include all.

Green: Nature

Although many queer spaces are urban, nature has a way of taking us out of the metropolis's frantic and frenzied pace, returning us to inner peace and joy. Connect to nature, even if it's a bath or surrounding yourself with plants. Nature reminds you that you too can move at a mindful pace.

Turquoise: Magic/Art

Producing art is one of the most magical things we could ever do. What's more surreal than creating something that never existed before? It's not unreasonable to assume those impulses to create, design, and perform don't come from this world—which is why they're magic. Draw, dance, sing, design, and love magically.

Indigo: Serenity

The choice to be serene is a decision your moon sign must make. A careful review of your deepest psychic needs allows you to find serenity's expression. A raging heart cannot bring about peace. A serene one can. Find serenity within so you are the most qualified instrument of serenity outside of you.

Violet: Spirit

To experience your natal chart is to experience the spirit within it. Aligning with the qualities of your spirit and identifying beyond the body, with the soul within, is the first step toward a spiritual life. You are a soul having a human experience, learning more about compassion, benevolence, and love given and received.

Fully engaging with spirit, serenity, magic/art, nature, sunlight, healing, life, and sex offers some of the most meaningful experiences in your hero's journey. Utilizing universal spiritual themes and astrology can help you engage with these arenas of the pride flag with shame resilience, worthiness, and courage.

I imagine a world where queer people can blend the best of spiritual and secular resources to liberate themselves from shame and earn relationships of the highest meaning.

If we're all spiritual beings having a human experience, I believe the universe's practice for us is to understand that what it means to be deeply human is found through relationship. It's a paradox, I know, but such is the nature of relationship. So why would the universe operate any differently?

Let's not forget that we cannot exist without each other. So the universe brings us relationships. *A Course in Miracles* teaches us that relationships are a spiritual practice. I know that the most difficult yet valuable arena for us to seek, to look within, and then to apply spiritual principles to is relationships. Our lives depend on it.

In other words—there is no proximity to the divine but through the people in front of you. From the most casual to the most intimate of connections, our relationship quality determines our individual competency around financial security and professional success. Not the other way around.

Astrology, relational intelligence, and other comparative spiritual tools can help queer people release their most authentic nature, and because nature supports nature and nature supports love, your authenticity will bring you into the arms of a lover.

Employing astrology as a complementary tool for self-acceptance, compassion, care, and relational intelligence gives queer-identified folks the chance to be seen and understood accurately, free from majority culture. With this framework, we can let the stardust in our soul come to life. It has to. We need it to, since our chart is the temple of our soul where we come to understand that we are made of stories, stars, myth, and magic.